2262B: Supporting Users Running Applications on a Microsoft® Windows® XP Operating System

Course Number: 2262B
Part Number: X11-14227
Released: 10/2004

END-USER LICENSE AGREEMENT FOR OFFICIAL MICROSOFT LEARNING PRODUCTS – STUDENT EDITION

PLEASE READ THIS END-USER LICENSE AGREEMENT ("EULA") CAREFULLY. BY USING THE MATERIALS AND/OR USING OR INSTALLING THE SOFTWARE THAT ACCOMPANIES THIS EULA (COLLECTIVELY, THE "LICENSED CONTENT"), YOU AGREE TO THE TERMS OF THIS EULA. IF YOU DO NOT AGREE, DO NOT USE THE LICENSED CONTENT.

1. **GENERAL.** This EULA is a legal agreement between you (either an individual or a single entity) and Microsoft Corporation ("Microsoft"). This EULA governs the Licensed Content, which includes computer software (including online and electronic documentation), training materials, and any other associated media and printed materials. This EULA applies to updates, supplements, add-on components, and Internet-based services components of the Licensed Content that Microsoft may provide or make available to you unless Microsoft provides other terms with the update, supplement, add-on component, or Internet-based services component. Microsoft reserves the right to discontinue any Internet-based services provided to you or made available to you through the use of the Licensed Content. This EULA also governs any product support services relating to the Licensed Content except as may be included in another agreement between you and Microsoft. An amendment or addendum to this EULA may accompany the Licensed Content.

2. **GENERAL GRANT OF LICENSE.** Microsoft grants you the following rights, conditioned on your compliance with all the terms and conditions of this EULA. Microsoft grants you a limited, non-exclusive, royalty-free license to install and use the Licensed Content solely in conjunction with your participation as a student in an Authorized Training Session (as defined below). You may install and use one copy of the software on a single computer, device, workstation, terminal, or other digital electronic or analog device ("Device"). You may make a second copy of the software and install it on a portable Device for the exclusive use of the person who is the primary user of the first copy of the software. A license for the software may not be shared for use by multiple end users. An "Authorized Training Session" means a training session conducted at a Microsoft Certified Technical Education Center, an IT Academy, via a Microsoft Certified Partner, or such other entity as Microsoft may designate from time to time in writing, by a Microsoft Certified Trainer (for more information on these entities, please visit www.microsoft.com). WITHOUT LIMITING THE FOREGOING, COPYING OR REPRODUCTION OF THE LICENSED CONTENT TO ANY SERVER OR LOCATION FOR FURTHER REPRODUCTION OR REDISTRIBUTION IS EXPRESSLY PROHIBITED.

3. **DESCRIPTION OF OTHER RIGHTS AND LICENSE LIMITATIONS**

   3.1 *Use of Documentation and Printed Training Materials.*

   3.1.1 The documents and related graphics included in the Licensed Content may include technical inaccuracies or typographical errors. Changes are periodically made to the content. Microsoft may make improvements and/or changes in any of the components of the Licensed Content at any time without notice. The names of companies, products, people, characters and/or data mentioned in the Licensed Content may be fictitious and are in no way intended to represent any real individual, company, product or event, unless otherwise noted.

   3.1.2 Microsoft grants you the right to reproduce portions of documents (such as student workbooks, white papers, press releases, datasheets and FAQs) (the "Documents") provided with the Licensed Content. You may not print any book (either electronic or print version) in its entirety. If you choose to reproduce Documents, you agree that: (a) use of such printed Documents will be solely in conjunction with your personal training use; (b) the Documents will not republished or posted on any network computer or broadcast in any media; (c) any reproduction will include either the Document's original copyright notice or a copyright notice to Microsoft's benefit substantially in the format provided below; and (d) to comply with all terms and conditions of this EULA. In addition, no modifications may made to any Document.

   Form of Notice:

   Copyright undefined.

   © 2004. Reprinted with permission by Microsoft Corporation. All rights reserved.

   Microsoft and Windows are either registered trademarks or trademarks of Microsoft Corporation in the US and/or other countries. Other product and company names mentioned herein may be the trademarks of their respective owners.

   3.2 *Use of Media Elements.* The Licensed Content may include certain photographs, clip art, animations, sounds, music, and video clips (together "Media Elements"). You may not modify these Media Elements.

   3.3 *Use of Sample Code.* In the event that the Licensed Content include sample source code ("Sample Code"), Microsoft grants you a limited, non-exclusive, royalty-free license to use, copy and modify the Sample Code; if you elect to exercise the foregoing rights, you agree to comply with all other terms and conditions of this EULA, including without limitation Sections 3.4, 3.5, and 6.

   3.4 *Permitted Modifications.* In the event that you exercise any rights provided under this EULA to create modifications of the Licensed Content, you agree that any such modifications: (a) will not be used for providing training where a fee is charged in public or private classes; (b) indemnify, hold harmless, and defend Microsoft from and against any claims or lawsuits, including attorneys' fees, which arise from or result from your use of any modified version of the Licensed Content; and (c) not to transfer or assign any rights to any modified version of the Licensed Content to any third party without the express written permission of Microsoft.

3.5   *Reproduction/Redistribution Licensed Content.* Except as expressly provided in this EULA, you may not reproduce or distribute the Licensed Content or any portion thereof (including any permitted modifications) to any third parties without the express written permission of Microsoft.

4.   **RESERVATION OF RIGHTS AND OWNERSHIP.** Microsoft reserves all rights not expressly granted to you in this EULA. The Licensed Content is protected by copyright and other intellectual property laws and treaties. Microsoft or its suppliers own the title, copyright, and other intellectual property rights in the Licensed Content. You may not remove or obscure any copyright, trademark or patent notices that appear on the Licensed Content, or any components thereof, as delivered to you. **The Licensed Content is licensed, not sold.**

5.   **LIMITATIONS ON REVERSE ENGINEERING, DECOMPILATION, AND DISASSEMBLY.** You may not reverse engineer, decompile, or disassemble the Software or Media Elements, except and only to the extent that such activity is expressly permitted by applicable law notwithstanding this limitation.

6.   **LIMITATIONS ON SALE, RENTAL, ETC. AND CERTAIN ASSIGNMENTS.** You may not provide commercial hosting services with, sell, rent, lease, lend, sublicense, or assign copies of the Licensed Content, or any portion thereof (including any permitted modifications thereof) on a stand-alone basis or as part of any collection, product or service.

7.   **CONSENT TO USE OF DATA.** You agree that Microsoft and its affiliates may collect and use technical information gathered as part of the product support services provided to you, if any, related to the Licensed Content. Microsoft may use this information solely to improve our products or to provide customized services or technologies to you and will not disclose this information in a form that personally identifies you.

8.   **LINKS TO THIRD PARTY SITES.** You may link to third party sites through the use of the Licensed Content. The third party sites are not under the control of Microsoft, and Microsoft is not responsible for the contents of any third party sites, any links contained in third party sites, or any changes or updates to third party sites. Microsoft is not responsible for webcasting or any other form of transmission received from any third party sites. Microsoft is providing these links to third party sites to you only as a convenience, and the inclusion of any link does not imply an endorsement by Microsoft of the third party site.

9.   **ADDITIONAL LICENSED CONTENT/SERVICES.** This EULA applies to updates, supplements, add-on components, or Internet-based services components, of the Licensed Content that Microsoft may provide to you or make available to you after the date you obtain your initial copy of the Licensed Content, unless we provide other terms along with the update, supplement, add-on component, or Internet-based services component. Microsoft reserves the right to discontinue any Internet-based services provided to you or made available to you through the use of the Licensed Content.

10.   **U.S. GOVERNMENT LICENSE RIGHTS**. All software provided to the U.S. Government pursuant to solicitations issued on or after December 1, 1995 is provided with the commercial license rights and restrictions described elsewhere herein. All software provided to the U.S. Government pursuant to solicitations issued prior to December 1, 1995 is provided with "Restricted Rights" as provided for in FAR, 48 CFR 52.227-14 (JUNE 1987) or DFAR, 48 CFR 252.227-7013 (OCT 1988), as applicable.

11.   **EXPORT RESTRICTIONS.** You acknowledge that the Licensed Content is subject to U.S. export jurisdiction. You agree to comply with all applicable international and national laws that apply to the Licensed Content, including the U.S. Export Administration Regulations, as well as end-user, end-use, and destination restrictions issued by U.S. and other governments. For additional information see <http://www.microsoft.com/exporting/>.

12.   **TRANSFER.** The initial user of the Licensed Content may make a one-time permanent transfer of this EULA and Licensed Content to another end user, provided the initial user retains no copies of the Licensed Content. The transfer may not be an indirect transfer, such as a consignment. Prior to the transfer, the end user receiving the Licensed Content must agree to all the EULA terms.

13.   **"NOT FOR RESALE" LICENSED CONTENT.** Licensed Content identified as "Not For Resale" or "NFR," may not be sold or otherwise transferred for value, or used for any purpose other than demonstration, test or evaluation.

14.   **TERMINATION.** Without prejudice to any other rights, Microsoft may terminate this EULA if you fail to comply with the terms and conditions of this EULA. In such event, you must destroy all copies of the Licensed Content and all of its component parts.

15.   **DISCLAIMER OF WARRANTIES. TO THE MAXIMUM EXTENT PERMITTED BY APPLICABLE LAW, MICROSOFT AND ITS SUPPLIERS PROVIDE THE LICENSED CONTENT AND SUPPORT SERVICES (IF ANY)** *AS IS AND WITH ALL FAULTS,* **AND MICROSOFT AND ITS SUPPLIERS HEREBY DISCLAIM ALL OTHER WARRANTIES AND CONDITIONS, WHETHER EXPRESS, IMPLIED OR STATUTORY, INCLUDING, BUT NOT LIMITED TO, ANY (IF ANY) IMPLIED WARRANTIES, DUTIES OR CONDITIONS OF MERCHANTABILITY, OF FITNESS FOR A PARTICULAR PURPOSE, OF RELIABILITY OR AVAILABILITY, OF ACCURACY OR COMPLETENESS OF RESPONSES, OF RESULTS, OF WORKMANLIKE EFFORT, OF LACK OF VIRUSES, AND OF LACK OF NEGLIGENCE, ALL WITH REGARD TO THE LICENSED CONTENT, AND THE PROVISION OF OR FAILURE TO PROVIDE SUPPORT OR OTHER SERVICES, INFORMATION, SOFTWARE, AND RELATED CONTENT THROUGH THE LICENSED CONTENT, OR OTHERWISE ARISING OUT OF THE USE OF THE LICENSED CONTENT. ALSO, THERE IS NO WARRANTY OR CONDITION OF TITLE, QUIET ENJOYMENT, QUIET POSSESSION, CORRESPONDENCE TO DESCRIPTION OR NON-INFRINGEMENT WITH REGARD TO THE LICENSED CONTENT. THE ENTIRE RISK AS TO THE QUALITY, OR ARISING OUT OF THE USE OR PERFORMANCE OF THE LICENSED CONTENT, AND ANY SUPPORT SERVICES, REMAINS WITH YOU.**

16.   **EXCLUSION OF INCIDENTAL, CONSEQUENTIAL AND CERTAIN OTHER DAMAGES. TO THE MAXIMUM EXTENT PERMITTED BY APPLICABLE LAW, IN NO EVENT SHALL MICROSOFT OR ITS SUPPLIERS BE LIABLE FOR ANY SPECIAL, INCIDENTAL, PUNITIVE, INDIRECT, OR CONSEQUENTIAL DAMAGES WHATSOEVER (INCLUDING, BUT NOT**

LIMITED TO, DAMAGES FOR LOSS OF PROFITS OR CONFIDENTIAL OR OTHER INFORMATION, FOR BUSINESS INTERRUPTION, FOR PERSONAL INJURY, FOR LOSS OF PRIVACY, FOR FAILURE TO MEET ANY DUTY INCLUDING OF GOOD FAITH OR OF REASONABLE CARE, FOR NEGLIGENCE, AND FOR ANY OTHER PECUNIARY OR OTHER LOSS WHATSOEVER) ARISING OUT OF OR IN ANY WAY RELATED TO THE USE OF OR INABILITY TO USE THE LICENSED CONTENT, THE PROVISION OF OR FAILURE TO PROVIDE SUPPORT OR OTHER SERVICES, INFORMATION, SOFTWARE, AND RELATED CONTENT THROUGH THE LICENSED CONTENT, OR OTHERWISE ARISING OUT OF THE USE OF THE LICENSED CONTENT, OR OTHERWISE UNDER OR IN CONNECTION WITH ANY PROVISION OF THIS EULA, EVEN IN THE EVENT OF THE FAULT, TORT (INCLUDING NEGLIGENCE), MISREPRESENTATION, STRICT LIABILITY, BREACH OF CONTRACT OR BREACH OF WARRANTY OF MICROSOFT OR ANY SUPPLIER, AND EVEN IF MICROSOFT OR ANY SUPPLIER HAS BEEN ADVISED OF THE POSSIBILITY OF SUCH DAMAGES. BECAUSE SOME STATES/JURISDICTIONS DO NOT ALLOW THE EXCLUSION OR LIMITATION OF LIABILITY FOR CONSEQUENTIAL OR INCIDENTAL DAMAGES, THE ABOVE LIMITATION MAY NOT APPLY TO YOU.

17.   **LIMITATION OF LIABILITY AND REMEDIES.** NOTWITHSTANDING ANY DAMAGES THAT YOU MIGHT INCUR FOR ANY REASON WHATSOEVER (INCLUDING, WITHOUT LIMITATION, ALL DAMAGES REFERENCED HEREIN AND ALL DIRECT OR GENERAL DAMAGES IN CONTRACT OR ANYTHING ELSE), THE ENTIRE LIABILITY OF MICROSOFT AND ANY OF ITS SUPPLIERS UNDER ANY PROVISION OF THIS EULA AND YOUR EXCLUSIVE REMEDY HEREUNDER SHALL BE LIMITED TO THE GREATER OF THE ACTUAL DAMAGES YOU INCUR IN REASONABLE RELIANCE ON THE LICENSED CONTENT UP TO THE AMOUNT ACTUALLY PAID BY YOU FOR THE LICENSED CONTENT OR US$5.00. THE FOREGOING LIMITATIONS, EXCLUSIONS AND DISCLAIMERS SHALL APPLY TO THE MAXIMUM EXTENT PERMITTED BY APPLICABLE LAW, EVEN IF ANY REMEDY FAILS ITS ESSENTIAL PURPOSE.

18.   **APPLICABLE LAW.** If you acquired this Licensed Content in the United States, this EULA is governed by the laws of the State of Washington. If you acquired this Licensed Content in Canada, unless expressly prohibited by local law, this EULA is governed by the laws in force in the Province of Ontario, Canada; and, in respect of any dispute which may arise hereunder, you consent to the jurisdiction of the federal and provincial courts sitting in Toronto, Ontario. If you acquired this Licensed Content in the European Union, Iceland, Norway, or Switzerland, then local law applies. If you acquired this Licensed Content in any other country, then local law may apply.

19.   **ENTIRE AGREEMENT; SEVERABILITY.** This EULA (including any addendum or amendment to this EULA which is included with the Licensed Content) are the entire agreement between you and Microsoft relating to the Licensed Content and the support services (if any) and they supersede all prior or contemporaneous oral or written communications, proposals and representations with respect to the Licensed Content or any other subject matter covered by this EULA. To the extent the terms of any Microsoft policies or programs for support services conflict with the terms of this EULA, the terms of this EULA shall control. If any provision of this EULA is held to be void, invalid, unenforceable or illegal, the other provisions shall continue in full force and effect.

Should you have any questions concerning this EULA, or if you desire to contact Microsoft for any reason, please use the address information enclosed in this Licensed Content to contact the Microsoft subsidiary serving your country or visit Microsoft on the World Wide Web at http://www.microsoft.com.

Si vous avez acquis votre Contenu Sous Licence Microsoft au CANADA :

DÉNI DE GARANTIES. Dans la mesure maximale permise par les lois applicables, le Contenu Sous Licence et les services de soutien technique (le cas échéant) sont fournis *TELS QUELS ET AVEC TOUS LES DÉFAUTS* par Microsoft et ses fournisseurs, lesquels par les présentes dénient toutes autres garanties et conditions expresses, implicites ou en vertu de la loi, notamment, mais sans limitation, (le cas échéant) les garanties, devoirs ou conditions implicites de qualité marchande, d'adaptation à une fin usage particulière, de fiabilité ou de disponibilité, d'exactitude ou d'exhaustivité des réponses, des résultats, des efforts déployés selon les règles de l'art, d'absence de virus et d'absence de négligence, le tout à l'égard du Contenu Sous Licence et de la prestation des services de soutien technique ou de l'omission de la 'une telle prestation des services de soutien technique ou à l'égard de la fourniture ou de l'omission de la fourniture de tous autres services, renseignements, Contenus Sous Licence, et contenu qui s'y rapporte grâce au Contenu Sous Licence ou provenant autrement de l'utilisation du Contenu Sous Licence. PAR AILLEURS, IL N'Y A AUCUNE GARANTIE OU CONDITION QUANT AU TITRE DE PROPRIÉTÉ, À LA JOUISSANCE OU LA POSSESSION PAISIBLE, À LA CONCORDANCE À UNE DESCRIPTION NI QUANT À UNE ABSENCE DE CONTREFAÇON CONCERNANT LE CONTENU SOUS LICENCE.

EXCLUSION DES DOMMAGES ACCESSOIRES, INDIRECTS ET DE CERTAINS AUTRES DOMMAGES. DANS LA MESURE MAXIMALE PERMISE PAR LES LOIS APPLICABLES, EN AUCUN CAS MICROSOFT OU SES FOURNISSEURS NE SERONT RESPONSABLES DES DOMMAGES SPÉCIAUX, CONSÉCUTIFS, ACCESSOIRES OU INDIRECTS DE QUELQUE NATURE QUE CE SOIT (NOTAMMENT, LES DOMMAGES À L'ÉGARD DU MANQUE À GAGNER OU DE LA DIVULGATION DE RENSEIGNEMENTS CONFIDENTIELS OU AUTRES, DE LA PERTE D'EXPLOITATION, DE BLESSURES CORPORELLES, DE LA VIOLATION DE LA VIE PRIVÉE, DE L'OMISSION DE REMPLIR TOUT DEVOIR, Y COMPRIS D'AGIR DE BONNE FOI OU D'EXERCER UN SOIN RAISONNABLE, DE LA NÉGLIGENCE ET DE TOUTE AUTRE PERTE PÉCUNIAIRE OU AUTRE PERTE

DE QUELQUE NATURE QUE CE SOIT) SE RAPPORTANT DE QUELQUE MANIÈRE QUE CE SOIT À L'UTILISATION DU CONTENU SOUS LICENCE OU À L'INCAPACITÉ DE S'EN SERVIR, À LA PRESTATION OU À L'OMISSION DE LA 'UNE TELLE PRESTATION DE SERVICES DE SOUTIEN TECHNIQUE OU À LA FOURNITURE OU À L'OMISSION DE LA FOURNITURE DE TOUS AUTRES SERVICES, RENSEIGNEMENTS, CONTENUS SOUS LICENCE, ET CONTENU QUI S'Y RAPPORTE GRÂCE AU CONTENU SOUS LICENCE OU PROVENANT AUTREMENT DE L'UTILISATION DU CONTENU SOUS LICENCE OU AUTREMENT AUX TERMES DE TOUTE DISPOSITION DE LA U PRÉSENTE CONVENTION EULA OU RELATIVEMENT À UNE TELLE DISPOSITION, MÊME EN CAS DE FAUTE, DE DÉLIT CIVIL (Y COMPRIS LA NÉGLIGENCE), DE RESPONSABILITÉ STRICTE, DE VIOLATION DE CONTRAT OU DE VIOLATION DE GARANTIE DE MICROSOFT OU DE TOUT FOURNISSEUR ET MÊME SI MICROSOFT OU TOUT FOURNISSEUR A ÉTÉ AVISÉ DE LA POSSIBILITÉ DE TELS DOMMAGES.

<u>LIMITATION DE RESPONSABILITÉ ET RECOURS.</u>   MALGRÉ LES DOMMAGES QUE VOUS PUISSIEZ SUBIR POUR QUELQUE MOTIF QUE CE SOIT (NOTAMMENT, MAIS SANS LIMITATION, TOUS LES DOMMAGES SUSMENTIONNÉS ET TOUS LES DOMMAGES DIRECTS OU GÉNÉRAUX OU AUTRES), LA SEULE RESPONSABILITÉ 'OBLIGATION INTÉGRALE DE MICROSOFT ET DE L'UN OU L'AUTRE DE SES FOURNISSEURS AUX TERMES DE TOUTE DISPOSITION DEU LA PRÉSENTE CONVENTION EULA ET VOTRE RECOURS EXCLUSIF À L'ÉGARD DE TOUT CE QUI PRÉCÈDE SE LIMITE AU PLUS ÉLEVÉ ENTRE LES MONTANTS SUIVANTS : LE MONTANT QUE VOUS AVEZ RÉELLEMENT PAYÉ POUR LE CONTENU SOUS LICENCE OU 5,00 $US. LES LIMITES, EXCLUSIONS ET DÉNIS QUI PRÉCÈDENT (Y COMPRIS LES CLAUSES CI-DESSUS), S'APPLIQUENT DANS LA MESURE MAXIMALE PERMISE PAR LES LOIS APPLICABLES, MÊME SI TOUT RECOURS N'ATTEINT PAS SON BUT ESSENTIEL.

À moins que cela ne soit prohibé par le droit local applicable, la présente Convention est régie par les lois de la province d'Ontario, Canada. Vous consentez Chacune des parties à la présente reconnaît irrévocablement à la compétence des tribunaux fédéraux et provinciaux siégeant à Toronto, dans de la province d'Ontario et consent à instituer tout litige qui pourrait découler de la présente auprès des tribunaux situés dans le district judiciaire de York, province d'Ontario.

Au cas où vous auriez des questions concernant cette licence ou que vous désiriez vous mettre en rapport avec Microsoft pour quelque raison que ce soit, veuillez utiliser l'information contenue dans le Contenu Sous Licence pour contacter la filiale de succursale Microsoft desservant votre pays, dont l'adresse est fournie dans ce produit, ou visitez écrivez à : Microsoft sur le World Wide Web à http://www.microsoft.com

Contents

About This Course

This section provides you with a brief description of the course, audience, suggested prerequisites, and course objectives.

Description

This course provides content on reacting to incident requests from users by troubleshooting and repairing end user problems with applications running on Microsoft® Windows® XP Professional and Windows XP Home Edition. This course discusses how to troubleshoot problems with Microsoft MS-DOS®–based, Microsoft Win32®, and Microsoft Win16 applications. This course also describes how to assist customers in customizing and configuring Internet Explorer, Microsoft Office Outlook®, Microsoft Office, and Microsoft Outlook Express to respond to issues that may occur with these applications.

Audience

Primary audience:

This course is primarily intended for people who have little or no job experience in the Internet technology (IT) industry. They will have experience working with Windows desktop operating systems and will be A+ certified, or have equivalent knowledge. The target students will be:

- New entrants to the IT field.
- Career changers entering the IT field.
- Academic students.

Secondary audience:

The secondary audience for this course consists of people who are currently working in the tier 1 job role and wish to obtain their MCDST credential. They will likely have most of the skills that are covered in this course, but will not have the formal education that may be required to pass the exams.

Student prerequisites

This course requires that students meet the following prerequisites:

- Basic understanding of Office applications and Windows accessories (including Internet Explorer).
- Course 2261: *Supporting Users Running the Microsoft Windows XP Operating System*

Course objectives

After completing this course, students will be able to:

- Explain the role of the Desktop Support Technician (DST) in desktop application support, the Windows XP system architecture in relation to application and operating system compatibility, and how application installation affects the computer and user settings.
- Troubleshoot issues related to desktop application support.
- Troubleshoot issues related to Internet Explorer.
- Troubleshoot issues related to Outlook.
- Troubleshoot issues related to Office.
- Troubleshoot issues related to Outlook Express.

Student Materials Compact Disc Contents

The Student Materials compact disc (CD) contains the following files and folders:

- *Autorun.inf*. When the compact disc is inserted into the compact disc drive, this file opens StartCD.exe.

- *Default.htm*. This file opens the Student Materials Web page. It provides you with resources pertaining to this course, including additional reading, review and lab answers, lab files, multimedia presentations, and course-related Web sites.

- *Readme.txt*. This file explains how to install the software for viewing the Student Materials compact disc and its contents and how to open the Student Materials Web page.

- *StartCD.exe*. When the compact disc is inserted into the compact disc drive, or when you double-click the **StartCD.exe** file, this file opens the compact disc and allows you to browse the Student Materials compact disc.

- *StartCD.ini*. This file contains instructions to launch StartCD.exe.

- *Flash*. This folder contains the installer for the Macromedia Flash browser plug-in.

- *Fonts*. This folder contains fonts that may be required to view the Microsoft Word documents that are included with this course.

- *Labfiles*. This folder contains files that are used in the hands-on labs. These files may be used to prepare the student computers for the hands-on labs.

- *Mplayer*. This folder contains the file to update the codecs for Microsoft Windows Media® Player.

- *Practices*. This folder contains files that are used in the hands-on practices.

- *Webfiles*. This folder contains the files that are required to view the course Web page. To open the Web page, open Windows Explorer, and in the root directory of the compact disc, double-click **StartCD.exe**.

- *Wordview*. This folder contains the Word Viewer that is used to view any Word document (.doc) files that are included on the compact disc.

Document Conventions

The following conventions are used in course materials to distinguish elements of the text.

Convention	Use
Bold	Represents commands, command options, and syntax that must be typed exactly as shown. It also indicates commands on menus and buttons, dialog box titles and options, and icon and menu names.
Italic	In syntax statements or descriptive text, indicates argument names or placeholders for variable information. Italic is also used for introducing new terms, for book titles, and for emphasis in the text.
Title Capitals	Indicate domain names, user names, computer names, directory names, and folder and file names, except when specifically referring to case-sensitive names. Unless otherwise indicated, you can use lowercase letters when you type a directory name or file name in a dialog box or at a command prompt.
ALL CAPITALS	Indicate the names of keys, key sequences, and key combinations—for example, ALT+SPACEBAR.
`monospace`	Represents code samples or examples of screen text.
[ ]	In syntax statements, enclose optional items. For example, [*filename*] in command syntax indicates that you can choose to type a file name with the command. Type only the information within the brackets, not the brackets themselves.
{ }	In syntax statements, enclose required items. Type only the information within the braces, not the braces themselves.
|	In syntax statements, separates an either/or choice.
▶	Indicates a procedure with sequential steps.
...	In syntax statements, specifies that the preceding item may be repeated.
. . .	Represents an omitted portion of a code sample.

Introduction

Contents

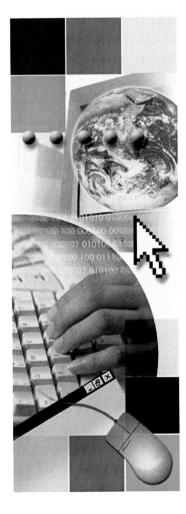

Introduction

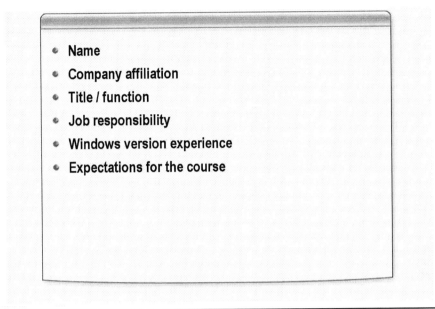

Course Materials

- • **Name card**
- • **Student workbook**
- • **Student Materials compact disc**

The following materials are included with your kit:

- ■ *Name card*. Write your name on both sides of the name card.

- ■ *Student workbook*. The student workbook contains the material covered in class, in addition to the hands-on lab exercises.

- ■ *Student Materials compact disc*. The Student Materials compact disc (CD) contains the Web page that provides you with links to resources pertaining to this course, including additional readings, review and lab answers, lab files, multimedia presentations, and course-related Web sites.

Note To open the Web page, insert the Student Materials CD into the CD-ROM drive, and then in the root directory of the CD, double-click **StartCD.exe**.

- ■ *Course evaluation*. You will have the opportunity to complete an online evaluation near the end of the course to provide feedback on the course, training facility, and instructor.

- ■ *Evaluation software*. If evaluation software is included in the product, please remove it.

To provide additional comments or feedback on the course, send e-mail to support@mscourseware.com. To inquire about the Microsoft Certified Professional (MCP) program, send e-mail to mcphelp@microsoft.com.

Prerequisites

- Basic experience using a Microsoft Windows operating system such as Microsoft Windows XP
- Basic understanding of Microsoft Office applications and Microsoft Windows accessories, including Microsoft Internet Explorer
- Basic understanding of core operating system technologies, including installation and configuration
- Basic understanding of hardware components and their functions

This course requires that you meet the following prerequisites:

- Basic experience using a Microsoft® Windows® operating system such as Microsoft Windows XP
- Basic understanding of Microsoft Office applications and Windows accessories, including Internet Explorer
- Basic understanding of core operating system technologies, including installation and configuration
- Basic understanding of hardware components and their functions

Prerequisites (*continued*)

- Basic understanding of the major desktop components and interfaces and their functions
- Basic understanding of TCP/IP settings
- Basic experience using command-line utilities to manage the operating system
- Basic understanding of technologies that are available for establishing Internet connectivity

---

- Basic understanding of the major desktop components and interfaces and their functions
- Basic understanding of Transmission Control Protocol/Internet Protocol (TCP/IP) settings
- Basic experience using command-line utilities to manage the operating system
- Basic understanding of technologies that are available for establishing Internet connectivity

Course Outline

* **Module 1: Introduction to Supporting Users Running Applications on Windows XP**
* **Module 2: Troubleshooting Desktop Application Support Issues**
* **Module 3: Troubleshooting Issues Related to Internet Explorer**
* **Module 4: Troubleshooting Issues Related to Outlook**
* **Module 5: Troubleshooting Issues Related to Office**
* **Module 6: Troubleshooting Issues Related to Outlook Express**

Module 1, "Introduction to Supporting Users Running Applications on Windows XP," describes the role and key skills required for a desktop support technician who is supporting users running applications on Windows XP. This module also explains the Windows system architecture and provides an overview of the application installation process. After completing this module, you will be able to describe the primary tools used in troubleshooting desktop operating systems, explain the Windows System Architecture as it relates to troubleshooting applications running on Windows desktops, and describe the application installation process.

Module 2, "Troubleshooting Desktop Application Support Issues," discusses how to troubleshoot Microsoft MS-DOS®–based applications, Microsoft Win16 applications, and Microsoft Win32® applications. This module also describes common application compatibility issues and security issues related to applications. After completing this module, you will be able to troubleshoot issues related to MS-DOS–based applications, Win16 applications, and Win32 applications; application compatibility; and application security.

Module 3, "Troubleshooting Issues Related to Internet Explorer," explains how to assist customers in configuring and customizing Internet Explorer settings. This module identifies key support topics related to Internet Explorer, such as how to help users configure content, security, and privacy settings. After completing this module, you will be able to troubleshoot issues related to Internet Explorer configuration and customization.

Module 4, "Troubleshooting Issues Related to Outlook," describes how to support customers who are configuring Microsoft Office Outlook® for Internet e-mail accounts and Microsoft Exchange e-mail accounts. This module identifies key support topics related to Outlook, such as how to help users configure junk mail filters and create rules to process and organize messages. After completing this module, you will be able to troubleshoot problems with Outlook e-mail, Exchange configuration, and Outlook data.

Module 5, "Troubleshooting Issues Related to Office," explains how to support customers who are using Microsoft Office products. This module describes how to install and activate Office, how to manage Office security, and how to recover and repair Office documents. It also discusses how to manage Office language tools, such as the custom dictionary and language packs. After completing this module, you will be able to troubleshoot issues related to Office installation, activation, security, recoverability, and the Office language tools.

Module 6, "Troubleshooting Issues Related to Outlook Express," describes how to support customers who are configuring Microsoft Outlook Express for e-mail. This module also explains how to manage Outlook Express data and configure Outlook Express for newsgroups. After completing this module, you will be able to troubleshoot problems with Outlook Express e-mail, data, and newsgroups.

Demonstration: Using Microsoft Virtual PC

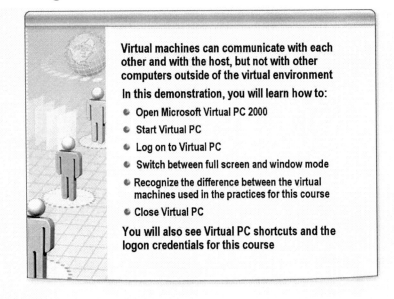

Virtual machines can communicate with each other and with the host computer, but they cannot communicate with other computers that are outside of the virtual environment. (For example, no Internet access is available from the virtual environment.) In this demonstration, your instructor will help familiarize you with the Microsoft Virtual PC 2004 environment, in which you will work to complete the practices in this course. You will learn:

- How to open Virtual PC.

- How to start Virtual PC.

- How to log on to Virtual PC.

- How to switch between full screen and window modes.

- How to tell the difference among the virtual machines that are used in the practices for this course.

- How to close Virtual PC and save changes.

- How to close Virtual PC and discard changes.

- How to pause and resume a virtual machine.

Your instructor will also show you some Virtual PC keyboard shortcuts.

Note   For more information about Virtual PC, see Microsoft Virtual PC Help.

Virtual PC keyboard shortcuts

While working in the virtual machine environment, you may find it useful to use keyboard shortcuts. All virtual machine shortcuts include a key that is referred to as the HOST key. By default, the HOST key is the ALT key on the right side of your keyboard.

Some useful shortcuts are included in this table.

Action	Keyboard shortcut
Log on to the virtual machine.	RIGHT ALT+DELETE
Switch between full screen mode and window modes.	RIGHT ALT+ENTER
Display the next virtual machine.	RIGHT ALT+RIGHT ARROW
Shut down the virtual machine.	RIGHT ALT+F4
Pause or resume a virtual machine.	RIGHT ALT+P

Important   When shutting down a virtual machine, pay close attention to the lab or practice instructions to determine whether you should save or discard changes.

Microsoft Learning

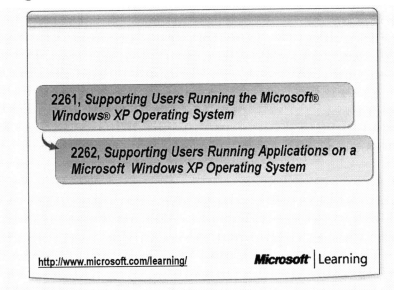

Introduction

Microsoft Learning develops Official Microsoft Learning Products for computer professionals who design, develop, support, implement, or manage solutions by using Microsoft products and technologies. These learning products provide comprehensive skills-based training in instructor-led and online formats.

Additional recommended courses

Each learning product relates in some way to another course. A related course may be a prerequisite, a follow-up course in a recommended series, or a course that offers additional training.

It is recommended that you take the following courses in this order:

- 2261: Supporting Users Running the Microsoft Windows XP Operating System
- 2262: Supporting Users Running Applications on a Microsoft Windows XP Operating System

Other related courses may become available in the future, so for up-to-date information about recommended courses, visit the Microsoft Learning Web site.

Microsoft Learning information

For more information, visit the Microsoft Learning Web site at http://www.microsoft.com/learning/.

Microsoft Certified Professional Program

Exam number and title	Core exam for the following track
70-272: *Supporting Users and Troubleshooting Desktop Applications on a Microsoft Windows XP Operating System*	MCDST

http://www.microsoft.com/learning/

Microsoft®
C E R T I F I E D
Professional

Introduction

Microsoft Learning offers a variety of certification credentials for developers and IT professionals. The Microsoft Certified Professional (MCP) program is the leading certification program for validating your experience and skills, keeping you competitive in today's changing business environment.

Related certification exam

This course helps students prepare for Exam 70-272: *Supporting Users and Troubleshooting Desktop Applications on a Microsoft Windows XP Operating System.*

Exam 70-272: *Supporting Users and Troubleshooting Desktop Applications on a Microsoft Windows XP Operating System* is a core exam for the Microsoft Certified Desktop Support Technician (MCDST) on Microsoft Windows XP certification.

MCP certifications

The Microsoft Certified Professional program includes the following certifications.

- MCDST on Microsoft Windows XP

    The Microsoft Certified Desktop Support Technician (MCDST) certification is designed for professionals who successfully support and educate end users and troubleshoot operating system and application issues on desktop computers running the Microsoft Windows operating system.

- MCSA on Microsoft Windows Server™ 2003

    The Microsoft Certified Systems Administrator (MCSA) certification is designed for professionals who implement, manage, and troubleshoot existing network and system environments based on the Windows Server 2003 platform. Implementation responsibilities include installing and configuring parts of systems. Management responsibilities include administering and supporting systems.

- MCSE on Windows Server 2003

  The Microsoft Certified Systems Engineer (MCSE) credential is the premier certification for professionals who analyze business requirements and design and implement the infrastructure for business solutions based on the Windows Server 2003 platform. Implementation responsibilities include installing, configuring, and troubleshooting network systems.

- MCAD

  The Microsoft Certified Application Developer (MCAD) for Microsoft .NET credential is appropriate for professionals who use Microsoft technologies to develop and maintain department-level applications, components, Web or desktop clients, or back-end data services, or work in teams developing enterprise applications. The credential covers job tasks ranging from developing to deploying and maintaining these solutions.

- MCSD

  The Microsoft Certified Solution Developer (MCSD) credential is the premier certification for professionals who design and develop leading-edge business solutions with Microsoft development tools, technologies, platforms, and the Microsoft Windows DNA (Digital Network Architecture) architecture. The types of applications MCSDs can develop include desktop applications and multi-user, Web-based, N-tier, and transaction-based applications. The credential covers job tasks ranging from analyzing business requirements to maintaining solutions.

- MCDBA on Microsoft SQL Server™ 2000

  The Microsoft Certified Database Administrator (MCDBA) credential is the premier certification for professionals who implement and administer Microsoft SQL Server databases. The certification is appropriate for individuals who derive physical database designs, develop logical data models, create physical databases, create data services by using Transact-SQL, manage and maintain databases, configure and manage security, monitor and optimize databases, and install and configure SQL Server.

- MCP

  The Microsoft Certified Professional (MCP) credential is for individuals who have the skills to successfully implement a Microsoft product or technology as part of a business solution in an organization. Hands-on experience with the product is necessary to successfully achieve certification.

- MCT

  Microsoft Certified Trainers (MCTs) demonstrate the instructional and technical skills that qualify them to deliver Official Microsoft Learning Products through a Microsoft Certified Partner for Learning Solutions.

Certification requirements

The certification requirements differ for each certification category and are specific to the products and job functions addressed by the certification. To become a Microsoft Certified Professional, you must pass rigorous certification exams that provide a valid and reliable measure of technical proficiency and expertise.

For More Information   See the Microsoft Learning Web site at http://www.microsoft.com/learning/.

You can also send e-mail to mcphelp@microsoft.com if you have specific certification questions.

Acquiring the skills tested by an MCP exam

Official Microsoft Learning Products can help you develop the skills that you need to do your job. They also complement the experience that you gain while working with Microsoft products and technologies. However, no one-to-one correlation exists between Official Microsoft Learning Products and MCP exams. Microsoft does not expect or intend for the courses to be the sole preparation method for passing MCP exams. Practical product knowledge and experience is also necessary to pass MCP exams.

To help prepare for MCP exams, use the preparation guides are available for each exam. Each Exam Preparation Guide contains exam-specific information such as a list of topics on which you will be tested. These guides are available on the Microsoft Learning Web site at http://www.microsoft.com/learning/.

Facilities

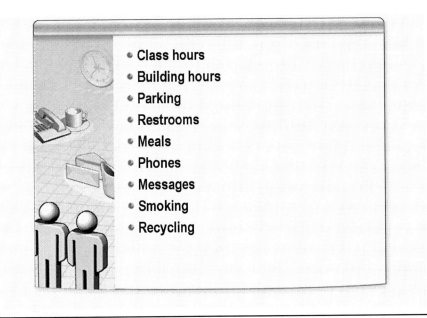

Microsoft®

Module 1: Introduction to Supporting Users Running Applications on Windows XP

Contents

Overview

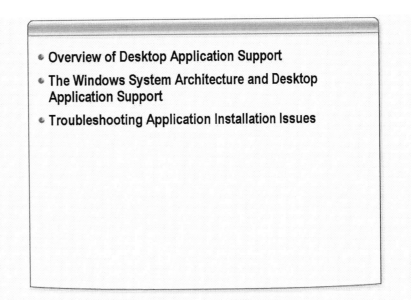

* Overview of Desktop Application Support
* The Windows System Architecture and Desktop Application Support
* Troubleshooting Application Installation Issues

Introduction

This module introduces you to desktop application support and teaches you how to best support end users running Microsoft® Windows® XP Professional in a corporate environment and Microsoft Windows XP Home Edition in a home or business environment. The module begins by describing the role of the desktop support technician (DST) in supporting users running applications on Windows XP and explains the skills required to be a successful DST. Finally, this module describes the tools you will use in this course to troubleshoot issues related to applications. At the end of this module, you should have a basic understanding of the skills and knowledge necessary to become a successful DST for applications running on Windows XP–based desktops.

Objectives

After completing this module, you will be able to:

- Describe the role of the DST in application support and the tools available for troubleshooting applications.

- Explain the importance of the Windows system architecture as it relates to troubleshooting applications running on Windows XP.

- Troubleshoot application installation issues.

Lesson: Overview of Desktop Application Support

* The Role of the DST in Desktop Application Support
* Skills Required for Desktop Application Support
* Key Terms and Definitions in Desktop Application Support
* Tools for Desktop Application Support

Introduction

In general, the role of the DST is to respond to users' technical questions. DSTs typically specialize in one of two areas: issues related to desktop applications or issues related to the operating system. This course focuses on supporting users running applications on Windows XP. This lesson provides an overview of desktop application support.

Lesson objectives

After completing this lesson, you will be able to:

- Describe the role of the DST in desktop application support.

- Describe the skills required to provide desktop application support.

- Explain key terms and definitions in desktop application support.

- Describe the tools available to assist in troubleshooting applications running on Windows-based desktops.

The Role of the DST in Desktop Application Support

Typical DST job duties:

✓ Performing general troubleshooting of installed applications

✓ Providing user support

✓ Installing, configuring, and upgrading applications

✓ Documenting calls and closing or escalating as required

Tier	Definition	DST
1: Help desk	Support: Categorizes and attempts to resolve issue	Yes
2: Administrator	Operational: Troubleshoots server and software	No
3: Engineer	Tactical: Analyzes and designs within a technology	No
4: Architect	Strategic: Analyzes and designs enterprises	No

Introduction

As a DST, your job is to help users be productive by troubleshooting and trying to solve issues that arise. To do this, you must understand your role in the support environment. The goal of this lesson is to describe the typical duties of a DST and to explain where DSTs fit within the technical support structure. Finally, this lesson describes how to determine when to escalate an issue.

Typical DST duties

As a DST supporting users running applications, you should be prepared to perform the following tasks:

- Perform general troubleshooting of installed applications.

- Provide user support, including listening to the user, defining and solving the problem, and educating the user on how to avoid the problem in the future.

- Install, configure, and upgrade applications.

- Document calls and close them or escalate them as required by company policy and time limits set by Service Level Agreements (SLAs). An *SLA* defines the parameters of service provided by a company to a user.

The DST within the technical support structure

Before you can understand when to escalate an issue, you must understand the technical support structure. Corporations frequently structure technical support into levels or tiers. This structure enables organizations to route requests based on the skill level of the DST and the complexity of the issue.

Organizations usually employ a three- or four-level tier in which the lowest level handles end-user issues and the highest level handles the most complex issues. For example, new requests are assigned to tier 1, where the DST categorizes the problem and attempts to resolve the issue. If the tier 1 technician cannot resolve the request, the request is escalated to tier 2. As a DST supporting users running applications, your position is located in tier 1, the help desk.

When to escalate an issue

As a DST, when a user presents you with an issue, you must quickly identify the problem and then determine if it is within the scope of your role. If it is outside the scope, you should escalate it to a higher tier. Although most companies set time limits and provide basic policies and guidelines for determining when to escalate an issue, there are times when the DST must make this determination. In general, you should escalate an issue when:

- The problem is beyond the scope of the DST's knowledge and training.
- The problem is beyond the scope of the DST's role in supporting users running applications, such as:
    - Operating system issues
    - Hardware issues
    - Server issues
- The problem is operational, such as system management and support.
- The problem is tactical, such as analyzing, designing, and implementing a technology, or performing complex troubleshooting.
- The problem is strategic, such as analyzing and designing enterprise technologies.

Skills Required for Desktop Application Support

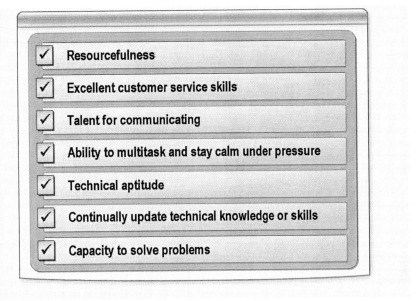

✓	**Resourcefulness**
✓	**Excellent customer service skills**
✓	**Talent for communicating**
✓	**Ability to multitask and stay calm under pressure**
✓	**Technical aptitude**
✓	**Continually update technical knowledge or skills**
✓	**Capacity to solve problems**

Introduction

Regardless of where you work or the specific responsibilities of your job, the skills you must attain as a DST involve much more than answering the phone and resolving a problem. They also involve understanding, communicating with, and pleasing the end user. You must be able to listen to a user, gather information from that user, diagnose and resolve or escalate the problem, and properly document the resolution of the problem in the manner dictated by company policy. The end user must also be satisfied with the solution and believe he or she was treated fairly and with respect. This section describes the skills necessary to succeed as a DST.

Resourcefulness

The primary skill of successful DSTs is the ability to quickly determine whether they have the answer for the user and, if not, where to find the answer. This includes determining whether they should research the issue using all resources available or escalate the issue to someone who knows the answer.

Excellent customer service skills

Successful DSTs have the ability and emotional intelligence to teach highly technical content to users with any level of experience. They can speak to any user about any problem and define that problem in terms the user can understand (without making the user feel inadequate). They have skills that any successful customer service employee has: They are polite, they are concerned for the customer, and they have a sincere desire to service the customer's needs. Beyond emotional intelligence, successful DSTs also have social intelligence, which is the ability to handle their (or others') anxieties, anger, and sadness; to be self-motivated; and to have empathy for others.

Talent for communicating

Qualified DSTs can communicate with end users of any level of experience, any personality, and any level of the corporate ladder. They can communicate technical information to nontechnical users and can acquire technical information from those who cannot explain the problem clearly. Qualified DSTs also take the time to explain in simple terms why the problem occurred, how it can be avoided in the future, and how and where to get help when no DST is available. Qualified DSTs document the problems, their communications with users, and the solutions they try, so that they can communicate even better with users the next time around.

Ability to multitask and stay calm under pressure

DSTs must deal with ongoing problems, multiple open troubleshooting tickets, deadlines for meeting SLAs, accountability to upper management and end users, and ambiguous problems. While dealing with these issues, DSTs must be able to work effectively and calmly under pressure. DSTs must also respond calmly when an end user becomes frustrated or angry, and must maintain a professional demeanor at all times.

Technical aptitude

DSTs have a natural aptitude for computers and software, and for configuring both. They enjoy working with technology, they have workstations at home at which they troubleshoot problems in their spare time, they welcome new technology, and they show a talent for visualizing how applications work and how to resolve various problems. Having the ability to visualize an issue is the first step to becoming an expert in your field.

Willingness to continually update technical knowledge or skills

DSTs are not necessarily required to have in-depth knowledge of an application, but they must have a basic understanding of the concepts involved with the pieces of the software, how the pieces work together, and common issues associated with the application.

Capacity to solve problems

Talented DSTs have the capacity to solve problems quickly. They are good at solving logic problems, operating mentally within the abstract, uncovering hidden clues, chasing leads, and discovering and attempting solutions without complicating the problem further. Communication and linear and logical troubleshooting abilities are skills employers look for. Technical skills can be taught much more easily than these skills, which have more to do with overall intelligence, personality, and social abilities than technical skills do. You must strive to develop your critical-thinking and problem-solving skills. The capacity to solve problems can be improved through training, experience, trial and error, observation, and working with higher-level DSTs.

Key Terms and Definitions in Desktop Application Support

Key term	Definition
Application	A program that performs specific tasks
Command line	The UI to a computer's operating system
DLL	A library of small programs that can be used by larger programs to communicate with a device
Escalation	The process of raising an issue to a higher level
Operating system	The software that performs fundamental tasks
Registry	A database of user and system settings
SLA	A contract that guarantees a level of service
Troubleshooting	The process of diagnosing and correcting an issue

Terms and definitions

Before you can support users running applications on Windows XP, you must understand the key terms described in the following table.

Key term	Definition
Application	A program, such as a word processor, spreadsheet, or database that performs a specific set of tasks.
Command line	The user interface (UI) to a computer's operating system, in which a command is typed, a response is received, another command is typed, and so on. The Windows command line enables a DST to quickly access troubleshooting tools and utilities. To access the command line, click **Start**, and then click **Run**. In the **Open** box, type **cmd** and then click **OK**.
Dynamic-link library (DLL)	A library of small programs that can be used by larger programs to communicate with a device such as a printer or a scanner.
Escalation	The process of raising an issue that cannot be resolved by a first-level DST to a higher-level support technician who has more experience with the problem.
Operating system	The software that performs fundamental tasks, such as maintaining files, running applications, and managing devices.
Registry	A database of user and system settings maintained by Windows. The registry is generally not meant to be modified.

(*continued*)

Key term	Definition
Service Level Agreement (SLA)	A contract between a customer and a company that identifies and commits the company to a required level of service. For example, an SLA usually identifies the type and level of service and support. From a support standpoint, it is very important to understand a customer's SLA. If an issue is not covered in the SLA, it is not the DST's responsibility to fix it. This does not mean that the issue can be rejected; instead, it means that you have a clear set of limits as to how far you can go to support the customer.
Troubleshooting	The process whereby a problem is diagnosed and corrected.

Tools for Desktop Application Support

Category	Tools	
Information-gathering	• Windows Task Manager • DirectX • Dependency Walker • System Information	• System Information in Help • Registry Editor
Debugging	• Online Crash Analysis • System Configuration Utility	• Dr. Watson • Error Reporting
Performance	• Device Manager • Performance Console • Memory Pool Monitor	
Application compatibility	• Program Compatibility Wizard • Windows Application Compatibility Toolkit	

Introduction

Windows XP Professional includes a number of tools that you can use to diagnose and troubleshoot applications. This section introduces the tools used in this course, categorized according to use.

Information-gathering tools

The following table lists the Windows XP information-gathering tools and where to access them.

Tool	Description	How to access
Windows Task Manager	View information about computer performance and details about programs and processes running on the computer.	Right-click an empty space on the taskbar, and then click **Task Manager**.
Microsoft DirectX®	View information about installed components and drivers. Test sound and graphics.	At the command prompt, type **dxdiag** and then press ENTER.
Dependency Walker	Examine a selected application or software component and determine the modules required to start it.	Download from http://support.microsoft.com.
System Information	View computer configuration information.	At the command prompt, type **systeminfo** and then press ENTER.
System Information in Help	Collect and display system information about hardware, system components, and software.	Click **Start**, and then click **Run**. In the **Open** box, type **msinfo32** and then click **OK**.
Registry Editor	Search, view, and edit contents of the registry.	At the command prompt, type **regedit** and then press ENTER.

Debugging tools

The following table lists the Windows XP debugging tools and where to access them.

Tool	Description	How to access
Online Crash Analysis	Sends kernel memory dump files to a Web site hosted by Microsoft for analysis. Searches database of known issues for matching issues.	Browse to http://oca.microsoft.com/en/windiag.asp.
System Configuration Utility	Enables or disables various settings for troubleshooting and diagnostic purposes.	Click **Start**, and then click **Run**. In the **Open** box, type **msconfig** and then click **OK**.
Dr. Watson	Detects information about system and program failures and records the information in a log file.	Click **Start**, and then click **Run**. In the **Open** box, type **drwtsn32** and then click **OK**.
Error Reporting	Monitors the system for problems that affect applications and components. When a problem occurs, you can send a report to Microsoft. Searches the database for matching conditions and responds with troubleshooting information.	In Control Panel, click **Performance and Maintenance**, and then click **System**. In the **System Properties** dialog box, on the **Advanced** tab, click **Error Reporting**.

Performance tools

The following table lists the Windows XP performance tools and where to access them.

Tool	Description	How to access
Device Manager	Provides graphical information about how a computer's hardware is installed and configured, and how the hardware interacts with the computer's software.	Right-click **My Computer**, click **Manage**, and then click **Device Manager**.
Performance Console	Provides data useful for detecting and diagnosing bottlenecks and changes in overall system performance.	At the command prompt, type **Perfmon** and then press ENTER.
Memory Pool Monitor	Detects and analyzes memory leaks.	Click **Start**, click **Help and Support**, click **Help and Support Resources**, click **Tools**, and then click **Windows Support Tools**.

Application compatibility tools

The following table lists the Windows XP application compatibility tools and where to access them.

Tool	Description	How to access
Program Compatibility Wizard	Test and resolve compatibility problems on running programs that worked correctly on earlier versions of Windows.	Click **Start**, point to **All Programs**, point to **Accessories**, and then click **Program Compatibility Wizard**.
Windows Application Compatibility Toolkit	Locate and solve application compatibility problems. The toolkit includes Microsoft Application Compatibility Analyzer, Windows Application Verifier, and Compatibility Administrator.	Download from http://msdn.microsoft.com/compatibility.

Practice: Installing Desktop Application Support Tools

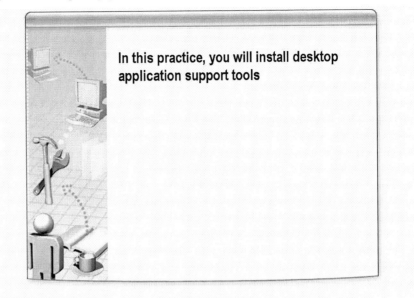

In this practice, you will install desktop application support tools

Objective

In this practice, you will install Windows desktop application support tools.

Scenario

You have been gathering a list of Web sites to help users with their problems. To prepare for user calls, you want to make sure that you can quickly access the Web sites in an organized manner.

Practice

Working with your classmates, develop a master list of support tools that each of you can take away from this course.

▶ **Install desktop application support tools**

1. Start the 2262_Bonn virtual machine, and log on locally as **Administrator** with the password **P@ssw0rd**.

2. Browse to C:\Program Files\Microsoft Learning\2262\Practices\ Mod01\Tools, and then double-click **SUPTOOLS**.

3. On the **Welcome to the Windows Support Tools Setup Wizard** page, click **Next**.

4. On the **End User License Agreement** page, click **I Agree**, and then click **Next**.

5. On the **User Information** page, click **Next**.

6. On the **Select An Installation Type** page, click **Complete**, and then click **Next**.

7. On the **Destination Directory** page, click **Install Now**.

8. On the **Completing the Windows Support Tools Setup Wizard** page, click **Finish**.

9. To view a list of the Windows support tools, click **Start**, point to **All Programs**, point to **Windows Support Tools**, and then click **Support Tools Help**.

10. Close all windows, log off, and then pause Bonn.

Lesson: The Windows System Architecture and Desktop Application Support

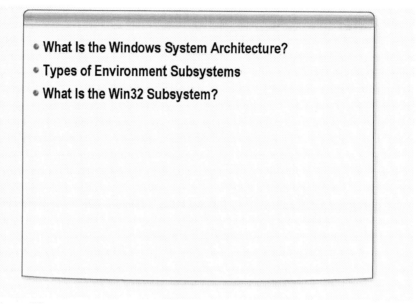

* What Is the Windows System Architecture?
* Types of Environment Subsystems
* What Is the Win32 Subsystem?

Introduction

Windows XP is built upon the foundation of Microsoft Windows NT®, in which the operating system and applications do not directly interact. This means that if an application ceases to function properly, it has little to no chance of interfering with the operating system and its services. Understanding the basics of the Windows system architecture will help you to better troubleshoot issues related to applications. This lesson provides an overview of the Windows XP architecture and explains its relevance to application support.

Lesson objectives

After completing this lesson, you will be able to:

- Explain the Windows system architecture and its relevance to troubleshooting applications.
- List the environment subsystems in the Windows system architecture and their relevance to troubleshooting applications.
- Describe the Microsoft Win32® subsystem and its relevance to troubleshooting applications.

What Is the Windows System Architecture?

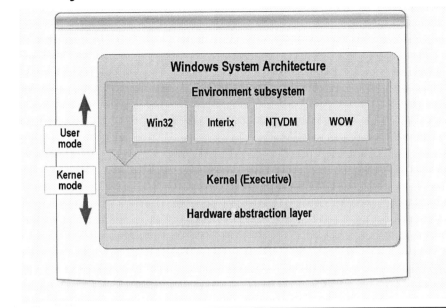

Introduction

This section describes the layers that make up the Windows XP architecture.

Hardware abstraction layer

The *hardware abstraction layer* (HAL) is a thin layer of software provided by the hardware manufacturer that hides, or abstracts, hardware differences from higher layers of the operating system. By means of the filter provided by the HAL, different types of hardware look alike to the rest of the operating system. This enables the operating system to be portable from one hardware platform to another. The HAL also provides routines that enable a single device driver to support the same device on all platforms.

Kernel

The *kernel* (also known as the executive) is the core of the layered architecture. The kernel manages the most basic operations of the operating system and the computer's processor. The kernel runs in *kernel mode*, which is the highly privileged mode of operations in which program code has direct access to all memory, including the address spaces of all user-mode processes and applications, and to hardware.

Environment subsystems

Environment subsystems enable applications written for different operating systems to run seamlessly on Windows XP. The Windows subsystem and the applications that run within it are *user-mode processes*; they do not have direct access to hardware or device drivers. User-mode processes run at a lower priority than kernel-mode processes. When the operating system needs more memory, it can *page* (or swap) to disk the memory that is used by user-mode processes.

Note Environment subsystems and Win32 are discussed in the following sections.

Types of Environment Subsystems

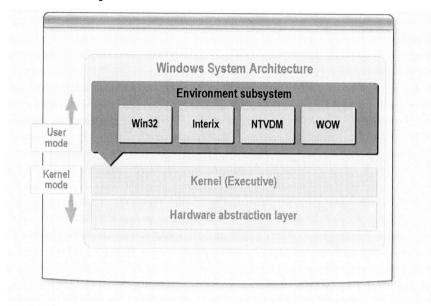

Introduction	Environment subsystems build on the services in the executive to produce environments that meet the specific needs of client applications. Implementing common operating system functions once (in the executive) and then separating the functions from environment-specific features (in the environment subsystems) reduces the effort required to develop new environment subsystems and makes it easier to maintain them.

Applications and environment subsystems have a client/server relationship. The subsystems (servers) provide services that applications (clients) utilize. Clients and servers communicate using messages that they send using the executive. |
| **Win32** | The Win32 subsystem is responsible for a large portion of Windows operations. In fact, the Win32 subsystem is really the main subsystem, for the following reasons:

■ Other subsystems use services provided by the Win32 subsystem.

■ The Win32 subsystem is the primary interface to the Executive Services from any applications. (The *Executive Services* are the common services available to all other components of the system.) |
| **Interix** | Interix provides both the tools and the application programming interface (API) libraries for porting applications to Windows XP Professional or Microsoft Windows 2000 Server. Inherent differences between UNIX variants require appropriate source code changes and recompilations. Interix minimizes these porting difficulties by using POSIX 1 and 2 specifications and tools, as well as a large number of UNIX programming interfaces. Interix enables you to either retain the original UNIX user interface for ported applications, or adapt the applications to use the Windows user interface. |

NTVDM

Windows NT Virtual DOS Machine (NTVDM) provides a simulated environment that supports MS-DOS®-based and Win16 applications. (*Virtual [MS-] DOS machines* [VDM] are special Win32 applications that provide MS-DOS and Win16 applications with an environment that looks like native MS-DOS.) NTVDM runs as a separate process on top of the existing operating system.

When you launch an MS-DOS-based application in Windows XP, the operating system creates a new NTVDM for that application. Each time you start another MS-DOS-based application, the operating system creates an additional NTVDM. Each NTVDM operates independently, with a single thread and its own address space.

WOW

Windows on Windows (WOW) is a Windows program that enables Win16 applications to run on 32-bit operating systems. WOW operates in the context of the NTVDM.

Subsystems used by MS-DOS-based and Win-16 applications

MS-DOS-based and 16-bit applications (Win16 applications) are not supported by their own environment subsystems running in separate user-mode processes. Instead, Win16 applications are supported by VDMs.

For MS-DOS applications, an NTVDM is created, and all calls by the application are translated by the NTVDM and passed along to the Win32 subsystem. Each MS-DOS application runs in a separate NTVDM.

All 16-bit Windows-based applications run in a single virtual machine. (A *virtual machine* is a self-contained operating environment that behaves as if it were a separate computer.) This can be problematic, because if a 16-bit application stops responding, it can potentially cause all other 16-bit Windows-based applications to fail as well.

The Win16-on-Win32 (WOW) shell is also run from an NTVDM. Many older Windows-based applications are designed to work with other Windows-based applications, but at the same time, they need a specific address space. As a result, there can be problems running multiple Win16 applications simultaneously. In this case, you can configure each Win16 application to run in its own memory address space.

When you launch a Win16 application in Windows XP, the operating system creates a new NTVDM. When you start additional Win16 applications after this, each of these applications will run in the same NTVDM.

What Is the Win32 Subsystem?

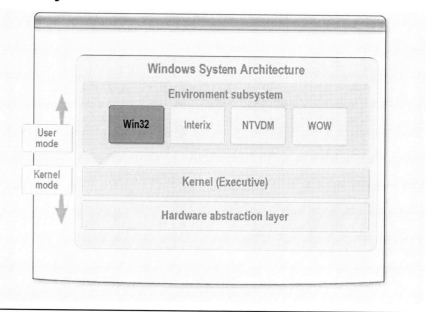

Introduction

The Win32 subsystem is responsible for the main components of what we generally think of as "Windows"—the kernel, the GDI (Graphics Device Interface), and USER. (USER.exe is the program that controls user interaction for Windows.) Together, these components handle user interaction from the keyboard and the mouse and how information is displayed to the user. These components also keep the system secure by interacting with the security functions of the operating system.

Applications

As discussed earlier, the ring structure prevents an application from having direct access to either the hardware or the kernel. To obtain this access, applications must communicate with the Win32 subsystem to request read/write access or hardware access.

When an application requests to write to the hard drive, that request is sent to the Win32 subsystem, which then passes that request along to the Executive Services. From there, the request is sent along to the kernel, and then is finally sent to the HAL.

The ring structure has definite ramifications for application support. For example, because applications are not permitted direct access to the hardware, if the user installs an older application—perhaps one that requires access to the video card—that application will either not work at all or will not work correctly.

Practice: Examining Environment Subsystems

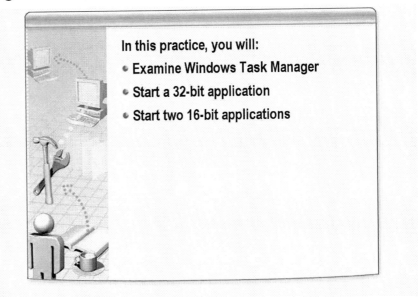

Objective

In this practice, you will examine environment subsystems. You will start a 16-bit application and a 32-bit application and examine how Windows accommodates each type of application.

Practice

▶ **Examine Windows Task Manager**

1. Resume the 2262_Bonn virtual machine.

2. Using the 2262_Bonn virtual machine, log on locally as **Administrator** with the password **P@ssw0rd**.

3. Click **Start** and then click **Run**. In the **Open** box, type **taskmgr** and then click **OK**.

4. Examine the information on the **Processes** tab to answer the following questions:

   a. How many processes are running?

   _20_

   b. In the **Image name** column, locate wowexec.exe and ntvdm.exe. Are they present in the list of processes? Why not?

   Because no Win16 or MS-DOS programs
   are running.

▶ **Start a 32-bit application**

1. Click **Start**, and then click **Run**. In the **Open** box, type **sol** and then click **OK**.

2. In Windows Task Manager, locate sol.exe.

3. Examine the information on the **Processes** tab to answer the following questions:

   a. How many processes are running?

   _n2_

   b. In the **Image Name** column, locate wowexec.exe and ntvdm.exe. Are they present in the list of processes?

   _No_

▶ **Start two 16-bit applications**

1. Click **Start**, and then click **Run**. In the **Open** box, type **sysedit** and then click **OK**.

2. Click **Start**, and then click **Run**. In the **Open** box, type **drwatson** and then click **OK**.

3. In Windows Task Manager, on the **Processes** tab, locate sysedit.exe and drwatson.exe.

4. Examine the information on the **Processes** tab to answer the following questions:

   a. In the **Image Name** column, locate wowexec.exe and ntvdm.exe. Are they present in the list of processes?

   YES

   b. How many processes are running? Did the number of processes increase as you expected? Why or why not?

   25 yes, because more programs are running

5. Close all windows, log off, and then pause Bonn.

Lesson: Troubleshooting Application Installation Issues

- The Application Installation Process
- System Changes Resulting from an Application Installation
- What Is the Registry?
- Common Causes of Application Installation Issues
- Tools for Troubleshooting Application Installation Issues
- Guidelines for Troubleshooting Application Installation Issues

Introduction

This lesson introduces the details of the application installation process and the changes that occur to a computer as a result of that installation.

Lesson objectives

After completing this lesson, you will be able to:

- Explain the application installation process.
- Describe changes to a computer resulting from the installation of an application.
- Describe the purpose and function of the registry in terms of application customization.
- List the common causes of application installation issues.
- List the tools for troubleshooting application installations.
- Apply guidelines for troubleshooting application installation issues.

The Application Installation Process

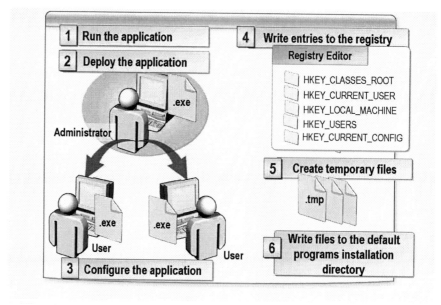

Application Installation

The exact sequence of events that occur in Windows XP when an application is installed is dictated by the developers of the application. Most applications are installed using the same general steps. This section describes this process.

Step 1: Run the application

Run the application by using Windows Installer or an executable. Windows Installer is a Windows XP component that simplifies the application installation process. It manages the installation and removal of applications by applying a set of centrally defined setup rules during the installation process. These setup rules define the installation and configuration of the installed application. You can also use this service to modify, repair, or remove an existing application. The Windows Installer technology consists of the Windows Installer service for the Windows operating systems and the package (.msi) file format used to hold information regarding the application setup and installation.

Windows Installer also manages the installation, addition, and deletion of software components; monitors file resiliency; and maintains basic disaster recovery with rollbacks. Windows Installer supports installing and running software from multiple sources, and can be customized by developers who want to install custom applications.

Step 2: Deploy the application

After the application is run, it is deployed by using Systems Management Server (SMS) or the Microsoft Active Directory® directory service.

Step 3: Configure the application

Ask the user configuration questions, or read parameters from a text file. This is how an unattended installation proceeds.

Step 4: Write entries to the registry

Write entries to the registry, typically to the **HKLM (HKEY_LOCAL_MACHINE)** or the **HKCU (HKEY_CURRENT_USER)** keys.

Step 5: Create temporary files

Copy DLL files to the default System32 directory (%systemroot%\system32).

Step 6: Write files to the programs directory

Finally, write the files to the default programs installation directory (C:\ProgramFiles).

System Changes Resulting from an Application Installation

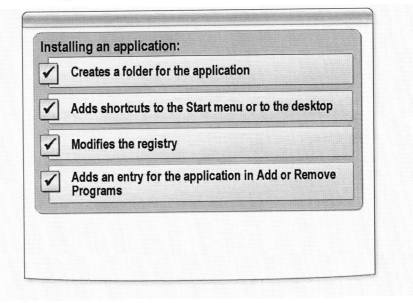

System changes

The application installation process can cause major changes to an operating system. Typically, when an application is installed, it makes the following system changes:

- Creates a folder for the application
- Adds shortcuts to the **Start** menu or to the desktop
- Modifies the registry
- Adds an entry for the application in Add or Remove Programs

What Is the Registry?

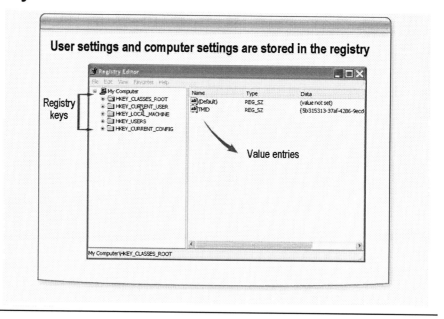

Introduction

After an application is installed, most users want to customize the application for their specific needs. The customization choices that are available to a user are determined by a variety of factors, including the user's permission level, whether the user is the owner of a particular file, and whether the user's computer is a part of a network or a domain.

Regardless of the actual customization choices that are available to users, all user settings and computer settings are stored in the registry. Although you will rarely need to make changes to the registry, it is important that you understand its function.

Definition

Windows stores its configuration information in a database called the *registry*. The registry contains profiles for each user of the computer, and information about system hardware, installed programs, and property settings. Windows continually references this information during its operation.

Registry Editors are available that enable you to inspect and modify the registry. However, you should not need to do so. Instead, allow Windows-based applications to modify the system registry as needed.

For example, if a user makes a change to the system, such as changing the screen resolution, that information is written to the **HKEY_CURRENT_USER** key in the registry. As a result, the next time the user logs on to that computer, the setting is retained. If someone else then logs on to the computer and also changes the screen resolution, that information is retained for that user.

Warning   Incorrectly editing the registry may severely damage the operating system. At the very least, you should back up any valued data on the computer before making changes to the registry.

How the registry is organized

The registry is organized hierarchically as a tree and is made up of the following components:

- *Key*. A folder that appears in the left pane of the Registry Editor window. A key can contain sub-keys and value entries.

- *Hive*. A section of the registry that appears as a file on the hard disk. A hive is a discrete body of keys, sub-keys, and values that is rooted at the top of the registry hierarchy. A hive is backed by a single file and a .log file, which are both located in the *systemroot*\System32\Config or in the *systemroot*\Profiles\username folders. By default, most hive files are stored in the *systemroot*\System32\Config folder. The *systemroot*\Profiles\username folder contains the user profile for each user of the computer.

- *Value entry*. The string of data that appears in the right pane of the Registry Editor window. The value entry defines the value of the currently selected key. A value entry has three parts: name, data type, and the value itself.

Types of registry keys

The following table lists the five keys in the registry.

Registry Key	Description
HKEY_CLASSES_ROOT	This key is where data on DLL files and applications is stored.
HKEY_CURRENT_USER	This key is where the current user's individual customizations are stored and tracked.
HKEY_LOCAL_MACHINE	This key contains information about all of the software installed on the computer. Virtually anything that the operating system might need to know about a particular application is stored here.
HKEY_USERS	This key is where all user data is stored. If multiple people use the same computer, all their user profiles are stored here. When a user logs on to the computer, the data is written to **HKEY_CURRENT_USER**.
HKEY_CURRENT_CONFIG	This key points to the current computer hardware configuration in the collection of configurations stored in **HKEY_LOCAL_MACHINE**. This enables the use of multiple computer hardware profiles.

Using the Registry Editor

An advanced user who is prepared to both edit and restore the registry can safely use the Registry Editor for such tasks as deleting entries for applications that have been uninstalled or deleted.

Note For more detailed information regarding the Windows Registry, see Knowledge Base (KB) article 256986.

Common Causes of Application Installation Issues

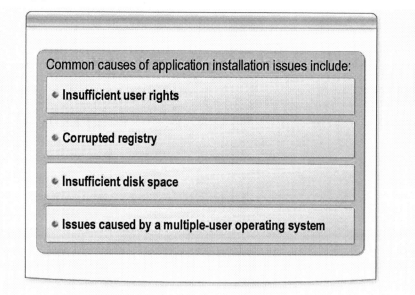

Common causes of application installation issues include:

- Insufficient user rights
- Corrupted registry
- Insufficient disk space
- Issues caused by a multiple-user operating system

Introduction

There are several common causes of application installation issues. As a DST, being aware of these common causes will help you to more quickly identify and solve a user's problem when the user is having trouble installing an application.

Insufficient user rights

Depending on the operating system, the user may have insufficient privileges to install an application. In Windows XP Professional, a user must either have administrative privileges or have a user profile with sufficient privileges to install applications to the hard drive. With Windows XP Home Edition, user accounts by default have Administrator privileges. Unless someone with Administrator privileges changes the other user accounts on the computer, this should not be an issue.

Corrupted registry

If the user has previously tried to install an application and had an unsuccessful installation, a further attempt can generate a corrupted registry, which in turn will prevent a successful installation.

Note For a description of this error as it pertains to Microsoft Internet Explorer, see KB article 221863.

Insufficient disk space

Many applications require not only enough disk space for program files, but also a large amount of space for temporary file creation during the installation process. Additionally, an application may require that the extra disk space be on the boot drive, even if the application itself is being installed to a different drive.

Issues caused by a multiple-user operating system

In addition to the user-rights issues mentioned above, there are other areas of particular concern to multiple-user operating systems. For example, security can be a consideration. If insufficient attention is paid to user privileges, all users may not have access to the application or users may be able to install an application and then find that they cannot actually run the application.

Windows XP includes a feature called Fast User Switching. This feature permits a user to "switch out" of a session without logging off of the computer. With multiple users all logged on to the same computer, resource problems can occur, particularly if an application installation happens to be running at the same time that other users are either trying to run the same installation application, or if so many other applications are running that there are no resources left for the install routine.

Tools for Troubleshooting Application Installation Issues

Category	Tools
General troubleshooting	• Programming Compatibility Wizard • Defragmentation tools • Knowledge Base • Microsoft Help and Support Center
Advanced troubleshooting	• Registry Editor • Safe mode • File Signature Verification
Debugging	• Dr. Watson • Setup switches and log files

Introduction

Windows XP Professional includes a wide variety of tools for troubleshooting application installation issues. The tools discussed in this section are particularly helpful to a DST.

General troubleshooting tools

The following tools are useful for troubleshooting issues related to applications:

■ *Program Compatibility Wizard.* Though most Windows-based applications install on any version of Windows, they may not run in the most efficient manner on every version. For example, while a 16-bit Windows 95 application will run on a computer running Windows XP Professional, it will not run as efficiently as it would on a computer running Windows 95. For this and similar situations, there is a Program Compatibility Wizard within Windows XP Professional and Windows XP Home Edition. The purpose of this six-step wizard is to improve how older applications run on later versions of Windows. The Program Compatibility Wizard is also useful for configuring MS-DOS-based applications to run more efficiently in Windows.

You can start the wizard from the Accessories folder on the **Start** menu. You can also access the wizard from Help and Support on the **Start** menu or by typing **hcp://system/compatctr/compatmode.htm** in the **Run** dialog box.

Important For additional information about the Program Compatibility Wizard, see KB articles 301911 and 292533.

- *Defragmentation tools.* Defragmentation is the process of rewriting parts of a file to contiguous sectors on a hard disk to increase the speed of access and retrieval. Windows XP Professional includes two methods for defragmenting volumes: the Disk Defragmenter snap-in (Dfrg.msc) and the Disk Defragmenter command-line tool (Defrag.exe). Both defragmentation tools rearrange files, folders, and programs so that they occupy contiguous space on the hard disk. The tools also reorder free space, moving it into a contiguous block at the end of each volume. As a result, the operating system can write files to the hard disk sequentially more often, which improves performance. You must be logged on as an administrator or a member of the Administrators group to use the defragmentation tools. Keep in mind that defragmentation tools take significant time to process. To start the Disk Defragmenter snap-in, at the command prompt, type **dfrg.exe** and then press ENTER. To start the Disk Defragmenter command-line tool, at the command prompt, type **defrag** and then press ENTER.

- *Knowledge Base.* The Knowledge Base (KB) contains thousands of technical articles, white papers, and case histories. When your user calls with a question about running applications on a computer running Windows XP, you can most likely find a document related to the issue in the KB.

- *Microsoft Help and Support Center.* This site provides comprehensive resources for practical advice, tutorials, and demonstrations on using Windows XP. You can use various services and perform important support tasks. Help and Support is useful for troubleshooting application-related issues because it enables you to:

  - Help users over the Internet by using Remote Assistance.

  - Research software that is compatible with Windows XP.

  - Get help online from a support professional by using Microsoft Online Assisted Support.

  - Stay current with the latest support information and Help news from sources such as Microsoft Product Support Services.

Advanced troubleshooting tools

The following advanced tools are useful for troubleshooting issues related to applications:

- *Registry Editor.* Advanced users can use the Registry Editor, Regedit.exe, to view or change system settings. Editing the registry directly is seldom required, and using the Registry Editor is typically a last-resort option. Use caution when editing the registry, because specifying incorrect values can cause instability. The Registry Editor is intended for advanced users who are familiar with registry concepts and want to configure settings for which a UI does not exist. However, because the articles in the Knowledge Base often refer to using the Registry Editor, it important that you are familiar with this tool and how it can be used.

Warning Incorrect use of the Registry Editor can cause the Windows operating system to stop functioning.

- *Safe mode.* Safe mode is a method of starting Windows when a problem prevents the operating system from starting normally. Safe mode allows you to troubleshoot the operating system to determine what is not functioning properly. For example, standard safe-mode troubleshooting procedures can detect and correct user profile issues that are associated with applications that launch at startup.

  In safe mode, you have access to only basic files and drivers (mouse, monitor, keyboard, mass storage, base video, and default system services), and no network connections. You can choose the Safe Mode with Networking option, which loads all of the above files and drivers and the essential services and drivers to start networking, or you can choose the Safe Mode with Command Prompt option, which is exactly the same as safe mode except that a command prompt is started instead of the graphical user interface. You can also choose Last Known Good Configuration, which starts your computer using the registry information that was saved at the last shutdown.

- *File Signature Verification.* When installing new software on a computer, system files and device driver files are sometimes overwritten by unsigned or incompatible versions, causing system instability. The system files and device driver files provided with Windows XP have a Microsoft digital signature, which indicates that the files are original, unaltered system files or that they have been approved by Microsoft for use with Windows. You can use File Signature Verification to identify unsigned files on your computer and view the following information about them: file name, file location, file modification date, file type, and file version number. To access File Signature Verification, click **Start** and then click **Run**. In the **Open** box, type **sigverif** and then click **OK**.

Debugging tools

The following debugging tools are useful for troubleshooting issues related to applications:

- *Dr. Watson.* Dr. Watson is a program error debugger. In the event of an application error, also known as a user-mode program exception, Dr. Watson writes information to a text-based log file named DrWtsn32.log in *systemdrive*\Documents and Settings\All Users\Application Data\ Microsoft\DrWatson (default folder location). This log contains the following information:

  - The file name of the program that caused the error

  - Information about the computer and user under which the error occurred

  - A list of programs and services active when the error occurred

  - A list of modules such as DLLs that were in memory when the error occurred

  - Information useful for diagnosing a program error for a computer running Windows

- *Setup switches and log files.* Many applications, including all versions of Microsoft Office, have a series of switches available for use with the setup program. Setup switches can be used for unattended installations and to specify alternate setup locations. Log files are useful for determining the cause of application-related problems.

Guidelines for Troubleshooting Application Installation Issues

- ✔ Apply a troubleshooting strategy
- ✔ Define the problem
- ✔ Use available resources to locate information
- ✔ Use sound troubleshooting techniques
- ✔ Follow general guidelines

Introduction

Troubleshooting is a skill in which problems are efficiently solved through a concise and well-planned series of steps. This applies to any kind of problem, from tying a shoelace, to piloting an airplane, to resolving computer problems. When approaching a user's application installation issue, use the following guidelines to move toward a resolution.

Apply a troubleshooting strategy

A sound troubleshooting strategy combines process, knowledge, and experience. A successful troubleshooter must:

- Understand the capabilities of the supported products.
- Know how to use the products.
- Have experience with a variety of problems associated with the products.
- Know when and where to seek answers from other sources.
- Have a healthy sense of curiosity and skepticism.

Often, a false premise builds upon itself. Starting out with a poorly developed troubleshooting strategy can result in prolonging the knowledge-acquisition process and even act to solidify poor troubleshooting habits. Conversely, correct knowledge also builds upon itself. This is why it is best to develop a sound troubleshooting strategy early in your career as a DST.

Define the problem

The first step in troubleshooting an issue is to gather enough information to define the problem. This requires skillful questioning of the user. It also requires skillful listening. After you have enough information, you can define the problem—though be prepared to backtrack if it turns out that you were premature in defining the problem.

Use available resources to locate information

Because a DST cannot know everything about computers and the applications that run on them, the ability to know how and where to locate the information to resolve an issue is an essential skill. Fortunately, there are many resources available to the DST. Key resources include:

- *Online Help and Support*. The Help system packaged with the operating system is an excellent resource, often overlooked.

- *The Microsoft Knowledge Base (KB)*. This database contains thousands of articles detailing resolutions to issues for nearly every Microsoft product. It is the single most useful source for retrieving information pertinent to an issue and should be the DST's primary source of information. If the KB does not contain information regarding a specific issue, it is either a new issue or the DST's perceived notion of the problem is not the actual problem and the DST may need to reevaluate the situation.

- *Microsoft TechNet*. This resource offers comprehensive help on applications, including installation, maintenance, and support. You can also access information on security, get downloads, read how-to articles, read columns, and access troubleshooting and support pages.

- *Other online resources*. Another useful resource is the Internet. You can use public search engines to search for other online resources, such as manufacturers' sites, driver sites, and newsgroups discussing information specific to a case.

The actual problem will generally dictate which of these should be your first choice. For example, with an unfamiliar problem, your first choice is probably going to be the Knowledge Base, while something you have handled numerous times is probably best served by your own experience.

Use sound troubleshooting techniques

Some of the common troubleshooting techniques include:

- *The linear approach*. A methodology that enables you to quickly determine the root cause of a problem by taking the user through a logical series of steps. Start with the problem statement, and proceed in a methodical manner until you uncover the source of the problem.

- *The subtractive approach*. In this approach, you form a mental picture of the system's components. Divide the system into two parts along a testable line. Test to see which side of the line has the problem, then continue in the same vein until you have isolated the problem component.

Follow general guidelines

Very few principles are universally applicable when it comes to troubleshooting application installations. Here are some common steps that apply to most situations:

- Close all other applications before you start the installation.

- Stop any virus programs that are running on the computer. Virus scanners can interfere with installation programs.

- Ensure that you have enough disk space before starting the installation.

- Remove all traces of any previous and/or failed installation attempts.

- Clean the CD prior to running the installation program.

Practice: Troubleshooting Application Installation Issues

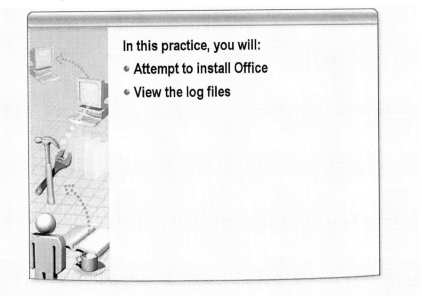

In this practice, you will:
* Attempt to install Office
* View the log files

Objective

In this practice, you will troubleshoot an application installation by analyzing application installation log files to determine the cause of a failed application installation.

To accomplish this objective, you will log on as a user and attempt to install Microsoft Office 2003 from the domain controller (London). Since this installation requires administrator privileges, the installation will fail and will generate log files that provide significant troubleshooting help. You will open these log files to identify the reason for the failure.

Practice

▶ **Attempt to install Office**

1. Resume the 2262_Bonn virtual machine.

2. Using the 2262_Bonn virtual machine, log on locally as **Samantha Smith** with the password **P@ssw0rd**.

3. In the 2262_Bonn – Microsoft Virtual PC 2004 window, on the **CD** menu, click **Capture ISO Image**.

4. In the Select CD Image to Capture window, navigate to C:\Program Files\ Microsoft Learning\2262\Drives, click **Office2003ProEval.iso** and then click **Open**.

5. Open **My Computer** and double-click the CD-ROM drive.

6. In the **Install Program As Other User** dialog box, click **Run the program as BONN\Samantha Smith**, and then click **OK**.

7. In the CD-ROM window, double-click **SETUP**.

8. In the **Install Program As Other User** dialog box, click **Run the program as BONN\Samantha Smith**, and then click **OK**.

   A dialog box appears stating the administrator has set policies to prevent this installation.

9. In the **Windows Installer** dialog box, click **OK**.

► **View the log files**

1. Click **Start**, and then click **Run**.

2. In the **Run** dialog box, type **C:\Documents and Settings\Samantha Smith\ Local Settings\Temp** and then click **OK**.

Note   The Local Settings folder is a hidden folder and will not auto-complete as you type in the Run dialog box.

---

3. In the Temp window, double-click **Microsoft Office 2003 Setup(0002).txt** to open this log file in Notepad.

4. In Notepad, scroll to the end of the log.

   Notice the line "RegCreateKeyEx returns Win32 Error == 5, Access is denied." This indicates that the user did not have adequate permissions to install the application.

5. Close Notepad.

6. In the Temp window, double-click **Microsoft Office 2003 Setup(0002)_Task(0001)** to open this file in Notepad.

7. In Notepad, at the end of the log file, notice the following information:

   - This installation is forbidden by system policy. Contact your system administrator.

   - Product: Microsoft Office Professional Edition 2003 -- Configuration failed.

8. In the 2262_Bonn – Microsoft Virtual PC 2004 window, on the CD menu, click **"Release Office2003ProEval.iso"**.

9. To close Bonn and delete changes, in the 2262_Bonn – Microsoft Virtual PC 2004 window, on the **Action** menu, click **Close**.

10. In the **Close** dialog box, select **Turn off and delete changes**, and then click **OK**.

Lab: Introduction to Supporting Users Running Applications on Windows XP

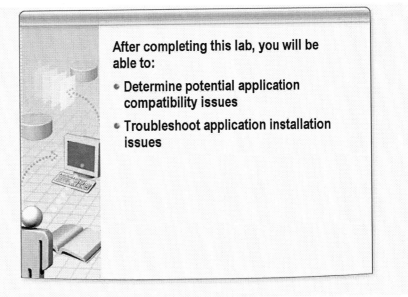

Objectives

After completing this lab, you will be able to:

- Determine potential application compatibility issues.
- Troubleshoot application installation issues.

Prerequisites

Before working on this lab, you must have an understanding of how to use Microsoft Virtual PC.

Before You Begin

For each exercise in this lab, use the password **P@ssw0rd**.

In Virtual PC, <RIGHT> ALT+DEL is the equivalent of CTRL+ALT+DEL.

Estimated time to complete this lab: 45 minutes

Exercise 1
Determining Potential Application Compatibility Issues

In this exercise, you will determine potential application compatibility issues.

Scenario

A home user calls and says she is considering purchasing an application; however, she is not sure if it will work with her existing computer configuration. The user is also concerned because the software does not indicate whether it is compatible with Windows XP. You need to ensure that the computer's processor, amount of RAM, and available hard disk space are more than adequate for the application installation, and then determine what, if any, compatibility issues the user is likely to face during application installation.

Tasks	Guidance for completing the task
1. Start the 2262_Acapulco virtual machine, and log on locally as **Administrator**.	■ Use the Virtual PC console.
2. Run the applicable tool or tools to determine the hardware resources available on the Acapulco virtual machine.	■ Refer to the section Tools for Troubleshooting Application Installation Issues and the section Tools for Desktop Application Support. ■ Successful completion of this exercise results in a text or graphic file displaying Acapulco's current RAM, total hard disk space, available hard disk space, and processor information.

Exercise 2
Troubleshooting Application Installation Issues

In this exercise, you will troubleshoot issues related to installing an application.

Scenario

Max Stevens is attempting to run a Windows application built on the .NET Framework and is receiving an error message stating the .NET Framework is not installed. Max then attempts to install the .NET Framework from the Windows XP Professional CD and receives an error message saying that he does not have permission to install the application. Max has asked you to install the .NET Framework on his computer and to explain why he is unable to do so himself.

Tasks	Guidance for completing the task
1. Start the Acapulco virtual machine, and log on locally as **Max Stevens**.	■ Use the Virtual PC console. ■ Log on to Acapulco(This Computer).
2. Reproduce the problem by running the Microsoft .NET Framework 1.1 setup program.	■ Browse to C:\Program Files\Microsoft Learning\2262\Labfiles\Lab01\ and double-click **dotnetfx**.
❓ Were you able to successfully install the application. _No, not an administrator_	
3. Resolve the application installation issue.	■ Refer to the section Guidelines for Troubleshooting Application Installations Issues. ■ Successful resolution of this issue enables Max to install the Microsoft .NET Framework.
4. Turn off the Acapulco virtual machine without saving changes.	■ To save time, you may interrupt the installation process at the License Agreement window.

Lab Discussion

After you have completed the exercises in this lab, take a moment to answer the following questions. When the entire class has finished the lab, the instructor will facilitate a lab discussion based on students' answers to these questions.

1. How did you determine the cause of the issue(s)?

2. How did you resolve the issue(s)?

3. What are some other ways the issue(s) could have been resolved?

Module 2: Troubleshooting Desktop Application Support Issues

Contents

Overview

- Troubleshooting Win32 Applications
- Troubleshooting Security Issues Related to Applications
- Troubleshooting Application Compatibility Issues
- Troubleshooting MS-DOS-Based and Win16 Applications

Introduction

As a desktop support technician (DST), you may receive calls from users who are using a variety of applications running on Microsoft® Windows® XP desktops. Some of these applications may have been designed for earlier operating systems, such as MS-DOS® or Windows 3.x.

Windows XP includes tools that enable Win32®, MS-DOS, and Win16 applications to run in these new environments. In many cases, your users may not know that they are running an earlier application. Your ability to identify these applications and potential compatibility issues with Windows XP will assist you in the troubleshooting process.

Objectives

After completing this module, you will be able to:

- Troubleshoot Win32 applications.

- Troubleshoot security issues related to applications.

- Troubleshoot application compatibility issues.

- Troubleshoot MS-DOS-based and Win16 applications.

Lesson: Troubleshooting Win32 Applications

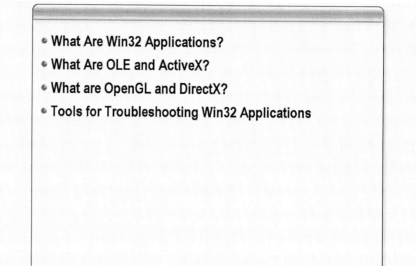

* What Are Win32 Applications?
* What Are OLE and ActiveX?
* What are OpenGL and DirectX?
* Tools for Troubleshooting Win32 Applications

Introduction

Windows 95, Windows 98, and Microsoft Windows NT® are all 32-bit operating systems that use the same Win32 application programming interface (API). Although the API has changed and expanded to encompass new features, most Win32 applications run without a problem on Windows XP. However, some Win32 applications display errors that are caused by a number of issues, such as limited memory access, outdated graphic languages, and incorrect or corrupted video and sound drivers. When you receive support calls regarding applications that are not functioning in Windows XP, your understanding of these issues will assist you in the troubleshooting process.

Objectives

After completing this lesson, you will be able to:

■ Describe the purpose and function of Win32 applications.

■ Describe the purpose and function of OLE and ActiveX®.

■ Describe the purpose and function of OpenGL and DirectX®.

■ Identify the tools for troubleshooting Win32 applications.

What Are Win32 Applications?

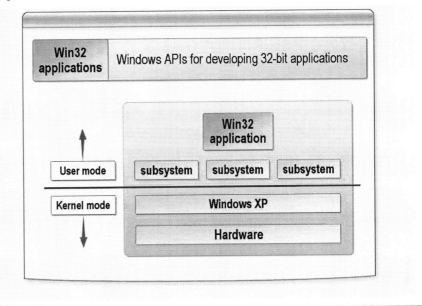

Introduction

The Windows operating system provides an *application programming interface* (API) that enables programmers to write applications that are consistent with the operating system. Win32 is the API for 32-bit Windows operating systems, which include Windows 95, Windows 98, Windows NT, and later Windows operating systems. (*32 bits* refers to the number of bits that can be processed or transmitted in parallel or the number of bits used for a single element in a data format.) When applications are written to the Win32 API, they are activating advanced functions not available from the 16-bit API (Win16).

If you use Windows 95 or later, you can run almost any Win32 application on your computer except for applications that include system-specific features that are unavailable in the operating system. For example, Windows NT provides security features that are not in Windows 95 or Windows 98; therefore, these features will not run on these two operating systems.

Windows XP provides several technologies that enable Win32-based applications to run regardless of operating system. These technologies include:

- Multithreading, to enhance system performance

- OLE and ActiveX technologies

- Open Graphics Language (OpenGL) and DirectX sets of APIs in Windows XP

Note OLE, ActiveX, OpenGL, and DirectX are discussed in more detail in the following sections.

What is multithreading?

Multithreading refers to the ability of an operating system to simultaneously run different parts of an application, called *threads*. For example, a Win32 Setup application can simultaneously run three threads:

- One that decompresses files

- One that copies files

- One that modifies the system configuration files

These threads are completely independent of each other. They run at the same time, thereby maintaining high system performance.

Win32 application reliability

Each Win32 application runs in its own 2-gigabyte (GB) address space. (An *address space* is the set of all addresses in memory for a given application.) For this reason, a Win32 application cannot corrupt the memory of another Win32 application. In other words, if one Win32 application fails, it does not affect other Win32 applications.

What Are OLE and ActiveX?

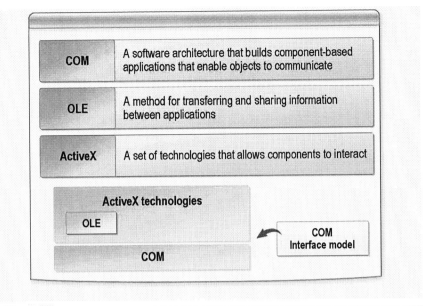

COM	A software architecture that builds component-based applications that enable objects to communicate
OLE	A method for transferring and sharing information between applications
ActiveX	A set of technologies that allows components to interact

ActiveX technologies
OLE
COM
COM Interface model

Introduction

Windows XP supports object linking and embedding (OLE) and ActiveX—two technologies that are based on the Component Object Model (COM). *COM* is a software architecture that builds component-based applications that enable *objects* (any items that can be selected or manipulated) to communicate with each other.

What is OLE?

COM is the interface model used in OLE programming. *OLE* is a method for transferring and sharing information between applications by copying information created in one application and pasting it into a document created by another application. In other words, OLE enables you to create objects using one application and then link or embed the objects in a second application. Embedded objects retain their original format and links to the application that created them. For example, if you create an OLE object in Microsoft Office Word that contains your business address, you can use the same object in Microsoft Office Excel without reentering information.

What is ActiveX?

ActiveX is a set of technologies that allows software components to interact with one another in a networked environment, regardless of the programming language in which the components were created.

Comparison of OLE and ActiveX functions and optimization

The following table compares OLE and ActiveX.

	OLE	ActiveX
Function	Provides application services, such as linking or embedding, for creation of compound documents	Enables controls to be embedded in Web sites and to respond interactively to events
Optimization	Optimized for usability and integration of desktop applications	Optimized for size and speed

What Are OpenGL and DirectX?

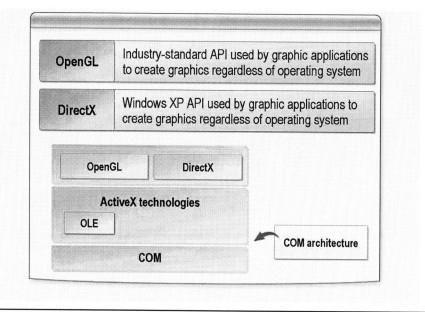

Introduction

Windows XP supports OpenGL and DirectX—two technologies that enable two-dimensional (2-D) and three-dimensional (3-D) graphics.

What is OpenGL?

OpenGL is the computer industry's software standard for producing still and animated 2-D and 3-D color graphic images. The 3-D screen savers included in Windows XP are examples of an OpenGL.

Prior to the implementation of OpenGL, developing a graphic application required rewriting the graphics portion of the application for each operating system platform. With OpenGL, an application can create the same effects in any operating system using any OpenGL-adhering graphics adapter.

Some graphics created using OpenGL use more CPU time than non-OpenGL graphics, which can negatively affect performance when they are used on a file, print, or application server.

Tip OpenGL issues are similar to DirectX issues in that they tend to be based on hardware compatibility. For example, some display drivers do not support OpenGL, so be sure to verify compatibility while troubleshooting this issue. For more information about running programs that require OpenGL support in Windows XP, refer to Microsoft Knowledge Base (KB) article 285912.

What is DirectX?

DirectX is the core technology included in Windows XP that drives high-speed multimedia and games on the computer. It provides a standard development platform for Windows-based computers by enabling software developers to access specialized hardware features without having to write hardware-specific code. This technology was first introduced in 1995 and is a recognized standard for multimedia application development on the Windows platform.

DirectX and APIs

At the core of DirectX are its APIs. The DirectX APIs allow multimedia applications to access the advanced features of high-performance hardware, such as 3-D graphics, acceleration chips, and sound cards. DirectX APIs control low-level functions, including 2-D graphics acceleration, support for input devices such as joysticks, keyboards, and mouse devices, and control of sound mixing and sound output.

Beginning with Microsoft Windows 95, DirectX has been integrated into all Windows operating systems. Later versions of Windows have included newer versions of the DirectX libraries. The current generation of Windows games and multimedia programs do not function properly without DirectX. Therefore, by design, you cannot remove DirectX.

What is the DirectX Diagnostic Tool?

Windows XP includes a utility called the DirectX Diagnostic Tool. This tool reports detailed information about the DirectX components and drivers installed on your system. It enables you to test multimedia driver compatibility and to display driver status and driver version information. You can use the tool to disable or reduce hardware acceleration levels to diagnose problems. Finally, you can use the tool to collect information that may be useful during a technical support call.

To access the DirectX Diagnostic Tool:

1. Click **Start**, and then click **Run**.

2. In the **Open** box, type **dxdiag** and then click **OK**.

Note   For more information about how to troubleshoot issues related to DirectX, refer to Frequently Asked Questions (FAQ) at http://www.microsoft.com/windows/directx/productinfo/overview/faq.asp.

For information about how to download and install DirectX, refer to KB article 179113.

Tools for Troubleshooting Win32 Applications

Tool	Use to
Dr. Watson	Diagnose program and system failures
MOCA	Determine the cause of a blue screen crash event or stop error
Windows Error Reporting	Track and address operating system and application interoperability errors
Event Viewer	View and manage event logs, monitor security events and gather information about hardware and software problems

Introduction

You can use a variety of tools to troubleshoot issues with Win32 applications. This section describes these tools: Dr. Watson, Microsoft Online Crash Analysis (MOCA), Windows Error Reporting, and Event Viewer.

What is Dr. Watson?

Dr. Watson is a program error debugger that gathers information about system and program failures and records the information in a log file that can be used by a DST to diagnose the problem. When an error is detected, Dr. Watson creates a text file (Drwtsn32.log) that can be delivered to support personnel by the method they prefer. There is an option to create a *crash dump file*, which is a binary file that a programmer can load into a debugger.

If a program error occurs, Dr. Watson for Windows starts automatically.

To start Dr. Watson:

1. Click **Start**, and then click **Run**.

2. In the **Run** box, type **drwtsn32** and then click **OK**.

By default, the log file created by Dr. Watson is named Drwtsn32.log and is saved in: C:\Documents and Settings\All Users \Application Data\Microsoft\Dr Watson.

Note   For more information about Dr. Watson, see KB article 308538.

What is MOCA?

MOCA is a Web tool designed to help users determine the cause of a blue screen crash event, or *stop error*, while using Windows XP. After an application or operating system stops responding, an error report is generated and the user is given the option of uploading the report to the MOCA site for analysis. If this option is chosen, MOCA attempts to determine the cause of the error and, if the cause is determined, MOCA displays information regarding the cause and suggests methods for resolving the issue.

Note   For more information about the Microsoft Online Crash Analysis service, see the FAQ section at http://oca.microsoft.com/EN/Welcome.asp. For more information about how to send a full or kernel dump to Microsoft Online Crash Analysis, see KB article 316450.

What is Windows Error Reporting?

Windows Error Reporting is a feature included with Windows XP that helps Microsoft track and address operating system and application interoperability errors. Along with applications such as Microsoft Office XP, Office 2003, Microsoft Office Visio® 2002, and Microsoft Visual Studio® .NET, Windows XP can send information about errors to Microsoft. This notification allows Microsoft to investigate the cause of the error and provide a solution to the user the next time a report is submitted.

When an error occurs, a dialog box is displayed, prompting users to indicate whether they want to report the problem. If the user clicks **For More Information**, details regarding the application that crashed, the module in which the crash occurred, the file version, and the memory address are displayed.

A Windows Error Report might look like the following example:

"Faulting application winword.exe, version 10.0.2627.0, faulting module mso.dll, version 10.0.2625.0, fault address 0x0001f65e."

When users choose to report the problem, technical information about the problem is collected and then sent to Microsoft over the Internet. If a similar problem has been reported by other users and more information is available, Microsoft provides a link to that information.

Note   For more information about how Microsoft uses the data collected in error reporting, see http://oca.microsoft.com/en/dcp20.asp.

What is Event Viewer?

Event Viewer is a component that can be used to view and manage event logs, gather information about hardware and software problems, and monitor security events. Event Viewer maintains logs about program, security, and system events reported by Windows Error Reporting. Use this tool to help users that do not have access to the Windows Error Reporting feature.

Practice: Troubleshooting Win32 Applications

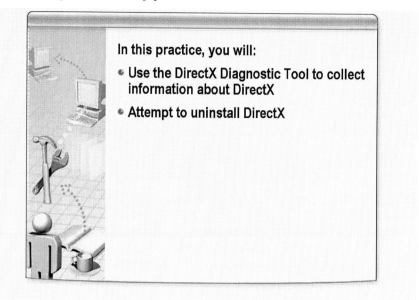

In this practice, you will:
- Use the DirectX Diagnostic Tool to collect information about DirectX
- Attempt to uninstall DirectX

Objective

In this practice, you will:

- Use the DirectX Diagnostic Tool to collect information about DirectX.
- Attempt to uninstall DirectX.

Practice

▶ **Use the DirectX Diagnostic Tool to collect information about DirectX**

1. Start the 2262_Bonn virtual machine.
2. Log on locally to Bonn as **Administrator** with the password **P@ssw0rd**.
3. Click **Start** and then click **Run**. In the **Open** box, type **dxdiag** and then click **OK**.
4. In the **DirectX Diagnostic Tool** dialog box, click **Yes**.
5. If a **Caution** dialog box is displayed indicating Virtual PC has disabled live resolution switching, click **OK**.
6. Use the **DirectX Diagnostic Tool** to answer the following questions:
   - On the **System** tab, determine the version of DirectX. Which version of DirectX is installed in the computer?

_9.0 c_

- On the **Display** tab, click **Test DirectDraw**, click **Yes**, and then click **OK** or **Yes** in all the subsequent dialog boxes. If a dialog box appears, stating Virtual PC has disabled live resolution switching, click **OK**. Were the tests successful?

  _____

- Verify that sound is enabled on your computer; then, on the Sound tab, click **Test Direct Sound**, click **Yes**, and then click **OK** or **Yes** in all the subsequent dialog boxes.. Were all tests successful?

  _____

7. In the DirectX Diagnostic Tool window, click **Exit**.

▶ **Attempt to uninstall DirectX**

1. Click **Start**, and then click **Control Panel**.
2. In Control Panel, click **Add or Remove Programs**.

   Can you remove Direct X?

   _____

3. Close Bonn and delete changes.

Lesson: Troubleshooting Security Issues Related to Applications

* Types of Application Security Issues
* What Are Security Updates?
* How to Install Security Updates
* Methods for Applying Security Updates
* What Are Application Security Options?
* How to Prevent Virus Attacks
* Guidelines for Recovering from a Virus Attack

Introduction

This lesson describes security issues and how they relate to applications. As a DST, you may receive calls from users about downloading security updates, identifying viruses, or configuring security firewalls. Your familiarity with each of these topics will assist you in the troubleshooting process.

Objectives

After completing this lesson, you will be able to:

- Describe the types of security issues related to applications.
- Explain the purpose and function of security updates for applications.
- Install security updates.
- Explain the methods for applying security updates.
- Describe the various types of application security options.
- Prevent virus attacks by using firewalls.
- Apply guidelines for recovering from virus attacks.

Types of Application Security Issues

Types of application security issues:
- ✓ Buffer overruns
- ✓ Registry access
- ✓ Installation issues
- ✓ Macros
- ✓ Viruses

Introduction

Without security, both public and private networks are subject to unauthorized monitoring and access. An application-layer attack targets application servers by causing a fault in a server's operating system or applications. This results in the attacker gaining the ability to bypass normal access controls and to gain control of an application, system, or network. The following table lists and describes key security issues related to applications.

Issue	Description
Buffer overruns	A *buffer* is an area of memory set aside for installation, which enables quick installs. When an application reads or writes large amounts of data, a buffer can be established that can be exploited by an attacker. This is a potential security issue that can result in your system becoming vulnerable to attack. For more information about buffer overruns, refer to KB article 308035.
Registry access	During an application installation, the setup routine has access to the registry. This is potentially a vulnerable time for the system.
Installation issues	Unless you install software from a trusted source, your computer and the data on it could be vulnerable to access by an attacker. If you are on a network, you may enable the attacker to access your entire network.
Macros	Many applications have a macro language, such as Microsoft Visual Basic® for Applications. These macro languages have very powerful command sets that allow them to manipulate the system in ways that may threaten security.
Viruses	Virus attacks are hitting the Internet with increasing frequency, which results in increased problems for your users. Without a virus scanner with up-to-date virus signatures installed, any system is vulnerable. For more information on computer viruses, refer to KB article 129972.

What Are Security Updates?

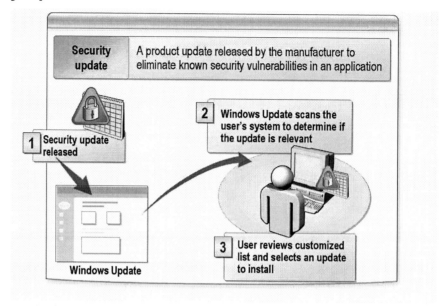

Introduction

A *security update* is a product update that is released by the manufacturer to eliminate known security vulnerabilities in an existing application. Security updates for applications are a relatively new concept. Previously, software companies released large incremental updates for the application that included multiple security updates.

In the last few years, however, companies have started to release security-related updates on an ongoing basis, as security gaps are discovered. By releasing updates on a case-by-case basis, companies are better able to manage and maintain the security of their applications over time.

What is Windows Update?

The Microsoft Windows Update Web site helps you to keep your computer up to date. Use Windows Update to choose updates for your computer's operating system, software, and hardware. Windows Update scans your computer and provides you with a customized selection of updates that apply only to the items on your computer. During the scan, a list of categories appears and the number of updates that are available in each category is noted in parentheses.

New content is added to the site regularly, so you can always get the most recent updates and fixes to protect your computer and keep it running smoothly. You can access the Windows Update Web site at http://v5.windowsupdate.microsoft.com/v5consumer/default.aspx?ln=en-us.

What are critical updates?

Any update that is critical to the operation of your computer is considered a *critical update*, and is automatically selected for installation during the scan for available updates. These updates are provided to help resolve known issues and to protect your computer from known security vulnerabilities. Whether a critical update applies to your operating system, software programs, or hardware, it is listed in the Critical Updates category.

How to Install Security Updates

On the Windows Update Web site, choose the installation method, and then click Install

What is Windows Update?

Windows Update is the online extension of Windows that helps you to keep your computer up to date. Use Windows Update to choose updates for your computer's operating system, software, and hardware.

How to install security updates for Windows XP

Advise your users to perform the following steps to install the latest security updates:

1. On the Microsoft Windows Update Web site at http://v5.windowsupdate.microsoft.com/v5consumer/default.aspx?ln=en-us, click **Express Install (Recommended): High Priority Updates for Your Computer** or **Custom Install: High Priority and Optional Updates for Your Computer.**

   The **Express Install (Recommended): High Priority Updates for Your Computer** option quickly scans for, downloads, and installs only critical updates and security updates.

   The **Custom Install: High Priority and Optional Updates for Your Computer** option scans for optional, critical, and security updates.

2. In the left pane, click **Install updates**.

   Windows Update scans for and then lists the available updates.

3. Browse through the available updates, click the name of update for information about the tool, and click **Details** for additional information about the tool.

4. Click **Install** to download the security update.

Note   Some updates may require that you restart your computer. Save your work and close any open programs before beginning the installation process.

What are Office Updates?

The Microsoft Office Online Web site includes Office Update, which enables you to check for updates that improve the stability and security of Microsoft Office applications. Office Update scans your computer and provides you with a tailored selection of updates that apply to the applications on your computer.

How to install security updates for Office

Advise your users to perform the following steps to install the latest Office updates:

1. On the Microsoft Office Online Web site at http://office.microsoft.com/officeupdate/default.aspx, click **Check for updates**.

   Windows Update scans for available updates and then lists any critical updates.

2. Browse through the available updates in each category, and then select the appropriate check boxes. To read a full description of each item, click **More information**.

3. When you have selected all the updates you want, click **Start Installation**.

Methods for Applying Security Updates

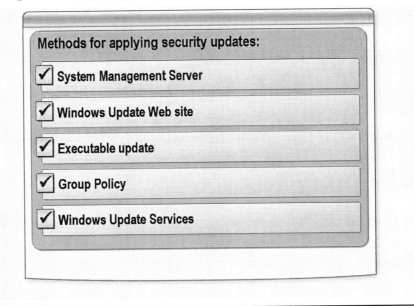

Introduction

There are several ways in which you can apply a security update to an application:

- *System Management Server*. Microsoft Systems Management Server is a Microsoft server application that automates network management. Systems Management Server enables administrators to control who can install, execute, or access network resources. Systems Management Server also notifies each local client when a security update is available.

- *Windows Update Web site*. As indicated in the previous section, the Microsoft Windows Update Web site enables users to install the latest security updates for Microsoft applications.

- *Executable update*. A security update can be applied by using an executable file or a compressed file (.zip). These files require you to manually decompress and extract compressed security updates.

- *Group Policy*. Group Policy can apply updates and update software that was deployed by the client through Group Policy. This is a procedure established by a network system administrator that provides any updates to the computers on the network.

- *Windows Update Services (WUS)*. WUS, previously known as Software Update Services (SUS), is a free add-on to Microsoft Windows Server 2003™ that is used to automate software distribution and update management infrastructure, such as security updates, in Windows.

What Are Application Security Options?

Security option	Description
File encryption	• Specifies how a file is encrypted
File sharing	• Protects a file by assigning a password • Configures a file to be read-only • Applies a digital signature • Protects a file for forms, tracked changes, or comments
Privacy	• Removes personal information • Warns before printing, saving, or sending • Stores random numbers
Macro security	• Adjusts the security level and specifies names of trusted macro developers

Introduction

You can determine an application's security level and how the application handles security-related issues by adjusting an application's security options. In Microsoft applications, you can specify how macros run, whether a file is password-protected, the level of protection applied to a file, and whether a digital signature is used. This section describes the security options in Microsoft Word 2003.

To configure application security settings in Word:

- On the **Tools** menu, click **Options**, and then click the **Security** tab.

File encryption options

The file encryption option allows you to specify how a file is encrypted. Several different cryptology API choices are available.

File sharing options

The file sharing option allows you to:

- Protect a file by assigning a password to it.

- Configure a file to be read-only.

- Apply a digital signature to a file that confirms that the file originated from the signer and has not been altered.

- Protect a file for forms, tracked changes, or comments, by assigning a password to it.

Privacy options

The privacy option allows you to:

- Remove personal information from a file.

- Warn before printing, saving, or sending a file that contains tracked changes or comments.

- Store random numbers to improve merge accuracy.

Macro security level   The macro security setting option allows you to adjust the security level for opening files that might contain macro viruses and specify the names of trusted macro developers. A *macro virus* is a computer virus that infects an application and causes a sequence of actions to be performed automatically when the application is started.

How to Prevent Virus Attacks

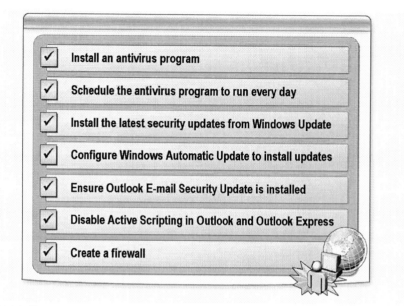

Introduction

With the frequency of new viruses, it may seem impossible to protect your computer from a virus attack. However, you can follow some basic guidelines to manage and maintain your computer's security.

General methods for protecting against a virus attack

To protect your computer, you can:

- Install an antivirus program.

- Schedule your antivirus program to download the latest updates every day and to scan the system while you sleep.

- Install the latest security updates from the Microsoft Windows Update Web site at http://v4.windowsupdate.microsoft.com/en/default.asp.

- Configure the Windows Automatic Update feature to download and install all critical updates. For a description of the Automatic Updates feature in Windows, see KB article 294871.

- Ensure that the Microsoft Outlook E-mail Security Update is installed.

  - Microsoft Office Outlook® 2000 post-Service Pack 2 and later includes this security update by default. For more information about how to apply the Outlook E-mail Security Update, see KB article 265627.

  - Configure Outlook Express 6 to block access to virus attachments.

- Disable Active Scripting in Outlook and Outlook Express.

  Note Active Scripting is disabled by default in Outlook Express 6 and Outlook 2002. See the Microsoft Knowledge Base (KB) for other versions.

■ Create a firewall. A *firewall* is a combination of hardware and software that is used to prevent unauthorized access from the outside to an internal network or intranet. By default, Windows XP Service Pack 2 (SP2) includes Windows Firewall, previously known as Internet Connection Firewall (ICF). Windows Firewall provides a level of protection from malicious users and programs that rely on unsolicited incoming traffic to attack computers on a network by dropping all unsolicited incoming traffic. Windows Firewall can be used also to protect non-networked computers, such as a single computer that uses a cable modem, DSL modem, or dial-up modem to connect to the Internet.

Caution When **Don't allow exceptions** is selected, the firewall also blocks unsolicited requests to share files or printers, and discovery of network devices.

Note For more information about security and firewalls, see http://www.microsoft.com/security/articles/firewall.asp. For more information about Windows Firewall, see http://www.microsoft.com/ technet/community/columns/cableguy /cg0204.mspx.

Important You must be logged on with administrator privileges to enable this service.

How to configure Windows Firewall

To configure Windows Firewall, you must be logged on to your computer with an owner account. After you have logged on correctly:

1. Click **Start**, click **Control Panel**, click **Security Center**, and then in the **Manage security settings for** section, click **Windows Firewall**.

2. In the **Windows Firewall** dialog box, on the **General** tab, click **On (Recommended)**.

Guidelines for Recovering from a Virus Attack

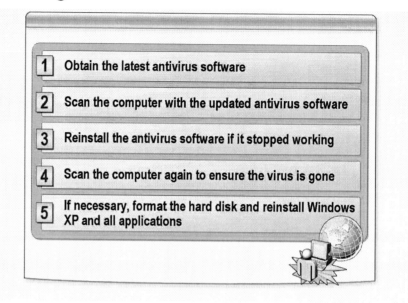

Introduction

A *computer virus* is an executable file that is designed to replicate itself and avoid detection by disguising itself as a legitimate program. Because viruses are frequently rewritten and adjusted, antivirus programs must be updated continuously to keep up with new or modified viruses. Most viruses arrive through e-mail and are disguised as something entertaining, such as a picture, music, or a greeting card. Viruses such as worms or Trojan horses can cause a great deal of damage to the infected computer.

Effects of viruses, worms, and Trojan horses

If you suspect or confirm that your computer is infected with a virus, obtain current antivirus software. When a virus infects your e-mail or other files, it may have the following effects on your computer:

- The infected file may make copies of itself, which can use all the free space in your hard disk.

- A copy of the infected file may be sent to all the addresses in your e-mail address list.

- The virus may reformat your disk drive, deleting your files and programs.

- The virus may install hidden programs, such as pirated software, which can be distributed and sold from your computer.

- The virus may reduce security to allow intruders to remotely access your computer or network.

Symptoms of viruses, worms, and Trojan horses

The following symptoms are indications that your computer may have been infected by a virus:

- You receive an e-mail message that has a strange attachment. When you open the attachment, dialog boxes appear or a sudden degradation of system performance occurs.

- There is a double extension on an attachment that you recently opened, such as .jpg.vbs or .gif.exe.

- An antivirus program is unexpectedly disabled and it cannot be restarted.

- An antivirus program cannot be installed on the computer or it will not run.

- Unexpected dialog boxes or message boxes appear onscreen.

- Someone tells you that they have recently received e-mail messages from you containing attached files (especially with .exe, .bat, .scr, or .vbs extensions) that you did not send.

- New icons appear on the desktop that you did not place there, or are not associated with any recently installed programs.

- You hear unexpected audio sounds.

- A program is no longer on the computer, and it was not intentionally uninstalled.

Guidelines for recovering from a virus attack

To recover from a virus attack:

1. Obtain the latest antivirus software from your antivirus vendor's Web site. For each new virus, antivirus vendors issue updates as inoculants against new viruses.

2. Scan your computer with the updated antivirus software.

3. Reinstall your antivirus program if it stopped working.

4. After the virus has been removed, scan your computer again to make sure that the virus has been removed completely.

5. You may have to format your computer's hard disk and reinstall Windows and all your computer programs if one or more of the following conditions are true:

    - Your antivirus software displays a message that it cannot fix or remove the virus.

    - The virus damaged or deleted some of the important files on your computer. This may be the case if Windows or some other programs do not start or they start with error messages indicating damaged or missing files.

    - The symptoms previously described persist even after your antivirus program scans your computer and you are sure the problems are caused by a virus.

Practice: Troubleshooting Security Issues Related to Applications

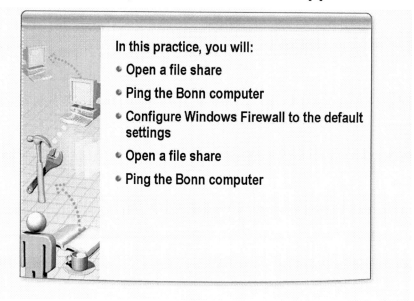

Objective

In this practice, you will test file sharing with different configurations of Windows Firewall.

Practice

▶ **Open a file share**

1. Start the 2262_London computer and, using London, log on to the domain as **Administrator** with a password of **P@ssw0rd**.

2. Start the 2262_Bonn computer.

3. Using London, click **Start**, and then click **Run**.

4. In the **Run** dialog box, type **bonn** then click **OK**.

   What happens?

   _____

5. Click **OK** to close the error message.

▶ **Ping the Bonn computer**

1. Using London, click **Start**, and then click **Run**.

2. In the **Run** dialog box, type **cmd** and then click **OK**.

3. At the prompt, type **ping bonn** and then press ENTER.

   What response did you receive?

   No network provider accepted the given network path

   Why are you not able to access the Bonn computer?

   bonn computer isnt on the network
   bonn has a firewall

4. Close the command window.

▶ **Configure Windows Firewall to the default settings**

1. Using Bonn, log on locally as Administrator with a password of **P@ssw0rd**.

2. Click **Start**, click **Control Panel**, and then click **Security Center**.

3. In the **Manage security settings for** section, click **Windows Firewall**.

4. On the **General** tab, clear the **Don't allow exceptions** check box and then click **OK**.

5. Close all windows.

▶ **Open a file share**

1. On London, click **Start**, and then click **Run**.

2. In the **Run** dialog box, type **\\bonn** and then click **OK**.

   What happens?

   it opens up bonn's C:\ fileshare

▶ **Ping the Bonn computer**

1. On London, click **Start**, and then click **Run**.

2. In the **Run** dialog box, type **cmd** and then click **OK**.

3. At the prompt, type **ping bonn** and then press ENTER.

   What happens to the packets?

   returned

4. Close London and delete changes.

5. Close all windows; log off and pause Bonn.

Lesson: Troubleshooting Application Compatibility Issues

* What Are Application Compatibility Issues?
* Common Causes of Application Compatibility Issues
* Tools for Troubleshooting Application Compatibility Issues
* How to Configure Application Compatibility
* Guidelines for Troubleshooting Application Compatibility Issues

Introduction

Many of the calls that you will receive as a DST will relate to application compatibility. You should be able to identify these issues quickly and suggest specific actions that your users can take to solve their problems. This lesson describes common application compatibility issues and provides information about how you can help your users optimize their applications to run on computers running Windows XP.

Objectives

After completing this lesson, you will be able to:

* Describe application compatibility issues.
* Identify common causes of application compatibility issues.
* Describe the tools used to troubleshoot application compatibility issues.
* Configure application compatibility.
* Apply guidelines for troubleshooting application compatibility issues.

What Are Application Compatibility Issues?

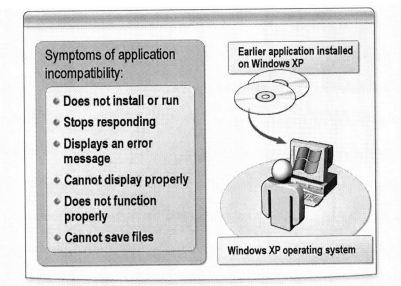

Symptoms of application incompatibility:

- Does not install or run
- Stops responding
- Displays an error message
- Cannot display properly
- Does not function properly
- Cannot save files

Earlier application installed on Windows XP

Windows XP operating system

Introduction	In general, applications are highly optimized for a specific operating system or operating system version. Application compatibility issues can arise when users try to run an earlier application on a later version of the Windows operating system. This may be especially true when migrating earlier applications to Windows XP, because Windows XP is built on the foundation of Windows NT and Windows 2000 and not the consumer-oriented line of operating systems, such as Windows 95, Windows 98, and Windows Millennium Edition. As a DST, you may receive calls from users about how to improve the performance of earlier applications running on Windows XP.
Symptoms of application compatibility issues	The specific symptoms of an application compatibility issue depend on the particular application that is running and the problem that is experienced; however, the following common symptoms include a program that:

- Does not install or run.
- Stops responding or hangs.
- Displays an error message.
- Displays a user interface (UI) improperly.
- Displays impaired functionality.
- Cannot save files.

What is Compatibility Mode?	*Compatibility Mode* is a feature of Windows XP that enables a computer to run programs written for a different operating system. It consists of a collection of individual fixes that enable Windows XP to emulate a specific operating system environment for that application. Compatibility Mode resolves several of the most common issues that prevent earlier programs from working correctly with Windows XP, such as problems related to the migration of an earlier application to Windows XP.

Common Causes of Application Compatibility Issues

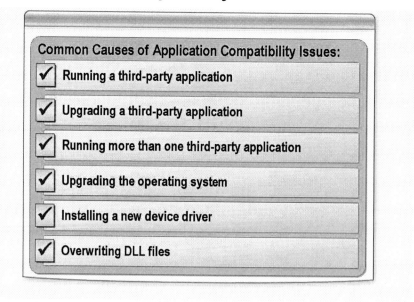

Common Causes of Application Compatibility Issues:
- ✓ Running a third-party application
- ✓ Upgrading a third-party application
- ✓ Running more than one third-party application
- ✓ Upgrading the operating system
- ✓ Installing a new device driver
- ✓ Overwriting DLL files

Common application compatibility issue scenarios

Application compatibility issues take many forms. Common scenarios include:

- Running a third-party application. For example, Office is running properly until the user installs a new third-party application. When this occurs, the user receives an error message when attempting to open an Office application.

- Upgrading a third-party application. For example, a user upgrades a third-party application and now cannot read the application's data files in Microsoft Office.

- Running more than one third-party application. For example, a third-party application runs properly on the user's computer unless the user runs another third-party application at the same time. When this occurs, the second application crashes.

- Upgrading the operating system. For example, a user upgrades her operating system and now a third-party application no longer runs, even though the third-party software company claims that the application will run on the new operating system. A user upgrades his operating system and now his earlier MS-DOS-based or Win16 application no longer works correctly.

- Installing a new device driver. For example, a user buys a new printer and loads its software. After the printer is installed, the user cannot print from Office applications. Third-party device drivers can create compatibility issues.

- Overwriting dynamic-link library (DLL) files. A user installs an application that writes over its own versions of system DLL files, creating multiple DLL versions. This problem, which used to be very common, results in applications that do not work correctly, if at all, and operating systems that suddenly become unstable. Fortunately, this particular issue is rapidly declining in frequency. Windows XP does not allow an application to overwrite system DLL files.

  A variation of this problem occurs when an application looks for a specific version of a DLL file. When the application cannot find the file, it generates error messages.

Tip When you attempt to install a program that is known to have compatibility problems in Windows XP, the operating system displays a message that indicates that the program is not compatible and may cause the system to become unstable. If your users receive this message, recommend that they contact the program manufacturer for an update, which they should download and install immediately. If an update is not available, recommend that they do not install the program.

Resources

For updated information about hardware and software compatibility for Windows XP, refer to the Windows Catalog at http://www.microsoft.com/windows/catalog/.

For updated information about hardware and software compatibility for Windows 2000, refer to the Windows 2000 Hardware Compatibility List at http://www.microsoft.com/whdc/hcl/search.mspx.

Tools for Troubleshooting Application Compatibility Issues

Tool	Use to
Program Compatibility Wizard	• Test an application in different modes or settings
Application Compatibility Toolkit	• Create a list of potential problem applications by using Application Compatibility Analyzer • Identify potential issues by using AppVerifier • Select and apply fixes by using Compatibility Administrator

Introduction

Windows XP includes two central tools that you can use to troubleshoot application compatibility issues: Program Compatibility Wizard and Windows Application Compatibility Toolkit.

Program Compatibility Wizard

If you experience problems with a program that worked correctly on an earlier version of Windows, the Program Compatibility Wizard helps you select and test compatibility settings that may fix these problems. For example, if the program was originally designed to run on Windows 95, set the Compatibility Mode to Windows 95 and try running the program again. If successful, the program will start in that mode each time. The wizard also prompts you to try different settings, such as switching the display to 256 colors and the screen resolution to 640 x 480 pixels.

Caution Changing compatibility options is a calculated risk, particularly when the program in question is a low-level utility such as an antivirus program or disk partitioning tool that was not specifically designed for Windows XP. Even a seemingly innocuous CD-burning program can cause problems if it tries to install an incompatible device driver. The safest practice is to do more research about the program before testing compatibility options.

Application Compatibility Toolkit

Use the Application Compatibility Toolkit Version 2.6. If your user's program does not run correctly after testing it with the Program Compatibility Wizard, suggest that the user perform the following steps:

1. Check the program manufacturer's Web site to see if an update is available.

2. Check the Windows Update Web site to see if a fix is available for the program.

3. If the program is a game that uses DirectX, ensure that the user is using the latest version of DirectX.

4. Check the Web sites of the video adapter manufacturer and the sound card manufacturer to see if newer drivers are available for either of these components.

When you try to use Compatibility Mode with a program, keep in mind that none of the options on the **Compatibility** tab are available unless you are an administrator or the program is on a network share or on a mapped network drive.

To use Compatibility Mode as a non-administrator, run the Program Compatibility Wizard and select the option to manually locate the program. When you do this, you can type the Universal Naming Convention (UNC) path of the program's executable file or you can browse for the program on a mapped network drive.

Note You cannot use Compatibility Mode with protected Windows XP components.

Note For more information on troubleshooting program compatibility issues in Windows XP, refer to KB article 285909.

AppVerifier

Available as part of the Application Compatibility Toolkit, the Application Verifier (AppVerifier) is a collection of tests used during the application development and testing process. It helps developers identify potential application compatibility, stability, and security issues.

The AppVerifier works by monitoring an application's use of the operating system, including the file system, registry, memory, and APIs, while the application is being run. The tool then provides guidance for source-code-level fixes of the issues it uncovers. The AppVerifier enables you to:

- Test for potential application compatibility errors caused by common programming mistakes.
- Examine an application for memory-related issues.
- Determine an application's compliance with various requirements of the Designed for Windows XP or Certified for Windows Server 2003 Logo Programs.
- Identify potential security issues in an application.

How to Configure Application Compatibility

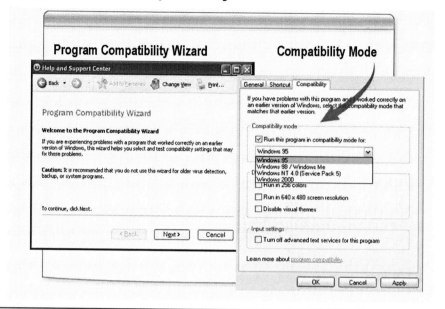

How to run the Program Compatibility Wizard

To start the Program Compatibility Wizard, click **Start**, point to **All Programs**, point to **Accessories**, and then click **Program Compatibility Wizard**.

How to run programs in Compatibility Mode

To run programs in Compatibility Mode:

1. Right-click the shortcut of the program that you want to fix, and then click **Properties**.

2. On the **Compatibility** tab, select the **Run this program in compatibility mode** check box, and then select one of these options:

    *   Windows 95

    *   Windows 98 / Windows Me

    *   Windows NT 4.0 (Service Pack 5)

    *   Windows 2000

3. Under **Display settings**, select the mode that you think is necessary for the program to work correctly:

    *   Run in 256 colors.

    *   Run in 640 x 480 screen resolution.

    *   Disable visual themes.

4. Click **Apply**.

5. Click **OK**, and then double-click the program.

Note   The **Compatibility** tab is available only for programs installed on the hard drive. Although you can run the Program Compatibility Wizard on programs or set up files on a CD-ROM or floppy disk, your changes will not remain in effect after you close the program. For more information about an option on the **Compatibility** tab, right-click the option and then click **What's This**.

Guidelines for Troubleshooting Application Compatibility Issues

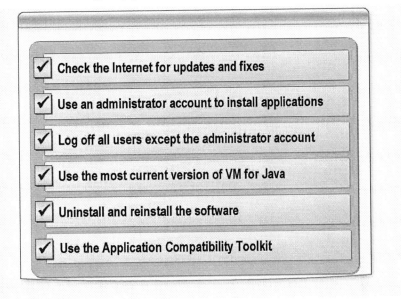

✓ Check the Internet for updates and fixes

✓ Use an administrator account to install applications

✓ Log off all users except the administrator account

✓ Use the most current version of VM for Java

✓ Uninstall and reinstall the software

✓ Use the Application Compatibility Toolkit

Guidelines

Although there are a great number of application compatibility problems that can occur and an equal number of possible solutions, refer to the following best practices when troubleshooting these issues.

Check the Internet for updates and fixes

Check the program manufacturer's Web site to see if an update is available. Check the Microsoft Windows Update Web site to see if a fix is available for the program.

Use an administrator account to install applications

Many applications must be installed by using an administrator account. This is because many programs were written for Microsoft Windows 95, Windows 98, Windows 98 Second Edition, or Windows Millennium Edition. These operating systems did not have administrator or limited user accounts.

Log off all users except the administrator account

The Fast User Switching feature is new to Windows XP, and because of this, earlier programs were not designed to support this feature.

Use the most current version of VM for Java

Use the most current version of the Microsoft Virtual Machine (VM) for Java. If the program uses the VM for Java, you may have to download the most current version of the VM.

Uninstall and reinstall the software

If your users upgraded to Windows XP from Windows 95, Windows 98, Windows 98 Second Edition, Windows Millennium Edition, Windows NT, or Windows 2000 Professional, and they are having problems with software that is listed as being compatible with Windows XP, have the users perform these steps:

1. Uninstall the software.

2. Reinstall the software.

3. If the issue is not resolved, recommend that the user contact the software manufacturer to inquire about how to manually uninstall the program. For example, the user would need to know how to delete the folder for the program and the registry entries that were made by the program. Also, recommend asking the software manufacturer about the availability of a fix for this issue, get the fix, and then install the program again.

Use the Application Compatibility Toolkit Version 2.6

The Application Compatibility Toolkit 2.6 contains documents and tools you can use to help diagnose and resolve program compatibility issues with Windows XP.

If your user's program does not run correctly after testing it with the Program Compatibility Wizard, suggest that the user perform the following steps:

1. Check the program manufacturer's Web site to see if an update is available.

2. Check the Windows Update Web site to see if a fix is available for the program.

3. If the program is a game that uses DirectX, ensure that the user is using the latest version of DirectX.

4. Check the Web sites of the video adapter manufacturer and the sound card manufacturer to see if newer drivers are available for either of these components.

Note   For more information on troubleshooting program compatibility issues in Windows XP, refer to KB article 285909.

Practice: Running Applications in Compatibility Mode

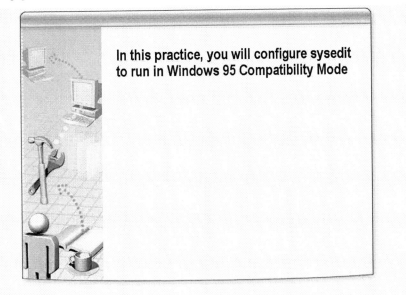

In this practice, you will configure sysedit to run in Windows 95 Compatibility Mode

Objective

In this practice, you will configure sysedit.exe, a 16-bit application, to run in a Windows 95 simulated environment. You will run the application in Compatibility Mode. In an earlier practice, you copied sysedit.exe to your desktop.

Practice

▶ **Configure sysedit to run in Windows 95 compatibility mode**

1. Resume Bonn and log on as **Administrator** with the password of **P@ssw0rd**.

2. Using Bonn, click **Start**, and then click **Run**.

3. In the **Open** box, type **c:\windows\system32** and then click **OK**.

4. Right-click **sysedit**, and then click **Copy**.

5. Close all windows.

6. Right-click the desktop, and then click **Paste**.

7. On the desktop, right-click **sysedit**, and then click **Properties**.

8. In the **sysedit Properties** dialog box, click the **Compatibility** tab.

9. In the **Compatibility Mode** box, select the **Run this program in compatibility mode for** check box, click **Windows 95**, and then click **OK**.

10. To run the application in Windows 95 Compatibility Mode, on the desktop, double-click **sysedit.exe**.

11. Close all windows and pause Bonn.

Lesson: Troubleshooting MS-DOS-Based and Win16 Applications

* What Are MS-DOS-Based and Win16 Applications?
* What Is an NTVDM?
* How to Configure an NTVDM
* What Is WOW?
* Advantages and Disadvantages of Multiple NTVDMs
* How to Start a Win16 Application in Its Own NTVDM
* Tools for Troubleshooting Win16 Applications
* Guidelines for Troubleshooting MS-DOS-Based and Win16 Applications

Introduction

As a DST, you may receive calls from users who are running MS-DOS or Win16 applications on computers running Windows XP. Although Windows XP is designed to run applications written for earlier operating systems, problems can occur. Your understanding of these types of applications will assist you in the troubleshooting process.

Objectives

After completing this lesson, you will be able to:

■ Describe the purpose and function of MS-DOS-based and Win16 applications.

■ Explain the purpose and function of a Windows NT Virtual DOS Machine (NTVDM).

■ Configure an NTVDM.

■ Explain the purpose and function of Windows on Windows (WOW).

■ Describe the advantages and disadvantages of multiple NTVDMs.

■ Start a Win16 application in its own NTVDM.

■ List the tools used to troubleshoot Win16 applications.

■ Apply guidelines for troubleshooting MS-DOS-based and Win16 applications.

What Are MS-DOS-Based and Win16 Applications?

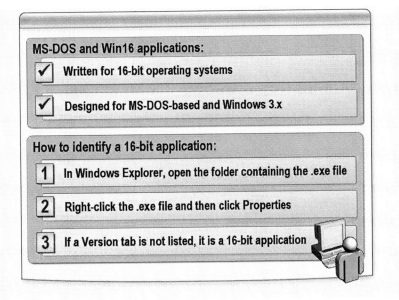

MS-DOS and Win16 applications:

☑ Written for 16-bit operating systems

☑ Designed for MS-DOS-based and Windows 3.x

How to identify a 16-bit application:

1 In Windows Explorer, open the folder containing the .exe file

2 Right-click the .exe file and then click Properties

3 If a Version tab is not listed, it is a 16-bit application

Introduction

The MS-DOS operating system is a 16-bit, non-graphical, line-oriented, command-driven operating system. 16-bit refers to the number of bits that are used to represent memory addresses, and the number of bits that can be transferred or processed in parallel. Windows 3.x is based on the MS-DOS operating system platform and is therefore also a 16-bit operating system. Most MS-DOS-based and Win16 software applications were originally written for 16-bit operating systems.

How to identify a 16-bit application

Because most 16-bit applications run without any problem in Windows XP, your users may not be able to tell whether an application is 16-bit or 32-bit.

To identify a 16-bit application:

1. In Windows Explorer, open the folder that contains the program's executable (.exe) file.

2. Right-click the .exe file, and then click **Properties**.

3. In the **Properties** dialog box, look for a **Version** tab. If there is no **Version** tab, the application is a 16-bit.

Note   For information about how to identify a 16-bit application, refer to KB article 320127.

What Is an NTVDM?

Definition	A simulated environment that allows MS-DOS-based and Win16 applications to run in a 32-bit environment
Function	Uses VDDs to enable MS-DOS-based applications to access system hardware
Components	• NTvdm.exe. Provides the virtual machine • NTis.sys. The equivalent of MS-DOS io.sys • NTdos.sys. The equivalent of MS-DOS.sys

Introduction

Although Windows XP is a 32-bit operating system, it will run earlier, 16-bit programs. To run these programs, Windows XP uses an application environment called a *Windows NT Virtual DOS Machine* (NTVDM). An NTVDM provides a simulated environment that supports MS-DOS-based and Win16 applications. It runs as a separate process on top of the existing operating system.

How NTVDM works

NTVDM uses *virtual device drivers* (VDDs) that allow MS-DOS-based applications to access system hardware. The VDD intercepts the application's hardware calls and interacts with the Windows NT–32-bit device driver. Windows NT provides VDDs for the mouse, keyboard, printer, and COM ports.

Key NTVDM components

MS-DOS drivers or executable files that attempt to directly access a device for which there is no VDD will fail. Windows protects the system from such failures. The following table describes key NTVDM components.

Component	Function
NTvdm.exe	The mechanism that provides the virtual machine
NTio.sys	The equivalent of the MS-DOS io.sys
NTdos.sys	The equivalent of the MS-DOS.sys

MS-DOS-based applications in Windows XP

When you launch an MS-DOS-based application in Windows XP, the operating system creates a new NTVDM for that application. Each time you start another MS-DOS-based application, the operating system creates an additional NTVDM. Each NTVDM operates independently, with a single thread and its own address space.

Win16 applications in Windows XP

When you launch a Win16 application in Windows XP, the operating system creates a new NTVDM. When you start additional Win16 applications after this, each of these applications will run in the same NTVDM.

How to Configure an NTVDM

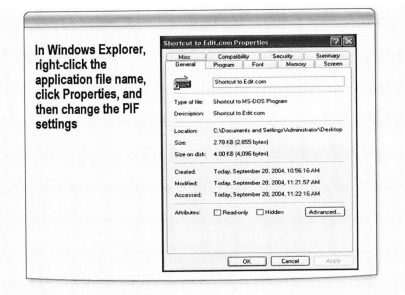

In Windows Explorer, right-click the application file name, click Properties, and then change the PIF settings

Introduction

To configure an NTVDM for a 16-bit application, you must change the settings in the application's *program information file* (PIF). A PIF is used to start a program written for MS-DOS or Windows 3.*x* from within Windows XP and can be used to configure a unique environment for individual programs that run in MS-DOS mode. PIFs allow you to set default properties for these programs, such as font size, screen colors, and memory allocation.

How to create and modify PIFs

To create and modify PIFs, in Windows Explorer, right-click the application file name and then click **Properties;** in the **Properties** dialog box, change any settings, and then click **OK**.

When you change a setting in a 16-bit program shortcut, a PIF is automatically created. The settings you specify are used each time you start the program by double-clicking its icon. If you start the program from the Command Prompt window, these settings are not used.

What are Autoexec and Config files?

When a 16-bit application starts, a new NTVDM starts, and it executes the Autoexec and Config files. The default files, Autoexec.nt and Config.nt, are located in *systemroot*\System32. Any changes to settings in either Autoexec.nt or Config.nt take effect when you save the changes and restart the application.

How to specify Autoexec and Config files

To specify Autoexec and Config files for a specific MS-DOS-based application, in the PIF for the application, on the **Program** tab, click **Advanced**. In the **Windows PIF Settings** dialog box, edit the PIF to specify different Config and Autoexec files for each application. PIFs can be created for MS-DOS-based applications by modifying the default properties for the applications.

Note   Windows XP supports the same commands in the Autoexec file that are supported by MS-DOS 5.0.

What Is WOW?

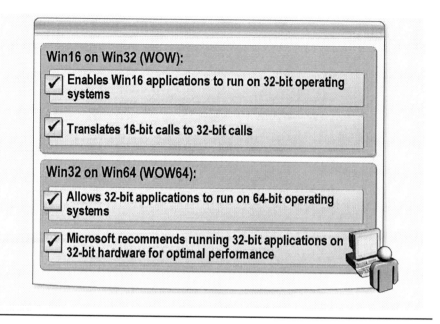

Introduction

Windows NT includes a program called Windows on Windows (WOW) that enables Win16 applications to run on 32-bit operating systems. WOW operates in the context of the NTVDM.

WOW components

The WOW environment is composed of the components described in the following table.

Component	Description
Wowexec.exe	Provides Windows 3.1 emulation for the NTVDM
Wow32.dll	Provides the DLL portion of the Windows 3.1 emulation layer
Win16 application	The 16-bit application running in WOW
Krnl386.exe	A modified version of the Windows 3.1 386 kernel for Intel $x86$-based computers that translates many operations to Win32 services
User.exe	A modified version of the Windows 3.1 User.exe that translates API calls to Win32 services
Gdi.exe	A modified version of the Windows 3.1 Gdi.exe that translates API calls to Win32 services

How WOW works

WOW translates 16-bit calls to 32-bit calls. When an application calls a Windows $3.x$ function, WOW intercepts the call and passes control to the equivalent Win32 function. As a result, Windows $3.x$-based applications use Win32 functions.

If the Win32 function needs to return anything to the calling application, it must be translated from 32 bits to 16 bits. Although these translations incur some overhead, the loss is offset by the speed gained in carrying out 32-bit instructions.

WOW provides the non-preemptive multitasking environment for which Win16 applications were designed.

By default, a single NTVDM starts when the first Win16 application is started, and then all Win16 applications run in that NTVDM.

How to determine if a 16-bit application is running

Your users may not know if they are currently running 16-bit programs. To determine if a 16-bit application is currently running:

1. Right-click a blank area on the taskbar, and then click **Task Manager**.

2. In the **Windows Task Manager** dialog box, on the **Processes** tab, note the contents of the **Image Name** column.

   If a 16-bit program is running, an entry is listed for Ntvdm.exe. You will also see wowexec.exe and the executable name of each 16-bit program that is running in that WOW virtual machine. As a helpful visual aid, wowexec.exe and the 16-bit executable file names are indented.

The limitations of WOW

The WOW environment has the following limitations:

- If one Win16 application fails, it can adversely affect all other Win16 applications running in the same NTVDM. For example, if a Win16 application does not release the microprocessor, the other Win16 applications cannot gain access to it. Other Windows NT applications can still access the microprocessor, but the failed Win16 application must be closed before other Win16 applications can gain access to the microprocessor.

- There is no shared memory between the applications running in WOW and other applications running under Windows NT. Win16 applications cannot call 32-bit DLLs, and Windows NT–based applications cannot call Win16 DLLs.

What is WOW64?

Windows on Windows 64 (WOW64) is a 32-bit subsystem that allows you to run 32-bit applications on 64-bit operating systems. Because 32-bit applications run in an emulation mode, Microsoft recommends running 32-bit applications on 32-bit hardware for optimal performance.

Advantages and Disadvantages of Multiple NTVDMs

Advantage of multiple NTVDMs:

- ✓ Reliability
- ✓ Interoperability
- ✓ Preemptive multitasking
- ✓ Multiprocessing

Disadvantage of multiple NTVDMs:

- ✓ Additional memory usage
- ✓ Lack of interoperability

Introduction

You can configure Win16 applications to run in their own memory spaces on an application-by-application basis, thereby creating multiple NTVDMs. Multiple NTVDMs prevent applications from interfering with each other.

When you configure a Win16 application to run in its own memory space, a new NTVDM is created when the application starts. Inside the NTVDM, a new WOW application environment starts. Each Win16 application that is configured to run in its own memory space creates its own WOW application environment within an NTVDM.

Note For more information about why Win16 applications run in a single VDM, see KB article 100318.

Advantages of multiple NTVDMs

There are several advantages to running Win16 applications in separate NTVDMs:

- *Reliability*. A single faulty Win16 application does not affect any other Win16 applications.

- *Interoperability*. If Win16 applications follow the OLE and Dynamic Data Exchange (DDE) specifications, they can interoperate with other applications in separate memory spaces.

- *Preemptive multitasking*. If several Win16 applications are running in a shared memory space, one busy application prevents the others from being used. Running each Win16 application in its own memory space, however, keeps all of the applications usable, even when one is busy.

- *Multiprocessing*. Multi-microprocessor computers enable multitasking and true multiprocessing of applications. This means that the processor can, in theory, run more than one application at a time. If each Win16 application is configured to run in a separate memory space, it can run them simultaneously, as long as the system has enough available microprocessors.

Disadvantages of multiple NTVDMs

There are also potential disadvantages to running Win16 applications in separate NTVDMs:

- *Additional memory usage.* Starting multiple Win16 applications in their own memory spaces introduces additional overhead into the system. Each Win16 application that is started in its own memory space starts another NTVDM and WOW application environment. This overhead can potentially be 2 megabytes (MB) of page file space and approximately 1 MB of RAM (random access memory) per separate memory space used. Depending on the amount of RAM in the computer, this overhead could affect system performance.

- *Lack of interoperability.* If Win16 applications do not follow the OLE and DDE specifications, or if they rely on shared memory to exchange data, they do *not* function correctly in separate memory spaces. To function properly, such applications must be run in the default (shared) NTVDM and WOW application environment.

How to close the NTVDM and WOW application environments

After it is started, the default (shared) NTVDM and WOW application environment remains open, even if all Win16 applications that were running in it are closed. Use Task Manager to close the shared NTVDM and WOW application environment, as needed, to regain system resources.

When a Win16 application is started in a separate memory space, an additional NTVDM and WOW application environment is started. When this Win16 application is closed, its NTVDM and WOW application environments are also closed. The default NTVDM is not affected.

How to Start a Win16 Application in Its Own NTVDM

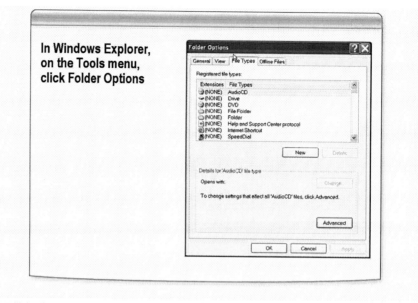

Introduction

Several options are available for starting a Win16 application in its own NTVDM.

- *At a command prompt.* Type **start /separate** [*path to application_executable*]

- *From a shortcut.* Create a shortcut, and, on the **Properties Shortcut** tab, select the **Run in Separate Memory Space** check box.

  If the **Run in Separate Memory Space** check box appears dimmed, the application is not a 16-bit Windows application, or the system cannot find the application.

- *By file association.* Start Win 16 in its own NTVDM by file association.

  In Windows XP Windows Explorer:

  1. On the **Tools** menu, click **Folder Options**.

  2. In the **Folder Options** dialog box, on the **File Types** tab, under **Registered file types**, select the application you want to edit, and then click **Advanced**.

  3. In the **Edit File Type** dialog box, in the **Actions** box, click **Open**, and then click **Edit**.

  4. In the **New Action** dialog box under **Application used to perform action**, add the **/separate** switch. An example follows:

     c:\windows\system32\notepad.exe /c start /separate %1

How to configure Win16 applications to start in separate NTVDMs by default

To configure a Win16 application to automatically start in a separate NTVDM, create a shortcut for the application. Right-click the shortcut, and then click **Properties**. In the **Properties** dialog box, on the **Shortcut** tab, select the **Run in Separate Memory Space** check box. Each time the application is started by using the shortcut, it is automatically in a separate NTVDM.

How to start a Win16 application in a shared memory space

To start a Win16 application in a shared memory space, edit the open line to read:

cmd /c start /shared *path\application_executable*

Tools for Troubleshooting Win16 Applications

Tool	Use to
Knowledge Base	Research technical articles, white papers, and case histories
Task Manager	List all the programs that are currently running
Windows Explorer	Set properties for MS-DOS-based programs
Regedit and Command.com	Locate corrupt registry values
Group Policy Editor	Centrally manage software installation, configuration, updates, and removal

Introduction

There are a variety of tools that you can use to troubleshoot issues with MS-DOS-based and Win16 applications, including:

- The Microsoft Knowledge Base (KB)
- Task Manager
- Windows Explorer
- Regedit and Command.com
- Group Policy Editor

The KB

The KB contains thousands of technical articles, white papers, and case histories. When your user calls with a question about running MS-DOS-based or Win16 applications on a computer running Windows XP, you can most likely find a document related to the issue in the KB.

To find general articles about 16-bit application troubleshooting, perform a search in the KB using the term "Windows XP 16-bit."

Tip KB article 314495 provides helpful hints on troubleshooting 16-bit applications in Windows XP.

To find articles on specific issues, enter additional keywords to narrow your search further. For example, if your user is having trouble installing Word version 2.0 for Windows on a computer running Windows XP, perform a search in the KB using the terms "Windows XP" and "Microsoft Word version 2.0."

The KB will return a list of articles that contain those keywords. Review the list to find the appropriate article.

Task Manager	Use Task Manager to determine if 16-bit applications are currently running. Task Manager lists all the programs that are currently running. If a 16-bit program is running, an entry exists for Ntvdm.exe. You will also see wowexec.exe and the executable name of each 16-bit program that is running in that WOW virtual machine. As a helpful visual aid, wowexec.exe and the 16-bit executable file names are indented. You can select applications from this list and shut them down if necessary.
Windows Explorer	Use Windows Explorer to set properties for individual MS-DOS-based programs.
Regedit and Command.com	The system registry contains settings for virtual display device drivers (VDDs) that are used by the NTVDM. If your users receive a "16-bit MS-DOS Subsystem" error when they attempt to install a new program, it may be caused by a corrupt registry value in the system registry. You can use the Regedit utility to locate and select the corrupt value. If the problem persists, the issue may have to do with the Command.com file. Verify that the proper version of this file is installed in the *systemroot*/System32 folder on your computer.
Group Policy Editor (GPMC)	Group Policy is a powerful feature of Windows XP that allows administrators to centrally manage software installation, configuration, updates, and removal. Administrators can also specify scripts to run at startup, shutdown, logon, and logoff, and redirect users' special folders, such as My Documents, to the network. In addition, administrators can customize settings to restrict users from being able to run 16-bit applications. However, it is important to note that commands that run in the Virtual DOS Machine (Ntvdm.exe) are not recognized by software restriction policies. See KB article 319458 for more information about NTVDM and software restriction policies.
Additional reading	For more information on these utilities, see KB articles 314452 and 314106.

Guidelines for Troubleshooting MS-DOS-Based and Win16 Applications

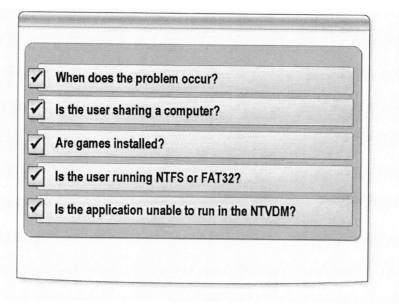

Introduction

As a DST, your main objective in troubleshooting any issue is to help users determine the cause of their problems. Remember that the troubleshooting process should be a logical process of elimination by which you will be able, in rapid order, to eliminate the possibilities that are *not* the issue. The pattern generally applied to the troubleshooting process is:

1. Determine what has changed.

2. Eliminate possible causes to determine probable causes.

3. Identify a solution.

4. Test the solution.

Focus your troubleshooting efforts

Although there are many possible problems that can occur when you run MS-DOS-based or Win16 applications on computers running Windows XP, remember that these applications depend on the NTVDM and WOW to operate successfully. Focus your initial troubleshooting efforts on these areas. Questions to ask the user include:

- When does the problem occur?

  If problems occur while the NTVDM or WOW is starting, follow the steps outlined in KB article 196453.

- Is the user sharing a computer?

  If your user is on a shared computer, the user may be encountering a Fast User Switching issue. The following KB articles detail the most common of these issues and their resolutions:

  301494   290249   298336   300820

- Are games installed?

  Games are a relatively common source of conflict, with many MS-DOS-based games requiring direct access to the computer's hardware. The following KB articles identify several game issues:

283576	327299	327979	310697	285912

  If the previously mentioned issues do not relate to your user's specific problem, your user may be experiencing an issue with Windows configuration. The following KB articles detail common troubleshooting steps for 16-bit applications.

320127	314106	254914	324767	314495	314452

Note   For more information, see KB article 314106.

Other considerations

Other considerations when troubleshooting MS-DOS-based and Win16 applications include:

- *File system*. If the user is running NTFS (NT file system), or FAT32 (file allocation system 32), there may be compatibility problems with particular applications. In this case, the user should contact the program vendor.

- *Hardware access*. Many earlier applications attempt to access hardware directly. Direct access is not allowed under Windows NT, Windows 2000 Professional, or Windows XP. If the application cannot run correctly in the NTVDM, the user may need to contact the program manufacturer for an updated version.

Practice: Configuring MS-DOS-Based and Win16 Applications

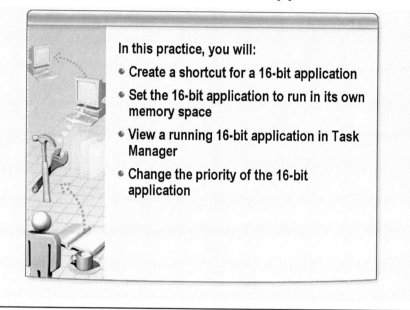

In this practice, you will:

● Create a shortcut for a 16-bit application

● Set the 16-bit application to run in its own memory space

● View a running 16-bit application in Task Manager

● Change the priority of the 16-bit application

Objective

In this practice, you will:

- Create a shortcut for a 16-bit application.

- Set the 16-bit application to run in its own memory space.

- View a running 16-bit application in Task Manager.

- Change the priority of the 16-bit application.

To complete this practice, you need to log on to the domain with an account that has local administrative rights on the computer.

Practice

▶ **Create a shortcut for a 16-bit application**

1. Resume Bonn.

2. Click **Start**, click **Run**, type **c:\windows\system32** in the **Open** box, and then click **OK**.

3. If the contents of the Windows folder are not displayed, in the **C:\windows** window, in the **System Tasks** pane, click **Show the contents of this folder**.

4. Right-click **sysedit**, click **Send To**, and then click **Desktop (create shortcut)**.

5. Close all windows.

► **Set the 16-bit application to run in its own memory space**

1. On the desktop, right-click **Shortcut to sysedit.exe**, and then click **Properties**.

2. In the **Shortcut to sysedit.exe Properties** dialog box, on the **Shortcut** tab, click **Advanced**.

3. In the **Advanced Properties** dialog box, select the **Run in separate memory space** check box, and then click **OK**.

4. Click **OK** to close the **Shortcut to sysedit.exe Properties** dialog box.

► **View a running 16-bit application in Task Manager**

1. On the desktop, double-click **Shortcut to sysedit.exe**.

2. Click **Start**, click **Run**, type **taskmgr** in the **Open** box, and then click **OK**.

   On the **Processes** tab, under **Image Name**, locate the entries for ntvdm.exe.

3. Start another instance of sysedit.exe. On the **Processes** tab, under **Image Name**, locate the entries for ntvdm.exe.

   How many ntvdm.exe instances are displayed in Windows Task Manager?

   _____

4. Close all instances of sysedit.

► **Change the priority of the 16-bit application**

1. Click **Start** and then click **Run**. In the **Open** box, type **sysedit** and then click **OK**.

2. In Task Manager, under **Image Name**, right-click **sysedit.exe**, and then point to **Set Priority**.

   Notice that you are unable to change the priority for this process. This is because it is running in an NTVDM. To change the priority of this process, you must change the priority of the NTVDM.

3. Under **Image Name**, right-click **ntvdm.exe**, point to **Set Priority**, and then click **High**.

4. Click **Yes** to close the warning message box.

   When running a process at high priority, other applications may run more slowly because the sysedit.exe is given first priority for CPU usage, forcing other applications to wait for access to the CPU.

5. Close Bonn and delete changes.

Lab: Troubleshooting Desktop Application Support Issues

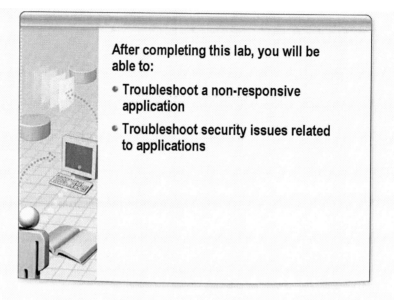

Objectives

After completing this lab, you will be able to:

- Troubleshoot a non-responsive application.
- Troubleshoot security issues related to applications.

Prerequisites

Before working on this lab, you must have an understanding of how to use Microsoft Virtual PC.

Before you begin

For each exercise in this lab, use the password **P@ssw0rd**.

In Virtual PC, <right> ALT+DEL is the equivalent of CTRL+ALT+DEL.

Scenario

You are a DST for Northwind Traders, a company whose workers use Windows XP Professional. Users call you for application troubleshooting assistance.

Estimated time to complete this lab: 15 minutes

Exercise 1
Troubleshooting a Non-Responsive Application

In this exercise, you will troubleshoot an application that no longer responds to commands or user activity.

Scenario

A user calls stating that one of her applications has stopped working. The application does not respond to mouse clicks or keyboard input. The user would like the DST to show her how to close the application without logging off or shutting down the computer.

Tasks	Guidance for completing the task
1. Start the 2262_London virtual machine.	▪ Use the Virtual PC console.
2. Start the 2262_Acapulco virtual machine and log on locally as **Administrator** with a password of **P@ssw0rd**.	▪ Use the Virtual PC console.
3. Open C:\Program Files\ Microsoft Learning\ 2262\Lab File|Lab02\ Bad Macro.doc and enable macros.	▪ To run the macro, on the **Tools** menu, point to **Macro** and then click **Macros**. Verify **BadMacro** is highlighted and then click **Run**. ▪ Wait a few seconds and then click inside the document several times.
4. Start Task Manager.	▪ One way to start Task Manager is to press \<right\> ALT+DEL and then click **Task Manager**.
5. Resolve the non-responsive application issue	▪ Refer to the Tools for Troubleshooting Win16 Applications topic. ▪ Successful resolution of this issue results in Microsoft Word not being listed as a process in the Task Manager.
6. Using Acapulco, close all windows and log off.	

Exercise 2
Troubleshooting Security Issues Related to Applications

In this exercise, you will troubleshoot application issues related to security.

Scenario

A user calls and says she cannot use her company database. Her company is using a Microsoft Access database. When she starts the database, she is unable to modify it. You talk to the database administrator and learn that the database is actually split into two files. One file resides on the client computer, Acapulco, and the other file resides on the server, London, in the RAHelp shared folder.

Tasks	Guidance for completing the task
1. Using Acapulco, log on to the domain as **AcapulcoUser**.	
2. Using Acapulco, browse to C:\Program Files\ Microsoft Learning\2262\ Labfiles\Lab02\ and double-click **Northwind_Client** and on the Main Switchboard window, click **Products**.	• This step introduces the problem. • Accept the default initials for AcapulcoUser. • In the **Security Warning** dialog box, click **Open**.
❓ Were you able to successfully open the Northwind Traders database and view the products window?	
3. Resolve the security issue.	• Refer to the Troubleshooting Security Issues Related to Applications lesson. • Successful resolution of this issue results in the user accessing the Northwind database and viewing Products from Acapulco using Northwind Client.mdb.
4. On both London and Acapulco, close the virtual machine and delete changes.	

Lab Discussion

After you have completed the exercises in this lab, take a moment to answer the following questions. When the entire class has finished the lab, the instructor will facilitate a lab discussion based on students' answers to these questions.

1. How did you determine the cause of the issue(s)?

2. How did you resolve the issue(s)?

3. What are some other ways the issue(s) could have been resolved?

Microsoft®

Module 3: Troubleshooting Issues Related to Internet Explorer

Contents

Overview

- • Configuring and Troubleshooting General Settings
- • Configuring and Troubleshooting Security and Privacy Settings
- • Configuring and Troubleshooting Content Settings
- • Configuring and Troubleshooting Connectivity Settings
- • Configuring and Troubleshooting Program Settings
- • Customizing Internet Explorer

Introduction

Users rely on the Internet as their primary method of accessing information, whether for communication, to perform transactions, for entertainment, or to accomplish a variety of other tasks. With Microsoft® Internet Explorer 6 and an Internet connection, users can search for and view information on the Internet. As a desktop support technician (DST), you must be able to support users running Internet Explorer on Microsoft Windows® XP Professional and Windows XP Home Edition.

To support your users, you must be familiar with the settings that are available in Internet Explorer and how to configure and customize these settings. For example, Internet Explorer enables users to specify the Web page that appears when the browser is started, delete temporary Internet files stored on the computer, block access to objectionable material, and set security levels. This module describes these Internet Explorer settings and explains how to configure and customize them.

Note   The Internet Explorer settings discussed in this module's lessons correspond to the seven tabs on the **Internet Options** dialog box in Internet Explorer. To open Internet Options, click **Start**, click **Control Panel**, click **Network and Internet Connections**, and then click **Internet Options**. The **Internet Options** dialog box displays the seven tabs.

Objectives

After completing this module, you will be able to:

- Configure and troubleshoot general settings.
- Configure and troubleshoot security and privacy settings.
- Configure and troubleshoot content settings.
- Configure and troubleshoot connectivity settings.
- Configure and troubleshoot program settings.
- Customize Internet Explorer.

Lesson: Configuring and Troubleshooting General Settings

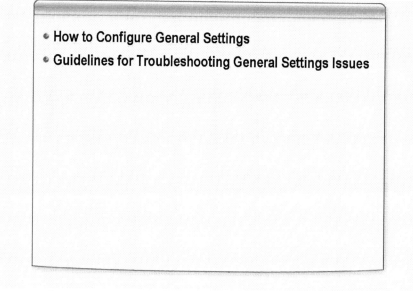

* How to Configure General Settings
* Guidelines for Troubleshooting General Settings Issues

This lesson provides information on how to configure and customize general settings and how to troubleshoot issues related to these settings.

Objectives

After completing this lesson, you will be able to:

- Configure settings on the General tab.
- Apply guidelines for troubleshooting issues related to general settings.

How to Configure General Settings

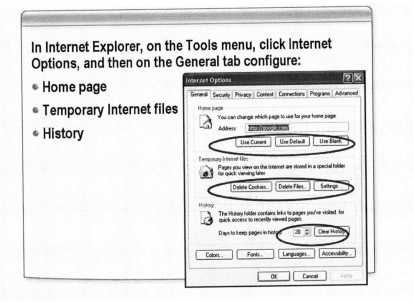

In Internet Explorer, on the Tools menu, click Internet Options, and then on the General tab configure:

● Home page

● Temporary Internet files

● History

Introduction

The General Settings options enable users to assign a home page, configure temporary Internet files, and increase access to recently viewed Web pages. This section describes these options.

To configure general settings:

1. In Internet Explorer, on the **Tools** menu, click **Internet Options**.

2. In the **Internet Options** dialog box, on the **General** tab, select the option to configure.

Home page options

The *home page* is the first page you see when you connect to Internet Explorer. The following table describes the Internet Explorer options for setting or changing your home page.

Option	Description
Use Current	Sets the home page using the URL (Uniform Resource Locator) currently displayed in Internet Explorer.
Use Default	Sets the home page using the setting configured during Internet Explorer installation. A system administrator can set the default page for users by using the Internet Explorer Administration Kit.
Use Blank	Sets the home page as a blank page not associated with a particular site.

Temporary Internet file options

The *Temporary Internet Files* (or cache) folder contains Web page content that is stored on a computer's hard disk for quick viewing. The cache permits Internet Explorer to download only the content that has changed since the user last viewed a Web page, instead of downloading all the contents for a page every time it is displayed. The following table describes the temporary Internet files options.

Option	Description
Delete Cookies	Deletes all cookies on the computer.
Delete Files	Deletes all the content archived in the Temporary Internet Files cache, including Hypertext Markup Language (HTML), graphic, and multimedia files. Cookies and History folder contents are not deleted.
Settings	Displays all the settings in the **Settings** dialog box, such as Check for newer versions of stored pages, amount of disk space to use, Move folder, View Files, View Objects.

History folder options

The History folder contains links to Web pages recently visited for enabling quick access to these pages. For example, if a user sets the history for one day, the folder will be cleared each day. This is useful for users who do not want others to know the Web sites they have visited, but it makes accessing the site slower.

Guidelines for Troubleshooting General Settings Issues

> ✓ What steps led to the problem?
>
> ✓ Is the computer a member of a network or domain?
>
> ✓ Is the computer running low on disk space?
>
> ✓ Identify a solution
>
> ✓ Test the solution

Introduction

Troubleshooting Internet Explorer general settings can be a challenge. This section describes the general troubleshooting questions you should ask your users when attempting to resolve issues regarding Internet Explorer general settings.

What steps led to the problem?

When a user calls you with a general settings issue, ask the user to clearly describe the problem and the steps that led up to the problem. Describe the problem back to the user. Make sure you know precisely what is supposed to happen, what is actually happening, and, most important, the detailed steps required to reproduce the problem. The following table lists the types of general settings issues you may encounter as DST:

Issue	Typical cause
Unexpected change of home page	• Visiting a Web site that changes the Internet Explorer home page • Installing a program that changes the Internet Explorer home page • A virus
Unable to change home page	• User does not know the procedure
Unable to delete temporary Internet files	• User does not know the procedure

Is the computer a member of a network or domain?

One of the most important questions to ask the user is if the computer is a member of a network or domain. If the computer is on a network or domain, the system administrator may have implemented policies or controls that determine the user's Internet Explorer settings. For example, the system administrator may have:

■ Reset user-defined settings to conform to company standards.

■ Enacted policies to prevent users from configuring particular settings.

Note   For information on how to determine if a user is a member of a domain, see Module 3, "Resolving Desktop Management Issues," in course 2261, *Supporting Users Running Microsoft Windows Desktop Operating Systems.*

Is the computer running low on disk space?

The Temporary Internet Files can use a large amount of disk space. The more sites a user visits, the larger the store of temporary Internet files on the hard disks becomes. If the size of the Temporary Internet Files cache exceeds the cache size limit, the Windows *swap file* (a storage area on a hard drive for data that is not used often) may run less efficiently, you may not be able to install other applications, and your hard disk may run out of space. If a user calls stating that they are running low on disk space, you can decrease the amount of disk space the Temporary Internet Files folder uses.

Note   For more information about the size of the Temporary Internet Files folder, see Knowledge Base (KB) article 301057.

Walk the user through the procedure

After you determine the cause of the user's problem, identify the solution.

Two possible scenarios include:

- If the user is a member of a network or domain and you determine that the system administrator has implemented network policies or controls, the user cannot configure his settings. Describe the reasons to the user.

- If the user is unable to change the home page because she does not know how to do it, walk the user through the procedure of changing the home page.

Test the solution

The final step in the troubleshooting process is to test and document the solution. Ask the user to repeat the step that she performed to cause the error, and then make sure that she is satisfied the problem is resolved. Finally, document and close the call, providing a good description of the problem and resolution.

For example, if the user calls and states that his home page changed and you step him through the procedures for changing the home page settings back to the page he wants, ask him to quit Internet Explorer and restart it. If the home page changed successfully, you succeeded in troubleshooting the problem. After you troubleshoot the user's issue, you must accurately document the user's issue and explain how you helped to resolve the problem.

Additional reading

For more information about troubleshooting settings on the **General** tab of the **Internet Options** dialog box, see KB articles 320159 and 260897.

Practice: Configuring General Settings

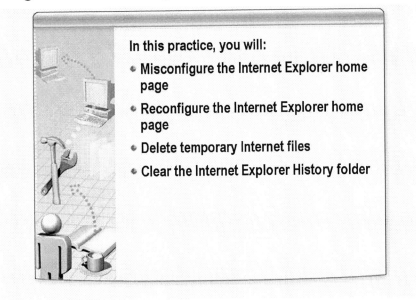

In this practice, you will:

* Misconfigure the Internet Explorer home page
* Reconfigure the Internet Explorer home page
* Delete temporary Internet files
* Clear the Internet Explorer History folder

Objective

In this practice, you will adjust general settings in Internet Explorer. After making these changes, you will need to find out how these settings affect Internet Explorer.

Practice

▶ **Misconfigure the Internet Explorer home page**

1. Start the 2262_London virtual machine.
2. Start the 2262_Acapulco virtual machine.
3. Using Acapulco, log on locally as **Administrator** with the password **P@ssw0rd**.
4. Start Internet Explorer.
5. In Internet Explorer, on the **Tools** menu, click **Internet Options**.
6. On the **General** tab, in the **Address** box, type **htp://london/exchange** (use htp instead of http) and then click **OK**.
7. On the **Internet Explorer** toolbar, click **Home** to verify that an error stating **The page cannot be displayed** appears in the browser.

▶ **Reconfigure the Internet Explorer home page**

1. Using Acapulco, in Internet Explorer, in the address bar, type **http://london/exchange** and then click **Go**.
2. In Internet Explorer, on the **Tools** menu, click **Internet Options**.
3. In the **Internet Options** dialog box, on the **General** tab, click **Use Current**, and then click **OK**.
4. On the **Internet Explorer** toolbar, click **Home** to verify Outlook Web Access is displayed.

▶ **Delete temporary Internet files**

1. Using Acapulco, in Internet Explorer, on the **Tools** menu, click **Internet Options**.

2. In the **Internet Options** dialog box, on the **General** tab, click **Settings**.

3. In **Settings**, click the **View Files** button.

4. In the Temporary Internet Files window, change to **Details** view, click the column heading **Type** to arrange the files in order of file type, and then scroll through the list to see the various kinds of files.

5. Close the Temporary Internet Files window.

6. In the **Settings** dialog box, click **OK**.

7. In the **Internet Options** dialog box, click **Delete Files**.

8. In the **Delete Files** warning box, select the **Delete all offline content** checkbox, and then click **OK**.

9. In the **Internet Options** dialog box, click **Settings**.

10. In the **Settings** dialog box, click **View Files**.

11. Scroll through the Temporary Internet Files window, and notice that all the files were deleted.

12. Close the Temporary Internet Files window.

13. In the **Settings** dialog box, click **OK**.

14. In the **Internet Options** dialog box, click **OK**.

▶ **Clear the Internet Explorer History folder**

1. Using Acapulco, on the **Internet Explorer** toolbar, click **History** to view a list of visited pages.

2. On the **History** taskbar, click **Today** to expand the Web sites viewed today.

3. In Internet Explorer, click **Tools**, and then click **Internet Options**.

4. In **Internet Options**, on the **General** tab, click **Clear History**.

5. In the **Internet Options** information box, click **Yes**.

6. In **Internet Options**, click **OK**.

7. Notice that the History pane is now blank, indicating that the contents of the History folder have been deleted.

8. Close Internet Explorer.

9. Using both Acapulco and London, close all windows, log off, and pause the virtual machine.

Lesson: Configuring and Troubleshooting Security and Privacy Settings

* What Are Cookies and ActiveX Controls?
* What Are Web Content Zones?
* How to Configure Security Settings
* How to Configure Privacy Settings
* Types of Security and Privacy Settings Issues

Introduction

Internet users are increasingly concerned about the security of their private information as they browse the Internet. Windows XP Service Pack 2 (SP2) introduces a number of new security features to Internet Explorer 6. As a DST, you need to understand how these enhancements affect the user interface (UI) and the user experience. For example, Internet Explorer provides immediate precautionary measures to secure browsing on the Internet, as well as security settings that users can configure to meet their particular security and privacy needs. Before you can support users in troubleshooting issues related to security and privacy, you need to understand the difference between these two features:

■ **Security** features prevent unauthorized users from gaining access to information and protect computers from unsafe software.

■ **Privacy** features protect personally identifiable information by allowing users to specify privacy settings.

The options on the **Security** tab and the **Privacy** tab in the **Internet Options** dialog box enable users to specify security settings and levels and to select privacy settings. This lesson explains how to configure and customize the security and privacy settings and how to troubleshoot these settings.

Objectives

After completing this lesson, you will be able to:

■ Explain the purpose and function of cookies and ActiveX® controls.

■ Explain the purpose and function of Web content zones.

■ Modify security settings.

■ Configure privacy settings.

■ Describe the types of issues related to security and privacy settings.

What Are Cookies and ActiveX Controls?

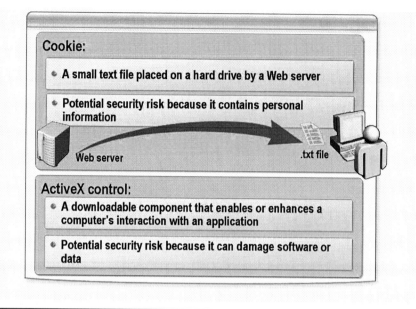

Introduction

Before you can assist Internet Explorer users in resolving their security and privacy issues, you need to understand some fundamental Internet technology concepts. This section describes cookies and ActiveX controls and explains that they are used by Web sites to store information and perform actions on the host computer, which can create a security risk to users.

What are cookies?

A *cookie* is a small text file placed on a computer hard drive (Web browser) by a Web server. The browser stores the message in a text file. The message is sent back to the server each time the browser requests a Web page from the server. The purpose of a cookie is to identify users and possibly prepare customized Web pages for them. For example, instead of viewing a generic Web page, you may see a Web page with your name on it.

Cookies contain various types of information about the user, such as the user's name and e-mail address. Often cookies are used to authenticate, or ensure that, the user is who he or she claims to be. For example, cookies can act as password authenticators so that users are not required to type their passwords every time they visit a particular site. Cookies are also used to maintain a "shopping basket" in an online store so that a user can close the browser and then reopen it at a later date to resume shopping.

Cookies are relevant to a user's security and privacy because they store personal information, such as credit card information, that a user has freely provided to a Web site. To increase user security and privacy, Web browsers today, such as Internet Explorer, enable users to extensively customize the way that cookies are managed.

What are ActiveX controls?

An *ActiveX control* is a reusable component (such as a small program or animation written to perform a specific action) that a Web site prompts you to download to enable or enhance a computer's interaction with an application. A single ActiveX control can contain one or more controls. *Controls* are items in a window or dialog box that are selected or manipulated, such as a scroll bar or a radio button.

Because ActiveX controls have full access to a computer's operating system, they provide tremendous positive potential as well as the potential risk of damaging the software or data on a computer. To control this risk, Microsoft created a registration system so that browsers can identify and authenticate an ActiveX control before downloading it.

What Are Web Content Zones?

Zone	Description
Internet	Contains anything that is not on a computer, on an intranet, or assigned to any other zone
Local intranet	Contains any addresses that do not require a proxy server
Trusted sites	Contains trusted sites
Restricted sites	Contains sites that are not trusted

Introduction

Preserving the security of your computer when you browse the Web is a balancing act. The more you download software and other content, the greater your exposure to risk; however, the more restrictive your settings, the less usable—and useful—the Web becomes.

What is a Web content zone?

The security features of Internet Explorer aim to strike an effective balance by providing four Web content zones: Internet, Local Intranet, Trusted, and Restricted. You can allocate Web sites to any zone you wish. You can also adjust each zone's security level. For example, you might put well-known entertainment or shopping sites in the Trusted zone, and set the security level lower on that zone than you would for unknown sites in the Internet zone. Descriptions of the four Web content zones in Internet Explorer follow.

Internet zone

Contains anything that is not on your computer or on an intranet, or is not assigned to any other zone. The default security level for the Internet zone is Medium. You can change your privacy settings for the Internet zone on the **Privacy** tab in the **Internet Options** dialog box.

Local intranet zone

Contains any addresses that do not require a proxy server to filter requests, as defined by the system administrator. These include sites specified on the **Connections** tab, network paths such as *computername**foldername*, and local intranet sites such as http://internal. You can add sites to this zone. The default security level for the Local intranet zone is Medium, which means that Internet Explorer allows all cookies from Web sites in this zone to be saved on your computer and read by the Web site that created them.

Trusted sites zone

Contains trusted sites from which you believe you can download or run files without damaging your computer or data. You can assign sites to this zone. The default security level for the Trusted sites zone is Low, which means Internet Explorer allows all cookies from Web sites in this zone to be saved on your computer and read by the Web site that created them.

Restricted sites zone

Contains sites you do not trust. Downloading or running files from these sites may damage your computer or data. You can assign sites to this zone. The default security level for the Restricted sites zone is High, which means Internet Explorer blocks all cookies from Web sites in this zone.

How to determine a Web page's security zone

When you attempt to open or download content from the Web, Internet Explorer checks the security settings for that Web site's zone. You can tell which zone the current Web page falls into by looking at the right side of the Internet Explorer status bar.

Note   Any files already on your local computer are assumed to be safe, so minimal security settings are assigned to them. You cannot assign a folder or drive on your computer to a security zone.

Tip   You can change the security level for a zone. For example, you might want to change the security setting for your Local intranet zone to Low. You can also customize settings for a zone by importing a privacy settings file from a certificate authority.

How to Configure Security Settings

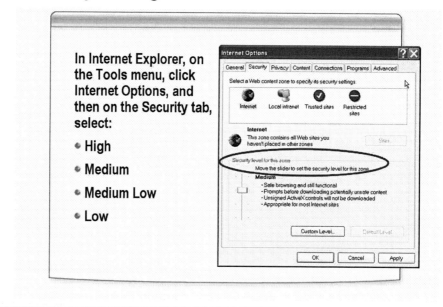

In Internet Explorer, on the Tools menu, click Internet Options, and then on the Security tab, select:

- High
- Medium
- Medium Low
- Low

Introduction

For each of the Web content zones, a default *security level* defines how Web sites in each zone are accommodated from a security standpoint. This section examines how different security levels affect your interaction with Web sites that fall into each of the various security levels and how to change the level of security in each Web content zone to suit your needs.

How to configure security settings levels

To configure the security settings level for a Web content zone:

1. In Internet Explorer, on the **Tools** menu, click **Internet Options**.

2. In the **Internet Options** dialog box, on the **Security** tab, click the zone on which you want to set the security level.

3. If the **Security level for this zone** is Custom, click **Default Level**.

4. Drag the slider to set the security level to High, Medium, Medium-low, or Low. Internet Explorer describes each option to help you decide which level to choose. You are prompted to confirm any reduction in security level.

5. Click **OK** to close the **Internet Options** dialog box.

Security levels

The following table describes the security levels available in Internet Explorer.

Security level	Description
High	The safest way to browse, but also the least functional. Less secure features are disabled. Appropriate for sites that might have harmful content.
Medium	Safe browsing and still functional. Prompts before downloading potentially unsafe content. Unsigned ActiveX controls are not downloaded.
Medium-low	Does not prompt before downloading potentially unsafe content. Most content runs without prompts. Unsigned ActiveX controls are not downloaded. Appropriate for sites on a local network (intranet).
Low	Minimal safeguards and warning prompts are provided. Most content is downloaded and run without prompts. Appropriate for sites that are absolutely trusted.
Custom	A security setting of your own design.

How to Configure Privacy Settings

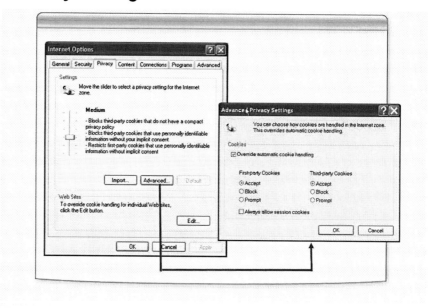

Introduction

Internet Explorer allows you to configure your computer's *privacy settings*. Privacy settings determine how much of your personal information can be accessed by Web sites and whether Web sites can save cookies on your computer.

To configure the privacy settings level for the Internet zone:

1. In Internet Explorer, on the **Tools** menu, click **Internet Options**.
2. In the **Internet Options** dialog box, on the **Privacy** tab, drag the slider to set the privacy level.

Internet Explorer describes each option to help you decide which level to choose. You are prompted to confirm any reduction in security level.

Privacy settings

The following table describes the security settings available in Internet Explorer.

Privacy setting	Description
Block All Cookies	Blocks cookies from all Web sites. Existing cookies on the computer cannot be read by Web sites.
High	Blocks cookies that do not have a compact privacy policy. Blocks cookies that use personally identifiable information (PIF) without explicit consent. (*PIF* is information that can be used to identify or contact you, such as your name, e-mail address, home or work address, and telephone number.)
Medium -High	Blocks third-party cookies that do not have a compact privacy policy. Blocks third-party cookies that use PIF without explicit consent. Blocks first-party cookies that use PIF without implicit consent.

(*continued*)

Privacy setting	Description
Medium	Blocks third-party cookies that do not have a compact privacy policy. Blocks third-party cookies that use PIF without implicit consent. Restricts first-party cookies that use PIF without implicit consent.
Low	Restricts third-party cookies that do not have a compact privacy policy. Restricts third-party cookies that use PIF without implicit consent.
Accept All Cookies	All cookies are saved on the computer. Existing cookies on the computer can be read by the Web sites that created them.

How to configure security settings for cookies

To configure security settings for cookies in each security zone:

1. In the **Internet Options** dialog box, on the **Privacy** tab, click **Advanced**.

2. In the **Advanced Privacy Settings** dialog box, select the **Override automatic cookie handling** check box, and then select one of the following options:

   - *First-party cookies*. These cookies originate on or are sent to the Web site you are currently viewing. These cookies are commonly used to store information such as your preferences when visiting that site.

   - *Third-party cookies*. These cookies originate on or are sent to a Web site different from the one you are currently viewing. Third-party Web sites usually provide some content on the Web site you are viewing. For example, many sites use advertising from third-party Web sites; those third-party Web sites may use cookies. For marketing purposes, these cookies are typically used to track the way in which you use the Web page.

Note   Changing your privacy preferences does not affect the cookie acceptance policy for cookies that have already been set unless you click **Accept All Cookies** or **Block All Cookies** on the **Privacy** tab.

Important   Privacy preferences are only applied to the Internet zone.

How to enable or block cookies

In Internet Explorer, you can allow or block cookies from individual Web sites. To override how cookies are handled for individual Web sites, in the **Internet Options** dialog box, on the **Privacy** tab, click **Sites**, type the address of the Web site that you want to manage, and then click **Allow** or **Block**.

Web site privacy policies

Many Web sites provide privacy statements that you can view on the Internet. A Web site's *privacy policy* tells you what kind of information the Web site collects, to whom it gives that information, and how it uses the information. Web sites also might provide a Platform for Privacy Preferences (P3P) privacy policy. If a Web site has a P3P privacy policy, Internet Explorer can display it. Internet Explorer can also compare your privacy settings to a representation of the P3P privacy policy and determine whether to allow the Web site to save cookies on your computer.

Additional reading

For more information about privacy settings, see KB article 283185.

Types of Security and Privacy Settings Issues

1	Focus troubleshooting efforts
2	Identify the solution

Issues a DST may encounter include:

Issue	Typical cause
Unable to open a Web page	The Web page may contain content that is not permitted by the security zone levels
Java error messages	A missing or incorrect version of the Java virtual machine
Prompted to enter a password	The change may have occurred in the user's security settings or privacy level
Prompted or not to save a cookie	
Security-related error messages	

Introduction

Security and privacy are two key concerns of Internet users today. Many of the calls you receive as a DST will relate to these issues. Refer to the following best practices when troubleshooting security and privacy settings in Internet Explorer.

Focus your troubleshooting efforts

The following table lists several privacy and security issues and their causes.

Issue	Typical cause
Unable to open a Web page	The Web page may contain content that is not permitted by your security zone levels.
Java error messages	The Java virtual machine may be missing or an incorrect version may be installed (either a third-party Java virtual machine or a Microsoft Java virtual machine).
Prompted to enter a password	A change may have occurred in the user's security settings or privacy level.
Prompted (or not being prompted) to save a cookie	A change may have occurred in the user's security settings or privacy level.
Security-related error messages	A change may have occurred in the user's security settings or privacy level.

Identify the solution

After you determine the cause of your users' problems, identify possible solutions, such as the following:

- Ask users to review their security zone level. Recommend that they set the security zone level back to the default.

- Ask users to review their privacy settings. Recommend that they reset the privacy settings to the default.

How to troubleshoot active content

Active content is content on a Web page that is either interactive or dynamic. Active content works by pushing action items to the computer, such as animated GIFs (Graphics Interchange Formats), Java (a high-level programming language used on the Web), JavaScript, streaming audio and video, or ActiveX controls.

Although most active content is safe, some Web pages contain active content that can cause security problems on your computer. For example, an ActiveX control that runs automatically when you load a particular Web page might damage your data or cause your computer to become infected with a virus. Internet Explorer uses security levels for active content to help prevent this situation. These levels are accessed and modified by customizing your Web content zone security settings.

If you are unable to load a particular Web page using Internet Explorer, the problem may be caused by active content on the Web page.

Note   For more information about troubleshooting active content, see KB article 154036.

How to troubleshoot Java

If at some point you receive a Java-related error message, the problem may be related to the implementation of Java that you have running on your computer. Java problems generally fall into three categories:

- Difficulty determining the scope of the Java problem
- Java problems on one Web site
- Java problems on all Web sites

Note   For more information about troubleshooting Java settings, see KB article 168806.

How to troubleshoot ICS problems

Internet Connection Sharing (ICS) is a feature of Windows XP. When you use ICS, you can share one Internet connection with two or more computers. If a user asks if she can use this feature, suggest she contact her Internet service provider (ISP) or read the ISP's Terms and Conditions of Use policy to determine if she is permitted to share a connection.

Note   For more information on ICS, see KB article 238135.

Practice: Configuring Security and Privacy Settings

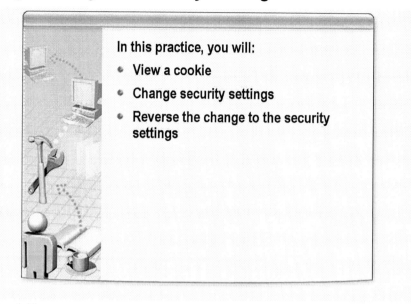

Objective

In this practice, you will adjust security and privacy settings in Internet Explorer. After making these changes, you will need to find out how these settings affect Internet Explorer.

Practice

▶ **View a cookie**

1. Resume London and Acapulco.

2. Using Acapulco, log on locally as **Administrator** with a password of **P@ssw0rd**.

3. Using Acapulco, navigate to **C:\Documents and Settings\ Administrator\Cookies**.

4. Double-click **administrator@microsoft[1]**.

5. In Notepad, view the contents of the file and, after viewing it, close Notepad.

6. Close the Cookies window.

▶ **Change security settings**

1. Using Acapulco, start Internet Explorer.

2. On the **Tools** menu, click **Internet Options**.

3. In the **Internet Options** dialog box, on the **Security** tab, click the **Local intranet** icon, and then click **Custom Level**.

4. In the **Security Settings** dialog box, under **Run ActiveX controls and plug-ins**, select **Disable**, and then click **OK**.

5. In the **Warning!** dialog box, click **Yes**.

6. In the **Internet Options** dialog box, click **OK**.

7. To view the impact of changing this security setting, type **http://london/mycalendar.htm** in the **Address** bar and press ENTER.

8. If the **Information Bar** dialog box is displayed, click **OK**.

▶ **Reverse the change to security settings**

1. In Internet Explorer, on the **Tools** menu, click **Internet Options**.

2. In the **Internet Options** dialog box, on the **Security** tab, click **Local intranet**, and then click **Default Level**, and then click **OK**.

3. Click **Refresh**.

    The calendar is displayed.

4. Close all windows, log off, and pause Acapulco and London.

Lesson: Configuring and Troubleshooting Content Settings

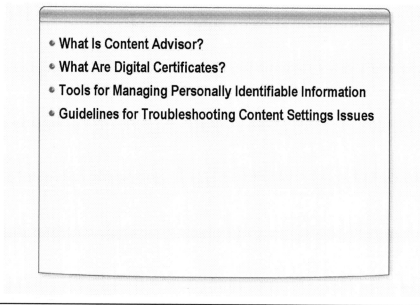

* What Is Content Advisor?
* What Are Digital Certificates?
* Tools for Managing Personally Identifiable Information
* Guidelines for Troubleshooting Content Settings Issues

Introduction

The Internet provides access to a wide variety of information, some of which is not suitable for viewers such as children. Many users have preferences regarding the kind of content that other users can view on their computer. The options on the **Content** tab in the **Internet Options** dialog box enables users to control the Internet content that can be viewed on the computer. This lesson provides information on how to configure and customize content settings and how to troubleshoot issues related to these settings.

Objectives

After completing this lesson, you will be able to:

■ Explain the purpose and function of Content Advisor.

■ Explain the purpose and function of digital certificates.

■ Use tools to manage personally identifiable information.

■ Apply guidelines for troubleshooting issues related to content settings.

What Is Content Advisor?

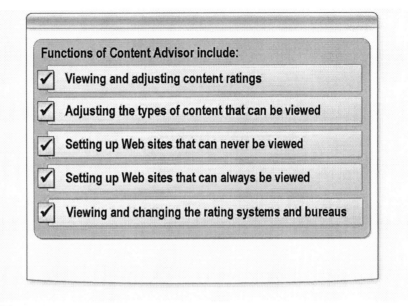

Functions of Content Advisor include:

✓ Viewing and adjusting content ratings

✓ Adjusting the types of content that can be viewed

✓ Setting up Web sites that can never be viewed

✓ Setting up Web sites that can always be viewed

✓ Viewing and changing the rating systems and bureaus

Introduction

Content Advisor is a feature of Internet Explorer that allows you to control the Internet content that can be viewed on a single computer. You must have administrator privileges to enable Content Advisor. An administrator can use the Content Advisor dialog box to configure which Web sites and content can and cannot be viewed based on the user's preferences and the guidelines of the Internet Content Rating Association (ICRA). ICRA's goal is to protect children from potentially harmful content while still preserving free speech on the Internet. Rating categories include Language, Nudity, Sex, and Violence. The Content Advisor also allows the user to specify customized and approved or disallowed sites.

Functions of Content Advisor

A password is required to change the settings in Content Advisor. After entering the password, you can use Content Advisor to:

- View and adjust the ratings to reflect what you think is appropriate content in each of four areas: Language, Nudity, Sex, and Violence.

- Adjust what types of content other people can view, with or without your permission. You can override content settings on a case-by-case basis.

  Note Enabling Content Advisor affects all user accounts on the computer, not just the initializing account.

- Set up a list of Web sites that other people can never view, regardless of how the sites' content is rated.

- Set up a list of Web sites that other people can always view, regardless of how the sites' content is rated.

- View and change the ratings systems and bureaus you use.

Important   If the password for Content Advisor is lost, Microsoft cannot help you recover it. For more information about Content Advisor, see KB article 189126.

When you first enable Content Advisor, the settings that are least likely to offend are in effect by default. You can adjust these settings to meet your own preferences.

Caution   Not all Internet content is rated. If you choose to allow other people to view unrated sites on your computer, some of those sites could contain material some users will regard as inappropriate.

What Are Digital Certificates?

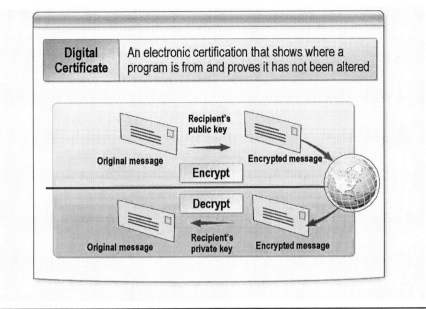

Introduction

A *digital certificate* is an electronic certification that shows where a program comes from and proves the installation package has not been altered. Digital certificates are a critical component of data security because they protect personally identifiable information on the Internet and help to protect computers from unsafe software. The most common use of a digital certificate is to verify the identity of the user sending the message and to provide a means for the receiver to encode a reply.

What is a CA?

Digital certificates are signed by the Certificate Authority (CA) that issues them. Essentially, a CA is a widely trusted third-party organization or company that guarantees that the individual granted the unique certificate is, in fact, who she or he claims to be. Digital certificates are used to create *digital signatures* (digital codes attached to e-mail messages that uniquely identify the sender) and public-private key pairs. Private and public keys are discussed later in this section.

Types of certificates

Four kinds of digital certificates are used on the Internet:

- *Personal certificates*. Used to identify individuals. This type of certificate is used to send personally identifiable information over the Internet to a Web site that requires a certificate to verify the user's identity. You can control the use of your own identity by having a private key on your computer that only you know. When used with e-mail programs, personal certificates with private keys are also known as *digital IDs*. Microsoft recommends exporting your personal certificates to a safe location as a form of backup in case your certificates are damaged.

- *Server certificates*. Used to identify servers that participate in secure communications with other computers that use communication protocols such as Secure Sockets Layer (SSL). These certificates allow a server to verify its identity to clients. Server certificates follow the X.509 certificate format that is defined by the Public-Key Cryptography Standards (PKCS).

- *Software publisher certificates.* Used to inform the user whether the software publisher is participating in the infrastructure of trusted publishers and CAs. These certificates are used to sign software that is distributed over the Internet.

  Microsoft Authenticode® requires a software publisher certificate to sign ActiveX and other compiled code. Internet Explorer is also capable of trusting software that is signed with a publisher's certificate.

  To view a list of trusted software publishers in Internet Explorer, on the **Tools** menu, click **Internet Options**, and then, on the **Content** tab, click **Publishers**. To remove a trusted publisher, click **Publishers**, and then, in the **Certificates** dialog box, click **Remove**.

- *Certificate Authority certificates* are divided into two categories:

  - *Root CAs.* Root CAs are self-signed, meaning that the subject of the certificate is also the signer of the certificate. Root CAs can assign certificates for Intermediate CAs.

  - *Intermediate CAs.* Intermediate CAs can issue server certificates, personal certificates, publisher certificates, or certificates for other Intermediate CAs.

How do digital certificates work?

Digital certificates work with two types of keys:

- A *public key* is an encryption/decryption key provided by an authority that, combined with a private key that is derived from the public key, can be used to encrypt messages.

- A *private key* is an encryption/decryption key known only by the parties that exchange messages. The key should be shared by the communicating parties so that each can encrypt and decrypt messages.

  For example, if User A wants to send a secure message to User B, User A uses User B's public key to *encrypt*, or translate, the data in the message into secret code. User B then uses his or her private key to decrypt the message.

A digital certificate, whether it is a personal certificate or a Web site certificate, associates an identity with a public key. Only the owner of the certificate knows the corresponding private key. The private key allows the owner to make a digital signature or decrypt information encrypted with the corresponding public key. When you send your certificate to other people, you are actually giving them your public key so that they can send you encrypted information that only you can decrypt and read with your private key.

The digital signature component of a security certificate is your electronic identity card. The digital signature tells the recipient that the information actually came from you and has not been forged or tampered with.

Before you can start sending encrypted or digitally signed information, you must obtain a certificate and set up Internet Explorer to use it. When you visit a secure Web site—a Web site whose address starts with *https*—the site automatically sends you its certificate.

Where to obtain security certificates

Security certificates are issued by independent certification authorities. There are different classes of security certificates, each providing a different level of credibility. You obtain your personal security certificate from certification authorities.

Note If you set Internet Explorer security settings to not allow certificates, the user cannot connect to secure Web sites and cannot download and install digitally signed software.

Note For more information about certificates, see KB article 195724, and go to http://www.microsoft.com/windows/ie/using/howto/security/digitalcert/using.mspx.

Tools for Managing Personally Identifiable Information

Introduction

Personally identifiable information is information that can be used to identify or contact you, such as your name, e-mail address, or home or work telephone number. Internet Explorer includes two tools to help you manage your personally identifiable information and preferences on the Internet: AutoComplete and Profile Assistant. These tools simplify the amount and type of information that you are required to enter when you are browsing Web sites or filling out Web-based forms.

What is AutoComplete?

The AutoComplete feature saves previous entries you have made for Web addresses, forms, and passwords. When you type information in one of these fields, AutoComplete suggests possible matches. These matches can include folder and program names you type into the Address bar, as well as search queries, stock quotes, or other information that you type in forms on Web pages. The information used for suggested matches is archived on your computer and is encrypted to protect your privacy.

Note   When typing information in Web forms, and when typing passwords, you can remove an item from the list of suggestions by clicking the item and then pressing the DELETE key.

What is Profile Assistant?

Profile Assistant stores personal information such as your e-mail address or e-mail alias on your computer. When you visit a new Web site that requests such information, Profile Assistant can enter it for you. This saves you from having to enter the same information every time you visit a new Web site. None of this information can be viewed on your computer or shared with others without your permission. When a Web site requests information from Profile Assistant, the request includes:

- The URL of the site requesting the information.

- What information the site is requesting from Profile Assistant, so that you can choose to exclude information.

- How this information will be used.

- Whether the site has a secure connection (SSL). If it does, you can verify the site's certificate.

How to configure AutoComplete and Profile Assistant settings

To configure AutoComplete and Profile Assistant settings:

1. In Internet Explorer, on the **Tools** menu, click **Internet Options**.

2. In the **Internet Options** dialog box, on the **Content** tab:

    - Click **AutoComplete**.

      You can use AutoComplete for Web addresses, forms, and user names and passwords. You can also clear the history of previous AutoComplete entries.

      – or –

    - Click **My Profile** and then, in the **Main Identity Properties** dialog box, click the appropriate tab to create a new profile or modify an existing profile.

Guidelines for Troubleshooting Content Settings Issues

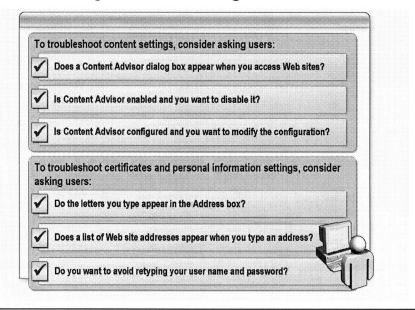

Introduction

Typically, calls from users or end users about Content settings concern unexpected activation of Content Advisor settings or an inability to deactivate or configure the settings to meet user needs. In addition, users or end users will have questions about certificates or AutoComplete settings and will want to know how to configure their settings differently.

It is critical that you determine exactly what users or end users want or are describing and then step them through the configuration process. To accomplish this, you must have a good understanding of the configuration settings available and how they might be described by an end user.

Sample questions to gather information

To troubleshoot Content settings, you need to determine how Internet Explorer is performing for the user and how the user expects or wants it to perform. To accomplish this, you need to elicit information from the user. Some questions you might want to ask the user include:

- Does a Content Advisor dialog box appear when you access Web sites?
- Is Content Advisor enabled and you want to disable it?
- Is Content Advisor configured and you want to modify the configuration?

For Certificate settings and Personal Information settings, you need to elicit the same type of information and then step the user through configuring Internet Explorer properties correctly. Some questions you might ask the user include:

- Do the letters you type appear in the Address box?
- Does a list of Web site addresses appear below the Address box when you type a Web site address?
- Do you want to save your user name and/or a password so that you do not have to retype it when you visit that page again?

Practice: Configuring and Troubleshooting Content Settings

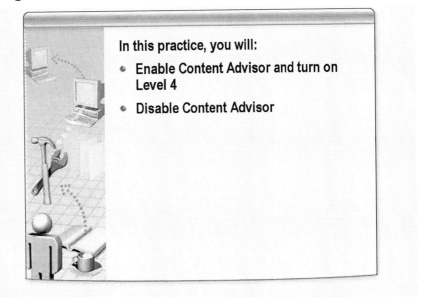

In this practice, you will:

- Enable Content Advisor and turn on Level 4
- Disable Content Advisor

Objective

In this practice, you will adjust Content Advisor settings in Internet Explorer.

Practice

▶ **Enable Content Advisor and turn on Level 4**

1. Resume London and Acapulco.

2. Using Acapulco, log on locally as **Administrator** with the password **P@ssw0rd**.

3. Click **Start**, and then click **Internet**.

4. In Internet Explorer, on the **Tools** menu, click **Internet Options**.

5. In the **Internet Options** dialog box, on the **Content** tab, click **Enable**.

6. In the **Content Advisor** window, select **Level 1** for each RSACi Category, and then click **OK**.

7. In the **Create Supervisor Password** window, when prompted for a password, type **P@ssw0rd** in the **Password** and **Confirm password** boxes, and then click **OK**.

8. In the **Content Advisor** dialog box requesting a hint, click **No**, and then, in the **Content Advisor** dialog box, click **OK**.

9. To close the **Internet Options** dialog box, click **OK**.

10. In Internet Explorer, in the **Address** bar, type **http://london** and then press ENTER.

    The **Content Advisor** dialog box is displayed stating http://london does not have a rating and prompts you for a password to gain access.

11. In the **Content Advisor** dialog box, click **Cancel**.

    Notice that canceling out of Content Advisor brought you back to your original site.

12. In the **Address** bar, type **http://london** and then press ENTER.

13. In Content Advisor, in the **Password** box, type **P@ssw0rd** and then click **OK**.

    The Under Construction page is displayed.

▶ **Disable Content Advisor**

1. In Internet Explorer, on the **Tools** menu, click **Internet Options**.

2. In the **Internet Options** dialog box, on the **Content** tab, click **Disable**.

3. In the **Supervisor Password Required** dialog box, in the **Password** box, type **P@ssw0rd** and then click **OK**.

4. In the **Content Advisor** dialog box, click **OK**.

5. In the **Internet Options** dialog box, click. **OK**.

6. Close all windows and log off.

7. Pause London and Acapulco.

Lesson: Configuring and Troubleshooting Connectivity Settings

- What Is a Dial-Up Connection?
- How to Configure a Dial-Up Connection
- What Is a VPN Connection?
- How to Configure a VPN Connection
- What Is a Proxy Server?
- How to Configure Internet Explorer to Use a Proxy Server
- Guidelines for Troubleshooting Connectivity Settings Issues

Introduction

A major area of concern—and occasional source of confusion—for end users is how to establish and maintain a connection to the Internet or to their organization's internal network or intranet. Before you can assist users in resolving these issues, you need to understand some fundamental Internet technology concepts related to connectivity. This lesson discusses dial-up, virtual private network (VPN), and local area network (LAN) settings, and how to configure and troubleshoot these settings.

The options on the **Connections** tab in the **Internet Options** dialog box enable users to set up an Internet connection and to help ensure that the connection is secure. This lesson provides information on how to configure and customize connectivity settings and how to troubleshoot issues related to this setting.

Objectives

After completing this lesson, you will be able to:

- Explain the purpose and function of a dial-up connection.
- Configure a dial-up connection.
- Explain the purpose and function of a VPN connection.
- Configure a VPN connection.
- Explain the purpose and function of a proxy server.
- Configure Internet Explorer to use a proxy server.
- Apply guidelines for troubleshooting issues related to connectivity settings.

What Is a Dial-Up Connection?

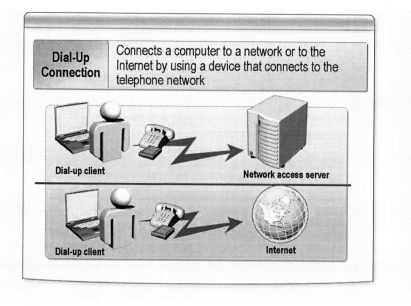

| Dial-Up Connection | Connects a computer to a network or to the Internet by using a device that connects to the telephone network |

Introduction

Dial-up settings are the settings that Internet Explorer uses to connect to the Internet when you are using a modem. *VPN settings* are the settings that Internet Explorer uses to configure a virtual private network (VPN) connection. This section examines how Internet Explorer interacts with the hardware you use to connect to the Web and how your user credentials determine the type of connection you make to the Web.

Definition

A *dial-up connection* connects a computer to a network or to the Internet by using a device that connects to the telephone network. This device can be a modem that uses a standard phone line, an ISDN (Integrated Services Digital Network) card with a high-speed ISDN line, or an X.25 network.

Most users have one or two dial-up connections, perhaps to the Internet and to a corporate network. However, in complex server scenarios, multiple dial-up connections are used to implement advanced routing. You can create multiple dial-up connections by copying them in the Network Connections folder. You can then rename the connections and modify their connection settings. By doing so, you can easily create various connections to accommodate multiple modems and dialing profiles.

Credentials required for dial-up connections

Credentials such as a user name and password are required to successfully connect to the Internet using dial-up connections. Based on your user profile, you have several choices regarding how your credentials are saved when you make a dial-up connection. Your user profile identifies you as having either administrator account privileges or user account privileges. If you have both administrator and user account privileges, only the privileges for the account on which you are currently logged on apply.

- *User account privileges.* If you log on with user account privileges, you can only make per-user dial-up connections, which are not accessible to other user accounts. For per-user dial-up connections, you can choose either to save your credentials for your use only, or to not save your credentials at all.

  If you save your credentials for your use only, the credentials are automatically supplied to complete a dial-up connection if you are logged on to the computer as the user who first saved the credentials. If you do not save your credentials, you are provided with a dialog box to enter your credentials before the connection is completed.

- *Administrator account privileges.* If you log on with administrator account privileges, you can make either a global connection or a per-user dial-up connection. Global connections are seen by any user who logs on to the computer that is hosting the connection; however, whether a connection is actually made is determined by how the credentials are saved. For global connections, you can save your credentials for all users, for your use only, or not at all. The following list describes these options:

  - If you save your credentials for all users, your credentials are automatically provided to any user attempting to connect to the Internet using the dial-up connection icon or on-demand dialing.

  - If you save your credentials for your use only, your credentials are used to complete the dial-up connection only if you are logged on to the computer. Other users are prompted for a user name and password; however, they cannot connect to the Internet unless they can provide the correct credentials.

  - If you do not save your credentials, a dialog box appears and prompts you to enter the correct credentials before the connection to the Internet is made.

How to Configure a Dial-Up Connection

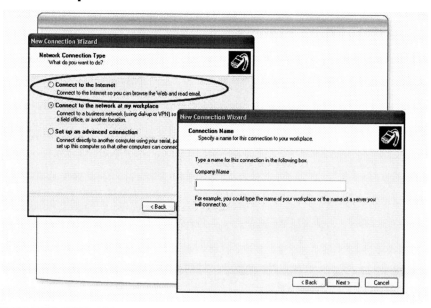

Procedure

▶ **To create a dial-up connection to connect to the Internet**

1. Click **Start**, click **Control Panel**, and then click **Network and Internet Connections**.

2. Click **Network Connections**.

3. Under **Network Tasks**, click **Create a new connection**, and then click **Next**.

4. Click **Connect to the Internet**, and then click **Next**.

5. On the **Getting Ready** page, click **Set up my connection manually** and then click **Next**.

6. On the **Internet Connection** page, click **Connect using a dial-up modem** and then click **Next**.

7. On the **Connection Name** page, in the **ISP Name** box, type the name of your ISP.

8. On the **Phone Number to Dial** page, in the **Phone number** box, type the phone number provided by your ISP and then click **Next**.

9. On the **Internet Account Information** page, provide the following information and then click **Next**:

    a. User name

    b. Password

    c. Password confirmation

10. On the **Completing the New Connection Wizard** page, click **Finish**.

What Is a VPN Connection?

Introduction

Data sent across the Internet generally is not protected, but you can use a VPN connection to make your Internet communications secure and to extend your private network. A VPN connection uses encryption and tunneling to transfer data securely on the Internet to a remote access VPN server on your workplace network. (*Tunneling* refers to a private, secure link between a remote user and a private network.)

To make a VPN connection, you must be connected to the Internet. You can make a VPN connection by first dialing an Internet service provider (ISP) or by using an existing connection to the Internet.

If you connect to the Internet using a dial-up connection, you must first connect to your ISP and then make a VPN connection to the private network's VPN server. After the VPN connection is established, you can access the private network.

If you are already connected to the Internet, whether on a local area network (LAN), a cable modem, or a digital subscriber line (DSL), you can make a VPN connection directly to the VPN server.

How to Configure a VPN Connection

Procedure

▶ **To create a VPN connection**

1. Click **Start**, click **Control Panel**, and then click **Network and Internet Connections**.

2. Click **Network Connections**.

3. Under **Network Tasks**, click **Create a new connection**, and then click **Next**.

4. Click **Connect to the network at my workplace**, and then click **Next**.

5. Click **Virtual Private Network connection**, and then click **Next**.

6. On the **Connection Name** page, in the **Company Name** box, type a name for the connection and then click **Next**.

7. On the **VPN Server Selection** page, in the **Host name** box, type the name of the host or its associated IP address, click **Next**, and then click **Finish**.

What Is a Proxy Server?

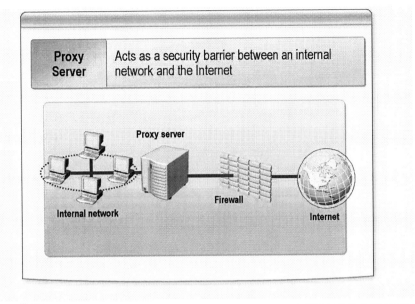

Introduction
Correctly configuring Internet Explorer for the hardware that you use to connect to the Web is just as important as configuring the software correctly. This section discusses proxy servers, ports, and settings, along with automatic configuration scripts and automatic settings detection.

Definition
A *proxy server* acts as a security barrier between your internal network and the Internet, helping to keep other users on the Internet from accessing information on your internal network. A proxy server also increases the efficiency with which Web pages are downloaded from the Internet because it maintains a cache of recently accessed Web pages.

How to Configure Internet Explorer to Use a Proxy Server

In the Internet Options dialog box, on the
Connections tab, click LAN settings

Local Area Network (LAN) Settings   ? X

Automatic configuration

Automatic configuration may override manual settings. To ensure
the use of manual settings, disable automatic configuration.

☐ Automatically detect settings

☐ Use automatic configuration script

Address

Proxy server

☑ Use a proxy server for your LAN (These settings will not apply to
dial-up or VPN connections).

Address: [   ]   Port: [   ]   (Advanced...)

☐ Bypass proxy server for local addresses

[OK] [Cancel]

Proxy Settings   ? X

Servers

Type   Proxy address to use   Port
HTTP: [   ] : [   ]
Secure: [   ] : [   ]
FTP: [   ] : [   ]
Gopher: [   ] : [   ]
Socks: [   ] : [   ]

☐ Use the same proxy server for all protocols

Exceptions

Do not use proxy server for addresses beginning with:

[   ]

Use semicolons (;) to separate entries.

[OK] [Cancel]

To configure proxy settings, in the LAN settings dialog box, select the
Proxy server check box and then click Advanced

Introduction

You can configure Internet Explorer to use a proxy server to help provide security when connecting to the Web.

How to configure Internet Explorer to use a proxy server

To configure Internet Explorer to use a proxy server:

1. Click **Start**, and then click **Internet Explorer**.

2. In Internet Explorer, on the **Tools** menu, click **Internet Options**.

3. In the **Internet Options** dialog box, on the **Connections** tab, click **LAN Settings**, and then select the **Use Proxy Server** check box.

4. In the Address field, type the Web address of the proxy server. (Use the format: http://*web_address*.)

5. In the Port field, type the port number that is assigned to the proxy server.

How to automate Internet Explorer configuration

Network administrators, ISPs, and others who want to automate the configuration of Internet Explorer settings can select the **Use Automatic Configuration Script** check box in the **LAN Settings** dialog box and then click **Advanced**.

The Automatic Configuration Script option entirely bypasses the user in the configuration process. For example, rather than having every user on a corporate network configure their own proxy server settings, a system administrator can use the Internet Explorer Administration Kit to construct an installation package that populates the automatic configuration options. Then, after the user installs Internet Explorer, the automatic configuration options take over and perform the configurations predetermined by the administrator.

Important   Most home users connect to the Internet using a dial-up, DSL, or Internet cable connection, rather than a LAN. Unless users have established home networks, they do not need to enable their LAN settings. Enabling LAN settings for these types of connections can make Internet Explorer appear as though it is either not responding or connecting very slowly.

Additional reading

For more information about Internet Explorer LAN settings, see KB article 220902.

Guidelines for Troubleshooting Connectivity Settings Issues

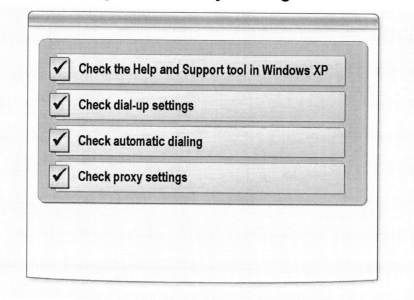

Introduction	This section describes the best practices you should consider when troubleshooting Internet Explorer connectivity issues.
Check the Help and Support tool in Windows XP	Windows XP Help and Support contains a tool for troubleshooting a variety of issues related to network and dial-up connections. This tool lists common problems, and their causes and solutions. To access this tool:

1. Click **Start**, and then click **Help and Support**.
2. In the Search field, type **troubleshooting network** and then press ENTER.
3. Select **Troubleshooting network and dial-up connections** in the **Overviews, Articles and Tutorials** section of the left pane.
4. Scroll to the appropriate problem, click the problem description, and review the cause(s) and solution(s).

Check dial-up settings	If the computer is part of a network, all dial-up selections are subject to the restrictions of a Group Policy. As a result, system administrators can choose whether to allow dial-up networking. If you are on a network, make sure that your system administrator has enabled this option.
Check automatic dialing	If you choose to enable automatic dialing, Internet Explorer may attempt to connect to the Internet when any application tries to access an Internet resource. For example, if a user inadvertently starts Instant Messenger, Internet Explorer attempts to establish a connection to the Internet. If you encounter this problem, disable automatic dialing.

Check proxy settings   If you use a backslash (\) instead of a forward slash (/) in the proxy server's address, the settings disappear from the Proxy Server field and Internet Explorer is unable to find the proxy server.

If you are using the Internet Protocol (IP) address of your proxy server, do not type leading zeros. For example, use 192.168.0.1 instead of 192.168.000.001.

If you do not know the Web address or port number of the proxy server, contact your network administrator. Also, if there are any Web servers on the local network for which you want to bypass the proxy, type the appropriate host names in the Don't Use Proxy For These Addresses field. For example, if you do not want to use the proxy server to obtain access to the "example.com" Web server on your LAN, type **example.com** in the Don't Use Proxy For These Addresses field.

Practice: Configuring and Troubleshooting Connectivity Settings

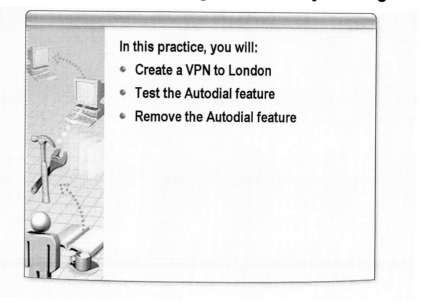

In this practice, you will:
- Create a VPN to London
- Test the Autodial feature
- Remove the Autodial feature

Objective

In this practice, you will configure a VPN connection, test the Autodial feature, and then remove the Autodial feature.

Practice

▶ **Create a VPN to London**

1. Resume London.

2. Resume Acapulco.

3. Using Acapulco, log on to locally as **Administrator** with the password **P@ssw0rd**.

4. Click **Start**, and then click **Internet**.

5. In Internet Explorer, on the **Tools** menu, click **Internet Options**.

6. In the **Internet Options** dialog box, on the **Connections** tab, click **Add**.

7. On the **Type of Connection** page, click **Connect to a private network through the Internet**, and then click **Next**.

8. In the **Host name or IP address** box, type **London** and then click **Next**.

9. On the **Finished** page, in the **Type a name you want for this connection** box, accept the default name for the connection, and then click **Finish**.

10. In the **Dial-up Settings** area of the **Virtual Private Connection Settings** dialog box, in the **User name** box, type **AcapulcoUser**. In the **Password** box, type **P@ssw0rd** and, in the **Domain** box, type **nwtraders.msft**. Click **OK**.

11. In the **Internet Options** dialog box, click **OK**.

▶ **Test the Autodial feature**

1. Using Acapulco, in Internet Explorer, type **London** in the **Address** bar, and then press ENTER.

   The **Dial-up Connection** dialog box appears.

2. In the **Dial-up Connection** dialog box, click **Work Offline**.

   The **Under Construction** page appears.

▶ **Remove the Autodial feature**

1. Using Acapulco, in Internet Explorer, on the **Tools** menu, click **Internet Options**.

2. In the **Internet Options** dialog box, on the **Connections** tab, click **Virtual Private Connection (Default)** and then click **Remove**.

3. In the **Internet Options** dialog box asking to confirm removal of the connection, click **OK**.

4. In **Internet Options** dialog box, click **OK**.

5. In Internet Explorer, on the **File** menu, click **Work Offline**.

6. Using Acapulco and London, close all windows, log off, and pause the virtual machine.

Lesson: Configuring and Troubleshooting Program Settings

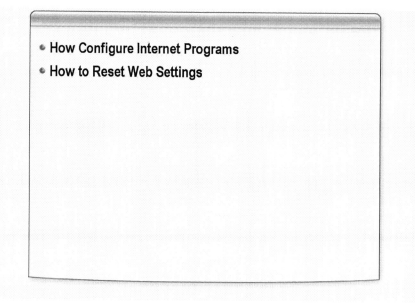

- How Configure Internet Programs
- How to Reset Web Settings

Introduction

The Program settings in Internet Explorer enable users to specify which program Windows XP automatically uses for each Internet service. This lesson provides information on how to configure and customize the program settings.

Objectives

After completing this lesson, you will be able to:

- Configure Internet programs.
- Reset Web settings.

How to Configure Internet Programs

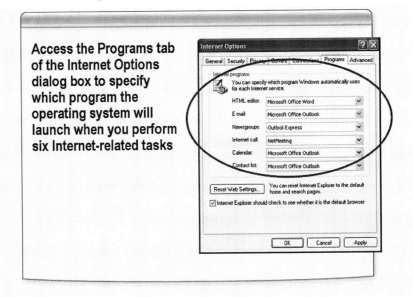

Access the Programs tab of the Internet Options dialog box to specify which program the operating system will launch when you perform six Internet-related tasks

Introduction

The list of programs displayed for each task is determined by the applications installed on your computer before you install Internet Explorer. For example, if you install Internet Explorer before you install Microsoft Office FrontPage®, an HTML editor, on your computer, Internet Explorer uses Notepad as the HTML editor. If Internet Explorer does not find the appropriate application, the list of program choices is blank. For example, if Microsoft Office is not installed on the computer, the **Calendar** drop-down list is blank.

How to configure Internet programs

To configure Internet programs:

1. In Internet Explorer, on the **Tools** menu, click **Internet Options**.

2. On the **Programs** tab, under **Internet programs**, select the program to use for each Internet service listed.

How to add programs to the program list

The programs choices listed on the **Programs** tab are reflected in the registry. If you want to add a program to the program list, you can install the proper string into the proper registry key. It may be necessary to do this if, for example, you want to add an older application as your news reader, or if your registry is damaged and you do not want to reinstall the applications after you repair it.

How to Reset Web Settings

To restore the default home and search pages in Internet Explorer, click Reset Web Settings.... on the Programs tab of the Internet Options dialog box

Introduction

One of the options on the **Programs** tab is to reset Web settings. This option enables you to reset Internet Explorer to the default home and search pages and determines if Internet Explorer is the default browser. For example, if you install a different Web browser after you have installed Internet Explorer, some of your Internet Explorer settings may change. You can reset your Internet Explorer settings to the original default settings without changing the settings in the other browser.

Note   These settings affect only the individual user, unless the user has administrative rights on the computer. If the user has administrative rights, the program settings that the user selects are put into effect on that computer, regardless of the user.

How to reset Web settings

To reset the Web settings to the default setting:

1. In Internet Explorer, on the **Tools** menu, click **Internet Options**.

2. On the **Programs** tab, click **Reset Web Settings**.

Practice: Configuring and Troubleshooting Program Settings

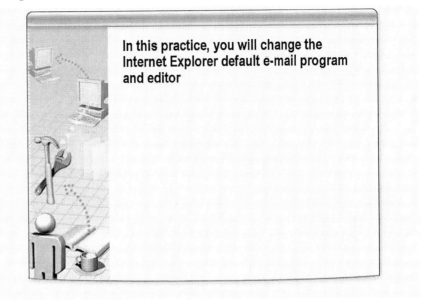

In this practice, you will change the Internet Explorer default e-mail program and editor

Objective

In this practice, you will adjust Program settings in Internet Explorer. After making these changes, you then determine how these settings affect Internet Explorer.

Practice

▶ **Change the Internet Explorer default E-mail program and Editor**

1. Resume Acapulco.

2. Using Acapulco, log on locally as **Administrator** with the password **P@ssw0rd**.

3. Start Internet Explorer.

4. In Internet Explorer, on the **Tools** menu, click **Internet Options**.

5. In the **Internet Options** dialog box, click the **Programs** tab.

6. On the drop-down list next to E-mail, select **Hotmail**, and then click **OK**.

7. On the **Tools** menu, point to **Mail and News**, and then click **Read Mail**.

   Internet Explorer attempts to load www.hotmail.msn.com.

8. Using Acapulco, close all windows, log off, and pause Acapulco.

Lesson: Customizing Internet Explorer

* What Is the Information Bar?
* How to Configure the Information Bar
* How to Save a Password for a Specific Web Site
* When to Synchronize Offline Web Pages
* How to Configure Offline Web Page Synchronization

Introduction

All users have different preferences and needs when it comes to their computer configuration. Internet Explorer provides a variety of customization options so that you can adapt Internet Explorer to fit your needs. This lesson focuses on the various customization options available in Internet Explorer.

Objectives

After completing this lesson, you will be able to:

* Explain the purpose and function of the Information Bar.
* Use the Information Bar to perform various tasks.
* Save a password for a specific Web site.
* Explain when to perform Web page synchronization.
* Configure offline Web page synchronization.

What Is the Information Bar?

> **The Information Bar:**
> - ✓ Provides information about downloads, blocked pop-up windows, and other status information
> - ✓ Use to avoid downloading potentially harmful files
>
> **The Information Bar provides notification when:**
> - ✓ Internet Explorer blocks a pop-up window
> - ✓ Internet Explorer blocks a control or active content on a Web page
> - ✓ Internet Explorer blocks a Web site from downloading a file

Introduction

In Windows XP SP2, Internet Explorer 6 displays an Information Bar just below the **Address** bar where you can see information regarding downloads, blocked pop-up windows, and other status information. This section describes the Information Bar and how it can be used to avoid downloading potentially harmful files that might otherwise be accepted from the Internet.

What is the Information Bar?

The Internet Explorer Information Bar in Windows XP SP2 replaces many of the common dialog boxes that prompt users for information and provides a common area for displaying information. Notifications such as blocked ActiveX installs, blocked pop-up windows, and downloads all appear in the Information Bar, which appears below the toolbars and above the main browsing window. Either clicking or right-clicking on the Information Bar brings up a menu that enables you to respond to the displayed notification.

The benefits of the Information Bar

The Information Bar notifies you:

- When Internet Explorer blocks a pop-up window. After the Information Bar is displayed, if you want to display the pop-up window, click the Information Bar and select either **Temporarily Allow Pop-ups** or **Always Allow Pop-ups from This Site**. You can also turn off the pop-up blocker.

- When Internet Explorer blocks a control or active content on a Web page. Internet Explorer allows the rest of the Web page to open, which lets you see how the Web page works without the control. Often you will not notice any difference, but your computer is less vulnerable when you do not install controls that you do not need.

- When Internet Explorer blocks a Web site from downloading a file to your computer. Internet Explorer still allows you to download a file, but it prevents the Web site from downloading any files without your knowledge or permission.

When is the Information Bar visible?

If Internet Explorer default settings are on, the Information Bar is visible when a Web site tries to:

- Install an ActiveX control on the computer.
- Open a pop-up window.
- Download a file to the computer.
- Run active content on the computer.
- Run an ActiveX control on the computer in a nonsecure manner.

How to Configure the Information Bar

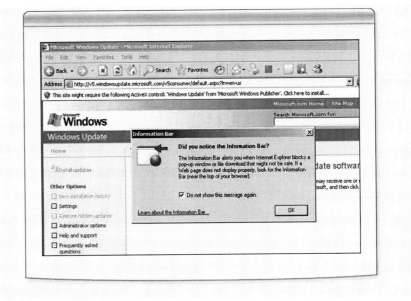

Introduction

This section describes how to configure the Information Bar.

How to use the Information Bar

When you see a message in the Information Bar, click the message to see more information or to take action.

How to turn off messages about blocked pop-up windows

Microsoft does not recommend turning off the Information Bar; however, if you do turn it off, you must turn it off for each type of message. You can, however, turn off Information Bar messages about blocked pop-up windows.

To turn off Information Bar messages about blocked pop-up windows:

1. On the **Tools** menu, point to **Pop-up Blocker**, and then click **Pop-up Blocker Settings**.

2. Clear the **Show Information Bar when a pop-up is blocked** check box.

How to enable the pop-up blocker in Internet Explorer

Pop-up windows are not only annoying to users; they can also cause instability in Internet Explorer. Windows XP SP2 introduces the first pop-up blocker built in to Internet Explorer.

To enable pop-up blocking in Internet Explorer:

1. Click **Start**, and then click **Control Panel**.

2. In **Control Panel**, click **Network and Internet Connections**.

3. In the **Network and Internet Connections** window, click **Internet Options**.

4. In the **Internet Properties** dialog box, on the **Privacy** tab, in the **Pop-Up Blocker** section, select the **Block Pop-Ups** check box.

5. Click **OK** to close the **Internet Properties** dialog box.

How to block or allow a Web site

Although the ability to block or allow a Web site regardless of Internet Explorer privacy settings is present in previous versions of Windows XP, the interface changes slightly when you install Windows XP SP2.

To block or allow a Web site in Internet Explorer:

1. In Internet Explorer, on the **Tools** menu, click **Internet Options**.
2. In the **Internet Properties** dialog box, on the **Privacy** tab, click **Sites**.
3. In the **Per Site Privacy Actions** dialog box, in the **Address Of Web Site** box, type the name of the site you want to block or allow.
4. Perform one of the following actions:
   - Click **Block** to block access to the site you typed even if Internet Explorer's privacy settings would otherwise allow the site.
   - Click **Allow** to allow access to the site you typed even if Internet Explorer's privacy settings would otherwise block the site.
5. Click **OK** to close the **Per Site Privacy Actions** dialog box.
6. Click **OK** to close the **Internet Options** dialog box.

How to stop blocking files and software downloads

You can enable Web sites to automatically prompt you when downloading files and software by bypassing the Information Bar.

To enable Web sites to prompt when downloading files and software:

1. Open Internet Explorer.
2. On the **Tools** menu, click **Internet Options**.
3. On the **Security** tab, click **Custom Level**.
4. Do one or both of the following:
   - To turn off the Information Bar for file downloads, in the **Downloads** section of the list, under **Automatic prompting for file downloads**, click **Enable**.
   - To turn off the Information Bar for ActiveX controls, in the **ActiveX controls and plug-ins** section of the list, under **Automatic prompting for ActiveX controls**, click **Enable**.

How to Save a Password for a Specific Web Site

Site-specific passwords are a function of the AutoComplete option

AutoComplete Settings

AutoComplete lists possible matches from entries you've typed before.

Use AutoComplete for

- ☑ Web addresses
- ☐ Forms
- ☑ User names and passwords on forms
  - ☑ Prompt me to save passwords

Clear AutoComplete history

[Clear Forms]   [Clear Passwords]

To clear Web address entries, on the General tab in Internet Options, click Clear History.

[OK]   [Cancel]

Introduction	Many Web sites require a password the first time that you visit the site. A common request made to DSTs by end users is how to avoid typing passwords when accessing Web sites. This section explains the purpose and function of password caching and how to use it to retain passwords.
What is password caching?	When you attempt to view a password-protected Web site, you are prompted to type your security credentials in the **Enter Network Password** dialog box. If you click **Save this password in your password list**, the computer saves your password so that you do not have to type the password again when you attempt to access the same site. This is known as *password caching*. Password caching is a function of the AutoComplete feature in Microsoft Office and it retains passwords for any site that you visit, as long as the function is enabled.
How to enable password caching	Password caching is enabled by default.

Note You can access AutoComplete configuration options on the **General** tab of the **Internet Options** dialog box.

How to disable password caching by using the Registry Editor

To disable password caching by using the Registry Editor:

1. In the Registry Editor, locate and click the following key in the registry:

   HKEY_CURRENT_USER\Software\Microsoft\Windows\ CurrentVersion\Internet Settings

2. On the **Edit** menu, click **Add Value**, and then add the following values:

   Value name: **DisablePasswordCaching**

   Data type: **REG_DWORD**

   Base: **Hexadecimal**

   Value data: **1**

Note   You can also disable password caching by using the Internet Explorer Administration Kit (IEAK) to create an executable file, and then attaching the file as an add-on component. When you use this method, Setup adds the **DisablePasswordCaching** value to the registry during the installation process.

When to Synchronize Offline Web Pages

View offline Web pages and not synchronize when:

✓ Using a laptop computer

✓ A network connection is not available

View offline Web pages and synchronize when:

✓ A connection is made to the Internet

Introduction

When you make a Web page available offline, you can read its content when your computer is not connected to the Internet and then update the page when you are back online. The process of updating an offline Web page to match its online version is referred to as *offline Web page synchronization*. This section describes circumstances in which it is useful to view Web pages offline and when to synchronize the offline content.

When to view offline Web pages and not synchronize

You might want to view Web pages offline if you are using a laptop computer and you do not have a network or Internet connection. Some users want to read Web pages at home without using a dial-up connection. You can specify how much content you want to view offline, such as only a page, or a page and all of its links. You can also choose how you want that content updated.

If you just want to view a Web page offline and you do not need to update the content, you can save the Web page onto your computer. There are several ways you can save the Web page, ranging from saving just the text to saving all of the images and text needed to display that page as it appears on the Web.

When to view offline Web pages and synchronize

Synchronization is the feature to use if you need to update the offline content the next time you connect your computer to the Internet.

How to Configure Offline Web Page Synchronization

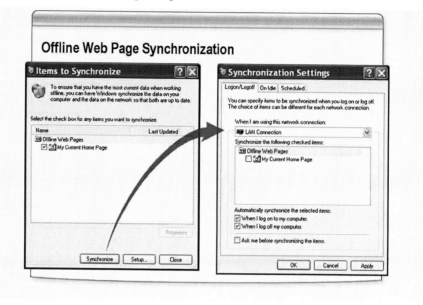

Offline Web Page Synchronization

Introduction	Windows XP includes a number of options that you can use to configure and customize Web page synchronization. This section describes these options and how to customize an offline Web page.

Web page synchronization options

The following table lists the options you can configure for Web page synchronization, what each option does, and when to use each option.

Use this option...	To do this...	When you...
Only when I choose Synchronize from the Tools menu	Manually synchronize your Web pages.	Are not concerned about keeping offline content up to date.
I would like to create a new schedule	Specify a synchronization time. You can give the schedule a unique name so that you can easily identify it.	Need offline access to content that changes on a regular basis, such as a Web site that provides sports scores.
Use this existing schedule	Choose a default daily, weekly, or monthly scheduled synchronization time. You can also choose from previously created custom schedules.	Need offline access to content that changes on a regular basis, and you have an existing schedule that you want to use.
Does this site require a password?	Specify a user name and password for the offline Web page, if it is required.	Will be receiving the content from a Web site that requires a user name and/or password, such as a newspaper Web site.

How to customize an offline Web page

To customize an existing offline Web page:

1. In Internet Explorer, on the **Favorites** menu, click **Organize Favorites**.

2. Select the offline Web page you want to modify, select **Make available offline**, and then click **Properties**.

The following table lists and describes the settings that you can configure on the **Schedule** tab of the **Properties** dialog box.

Setting	Description
Only when I choose Synchronize from the Tools menu	Manually synchronizes Web pages.
Using the following schedule(s)	Specifies a default schedule.
Add	Specifies a synchronization time and a unique name for a schedule.
Remove	Removes a schedule.
Edit	Allows you to customize settings on the following tabs: • **Synchronization Items**. Use the options on this tab to specify the network connection to use for the selected schedule or to select which offline Web pages to synchronize with this schedule. • **Schedule**. Use the options on this tab to modify the time settings for the selected schedule and to choose advanced schedule options such as start date, end date, and how often the task can be repeated. • **Settings**. Use the options on this tab to specify what to do with a task after it is completed, whether the computer has to be idle when the task is started, and power management settings.

The following table lists and describes the settings that you can configure on the **Download** tab of the **Properties** dialog box.

Setting	Description
Download pages *<number>* links deep from this page	Specifies how many links deep, up to a maximum of three, Internet Explorer will download Web pages for offline use. You can choose to follow links outside of the page's Web site and limit the amount of hard disk space allocated to the Web page. You can also specify what type of content to download or omit from your Web pages by clicking the **Advanced** button.
When this page changes, send e-mail to	Sends you e-mail when the content of the offline Web page changes.
Logon	Allows you to specify a user name and password for sites that require you to log on.

How to remove synchronized Web pages

If you want to remove your synchronized Web pages, you need to delete the files in the Temporary Internet Files folder.

To delete the files in the Temporary Internet Files folder:

1. In the **Internet Options** dialog box, on the **General** tab, under **Temporary Internet files**, click **Delete Files**.

2. In the **Delete Files** dialog box, select **Delete all offline content** if you want to delete all Web page content that you have made available offline, and then click **OK**.

Practice: Customizing Internet Explorer

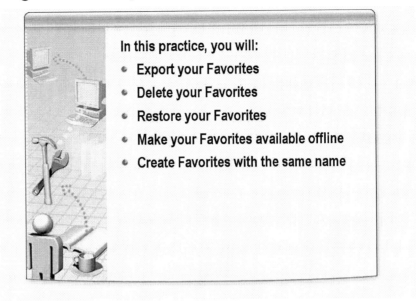

In this practice, you will:

• Export your Favorites

• Delete your Favorites

• Restore your Favorites

• Make your Favorites available offline

• Create Favorites with the same name

Objective

In this practice, you will customize your Favorites in Internet Explorer and practice importing and exporting these Internet shortcuts.

Practice

▶ **Export your Favorites**

1. Resume Acapulco.

2. Using Acapulco, log on locally as **Administrator** with the password **P@ssw0rd**.

3. Start Internet Explorer.

4. In Internet Explorer, click **File**, and then click **Import and Export**.

5. On the **Welcome to the Import/Export Wizard** page, click **Next**.

6. On the **Import/Export Selection** page, under **Choose an action to perform**, click **Export Favorites**, and then click **Next**.

7. On the **Export Favorites Source Folder** page, verify that the **Favorites** folder is selected, and then click **Next**.

8. On the **Export Favorites Destination** page, under **Export to a File or Address**, notice that the default path for the bookmark file is C:\Documents and Settings\Administrator\My Documents\bookmark.htm, and then click **Next**.

9. On the **Completing the Import/Export Wizard** page, click **Finish**.

10. In the **Export Favorites** dialog box, click **OK**.

▶ **Delete your Favorites**

1. In Internet Explorer, on the **Favorites** menu, click **Organize Favorites**.

2. In the **Organize Favorites** dialog box, click **MSN.com**, and then click **Delete**.

3. In the **Confirm File Delete** dialog box, click **Yes**.

4. Repeat steps 2 and 3 to delete all shortcuts and folders and then click **Close**.

▶ **Restore your Favorites**

1. In Internet Explorer, click **File**, and then click **Import and Export**.

2. On the **Welcome to the Import/Export Wizard** page, click **Next**.

3. On the **Import/Export Selection** page, under **Choose an action to perform**, click **Import Favorites**, and then click **Next**.

4. On the **Import Favorites Source** page, under **Import from a File or Address**, click **Next** to accept the default path.

5. On the **Import Favorites Destination Folder** page, verify that **Favorites** is selected, and then click **Next**.

6. Click **Finish**.

7. In the **Import Favorites** message box, click **OK**.

8. In Internet Explorer, on the toolbar, click **Favorites** to verify that your favorites were imported.

▶ **Make your Favorites available offline**

1. Resume London.

2. Using Acapulco, in Internet Explorer, in the address bar, type **http://london/mycalendar.htm** and press ENTER.

3. On the **Favorites** menu, click **Add to Favorites**.

4. In the **Add Favorite** dialog box, select the **Make available offline** check box; in the **Name** box, type **My Calendar** and then click **OK**.

5. After synchronization finishes, pause London.

6. Using Acapulco, on the **File** menu, click **Work Offline**.

7. On the **Favorites** menu, click **My Calendar**.

   The calendar is displayed even though you are disconnected from London.

▶ **Create Favorites with the same name**

1. Using Acapulco, in Internet Explorer, on the **Favorites** menu, click **Add to Favorites**.

2. In the **Name** box, type **My Calendar** and then click **OK**.

   What happens?

   _____

   _____

3. In the **Add Favorite** dialog box, click **No**.

4. In the **Add Favorite** dialog box, click **Cancel**.

5. Close London and Acapulco without saving changes.

Lab: Troubleshooting Issues Related to Internet Explorer

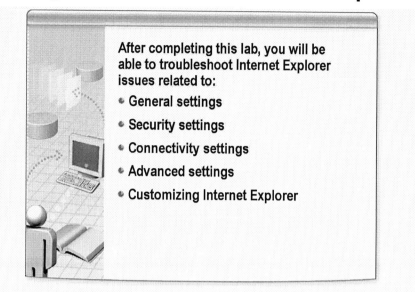

Objectives

After completing this lab, you will be able to:

- Troubleshoot Internet Explorer issues related to general settings.
- Troubleshoot Internet Explorer issues related to security settings.
- Troubleshoot Internet Explorer issues related to connectivity settings.
- Troubleshoot Internet Explorer issues related to advanced settings.
- Troubleshoot issues related to customizing Internet Explorer.

Prerequisites

Before working on this lab, you must have an understanding of how to use Microsoft Virtual PC.

Before you begin

For each exercise in this lab, use the password **P@ssw0rd**.

In Virtual PC, <right> ALT+DEL is the equivalent of CTRL+ALT+DEL.

Scenario

You are a DST for Northwind Traders, a company whose workers use Windows XP Professional. Two users call with various Internet Explorer configuration and customization questions.

Estimated time to complete this lab: 30 minutes

Exercise 1
Troubleshooting Internet Explorer Issues Related to General Settings

In this exercise, you will troubleshoot issues related to general settings.

A user calls and says he is experiencing a greater than normal delay when viewing his most frequently used sites. Many of his frequently visited sites contain large graphic files. He has plenty of disk space available and would like these frequently visited sites to appear faster. He also complains that his home page has unexpectedly changed and he would like to change it back to http://london/exchange/AcapulcoUser/Inbox.

Tasks	Guidance for completing the task
1. Start the London and Acapulco virtual machines and, using Acapulco, log on as **NWTRADERS\ AcapulcoUser**.	▪ Use the Virtual PC console. ▪ Wait for London to display the logon screen before starting Acapulco. ▪ If necessary, click **Show the contents of this folder**.
2. Using Acapulco, browse to C:\Program Files\ Microsoft Learning\2262 \Labfiles\Lab03\ and run 2262_Lab03_Ex01.	▪ This step introduces the problem.
3. Resolve the home page issue.	▪ Refer to the Guidelines for Troubleshooting General Setting Issues topic. ▪ Successful resolution of this issue will result in the user's home page being set to http://london/exchange/AcapulcoUser/Inbox.
4. Resolve the unnecessary need to constantly download images.	▪ Refer to the Guidelines for Troubleshooting General Setting Issues topic.
5. Close all windows and log off Acapulco.	

Exercise 2
Troubleshooting Internet Explorer Issues Related to Security Settings

In this exercise, you will troubleshoot issues related to Internet Explorer security settings.

Scenario

A user calls and says she is no longer able to view or send messages using Microsoft Outlook® Web Access and that someone recently updated her security settings in Internet Explorer. The Information Bar shows a message, "Internet Explorer has blocked this site from using an ActiveX control in an unsafe manner. As a result, this page may not display correctly." After reviewing Northwind Trader's security policy, you learn it is not necessary to block ActiveX controls.

Tasks	Guidance for completing the task
1. Logon to Acapulco as **NWTRADERS\ AcapulcoUser**, browse to C:\Program Files\ Microsoft Learning\2262 \Labfiles\Lab03\ and run 2262_Lab03_Ex02.	▪ This step introduces the problem.
2. Using Acapulco, in Internet Explorer connect to Outlook Web Access and send a message to yourself (AcapulcoUser).	▪ http://london/exchange/acapulcouser/inbox.
❓ Were you able to successfully send an e-mail message to yourself? _____ _____	
3. Resolve the security issue.	▪ Successful resolution of this issue will enable the user to send and receive an e-mail, and display the contents of the inbox by using Outlook Web Access.
4. For all virtual machines, close all windows and log off.	

Exercise 3
Troubleshooting Internet Explorer Issues Related to Connectivity Settings

In this exercise, you will troubleshoot issues related to Internet Explorer Connectivity Settings.

Scenario

A user calls and says he is unable to open a Web page. When attempting to view the Web page, he receives an error that the page contains ActiveX controls and may not be displayed properly.

Tasks	Guidance for completing the task
1. Using Acapulco, log on to the domain as **NWTRADERS\ Administrator**.	▪ Use the Virtual PC console.
2. Using Acapulco, browse to C:\Program Files\ Microsoft Learning\2262 \Labfiles\Lab03\ and run 2262_Lab03_Ex03.	▪ This step introduces the problem.
3. Using Internet Explorer, browse to Outlook Web Access.	▪ The Outlook Web Access URL is http://london/exchange.
❓ Were you able to successfully connect to Outlook Web Access?	
4. Resolve the connectivity settings issue.	▪ Refer to the Guidelines for Troubleshooting Connectivity Settings Issues.
5. For all virtual machines, close all windows and log off the virtual machine.	

Exercise 4
Troubleshooting Internet Explorer Issues Related to Advanced Settings

In this exercise, you will troubleshoot issues related to privacy.

Scenario

A user calls and says that Web pages are not downloading correctly, and when browsing to https://london/exchange/acapulcouser/inbox, none of the icons or other images are displayed.

Tasks	Guidance for completing the task
1. Using Acapulco, log on as **NWTRADERS\ Administrator**.	▪ Use the Virtual PC console.
2. Using Acapulco, browse to C:\Program Files \ Microsoft Learning\2262 \Labfiles\Lab03\ and run 2262_Lab03_Ex04.	▪ This step introduces the problem.
3. Using Internet Explorer, browse to the Administrator's Exchange inbox and, on the Internet Explorer status bar, note the error icon.	▪ http://London/exchange/administrator/inbox.
❓ Were you able to successfully connect to Outlook Web Access? _____ _____	
4. Resolve the advanced settings issue.	
5. For all virtual machines, close all windows and log off.	

Exercise 5
Troubleshooting Issues Related to Customizing Internet Explorer

In this exercise, you will troubleshoot issues related to customizing Internet Explorer.

Scenario

A user calls and says that no matter what she tries, she cannot modify the Internet Explorer bar. She has tried updating Internet Explorer from the Windows Update Site and reapplying Windows XP Service Pack 2. Just above the main browser window, the user says she sees the Links toolbar. She has viewed the Customizing the Links help file and is able to show and hide the Links toolbar but is unable to move it. The Microsoft Windows Media® link is one of her favorites and she would like to access it more easily. She has asked you to fix the Links toolbar so that it is more visible.

Tasks	Guidance for completing the task
1. Using the Acapulco virtual machine, log on to the domain as **NWTRADERS\ AcapulcoUser**.	▪ Use the Virtual PC console.
2. Open Internet Explorer and reproduce the problem.	▪ Verify that you cannot move the Links toolbar, but that you can display or hide it.
3. Resolve the customization issue.	▪ Successful resolution of this issue results in the Links toolbar being more easily accessible to the user so that she can click Windows Media.
4. Close all virtual machines and delete changes.	

Lab Discussion

After you have completed the exercises in this lab, take a moment to answer the following questions. When the entire class has finished the lab, the instructor will facilitate a lab discussion based on students' answers to these questions.

1. How did you determine the cause of the issue(s)?

2. How did you resolve the issue(s)?

3. What are some other ways the issue(s) could have been resolved?

Microsoft®

Module 4: Troubleshooting Issues Related to Outlook

Contents

Overview

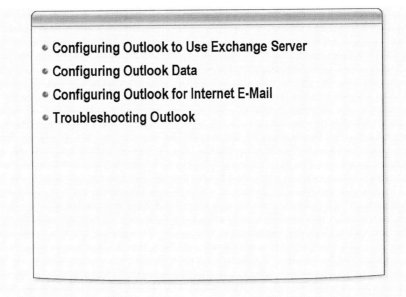

* Configuring Outlook to Use Exchange Server
* Configuring Outlook Data
* Configuring Outlook for Internet E-Mail
* Troubleshooting Outlook

Introduction

Microsoft® Office Outlook® 2003 provides an integrated solution for managing and organizing e-mail messages, schedules, tasks, notes, contacts, and other information. Many of the calls that you will receive as a desktop support technician (DST) will relate to everyday tasks that users are trying to perform in Outlook, such as configuring e-mail settings or archiving old data. Your understanding of how to perform these tasks in Outlook will greatly assist you in troubleshooting user issues.

The purpose of this module is to teach you to support end users who run Microsoft Windows® XP Professional or Microsoft Windows XP Home Edition, use Microsoft Exchange Server 2003 as their e-mail server, and use Outlook 2003 as their e-mail client. In this module, you will learn how to create, configure, and troubleshoot e-mail accounts; keep Outlook running smoothly by maintaining the stored data; and perform common troubleshooting tasks in Outlook, such as repairing corrupt Outlook data and using RPCPing.

Objectives

After completing this module, you will be able to:

- Configure Outlook to use Exchange Server.
- Configure Outlook data.
- Configure Outlook for Internet e-mail.
- Apply guidelines for troubleshooting Outlook.

Lesson: Configuring Outlook to Use Exchange Server

- **Outlook Components and Requirements**
- **How Outlook and Exchange Server Work Together**
- **How to Connect to Exchange Server Using Outlook**
- **What Is RPC over HTTP?**
- **How to Remotely Connect to Exchange Server Using RPC over HTTP**
- **How to Create and Synchronize an .ost File**
- **What Is Cached Exchange Mode?**
- **How to Configure Outlook to Use Cached Exchange Mode**
- **Common Issues in Troubleshooting Exchange Server Configuration**

Introduction

If you work in a corporate environment, it is likely that your company will use an internal mail server such as Exchange Server 2003 to provide e-mail service. Companies that use Exchange Server to provide e-mail service typically use Outlook as their default e-mail client. Used together, Outlook and Exchange Server offer advanced functionality that enables users to better manage e-mail and personal information while making it easier to share and create information with other users. This lesson describes the primary function of Outlook and Exchange Server and explains how to connect to a computer running Exchange Server by using Outlook. This lesson also describes how to remotely connect to a computer running Exchange Server by using Remote Procedure Call over Hypertext Transfer Protocol (RPC over HTTP) and how to configure offline folder access for those times when remote access is not feasible. Finally, this lesson discusses how to use Cached Exchange Mode to enable mobile users to easily switch from online to offline without encountering network- or server-connection issues.

Lesson objectives

After completing this lesson, you will be able to:

- Describe Outlook components and configuration requirements.
- Describe how Outlook and Exchange Server work together.
- Connect to a computer running Exchange Server using Outlook.
- Explain the purpose and function of RPC over HTTP.
- Remotely connect to a computer running Exchange Server using RPC over HTTP.
- Create and synchronize an .ost file.
- Explain the purpose and function of Cached Exchange Mode.
- Configure Outlook to use Cached Exchange Mode.
- Troubleshoot common issues in Exchange Server configuration.

Outlook Components and Requirements

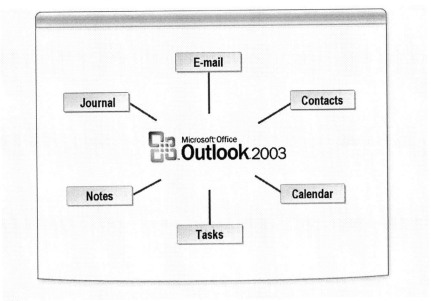

Introduction	Many users use Outlook to provide a single, integrated solution for organizing and managing their digital communication tools, such as e-mail and instant messaging, and their day-to-day information, such as calendars, contacts, tasks, and notes. Outlook helps users to manage their time and tasks more effectively, making it easier to synthesize information and share it with others.
Outlook components	The primary components of Outlook are:

- *E-mail*. Enables users to send and receive e-mail messages.

- *Contacts*. Enables users to store names, addresses, phone numbers, e-mail addresses, and other information about coworkers, friends, and family.

- *Calendar*. Enables users to organize meetings and appointments, store and share appointments, and generate reminders of upcoming appointments.

- *Tasks*. Enables users to organize assignments, responsibilities, or errands. Users can also track their progress on a task and set up a recurring task.

- *Notes*. Enables users to create notes that they can display on the screen or list in the notes area of Outlook.

- *Journal*. Enables users to record interactions with other people. Journal automatically records actions that you choose relating to the contacts that you choose and places the actions in a timeline view. In addition to recording Outlook items, such as e-mail, or other Microsoft Office documents, such as Microsoft Office Word or Microsoft Office Excel files, users can keep records of any interactions that they want to remember, such as phone conversations or handwritten letters that they mailed or received.

Outlook configuration requirements

To configure an e-mail account in Outlook, you must know:

- Your account name, password, and e-mail server.
- How your computer will connect to your e-mail server.
- When and how to get your e-mail from the server.
- Where to keep your e-mail messages.

How Outlook and Exchange Server Work Together

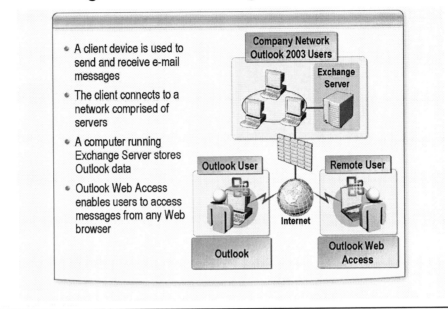

Introduction

Exchange Server, a Microsoft messaging and collaboration server, is software that runs on servers. Exchange Server enables you to send and receive e-mail and other forms of interactive communication through computer networks. Designed to interoperate with a software client application such as Outlook, Exchange Server also interoperates with Outlook Express and other e-mail client applications.

The benefits of Exchange Server and Outlook interoperability

Connecting Outlook 2003 to a computer running Exchange Server enables you to:

- Create junk-mail filters and block unsolicited e-mails.

- Connect to Exchange Server 2003 by using HTTP protocols.

- Use Cached Exchange Mode.

- With the appropriate permissions, create public folders that allow you to share information with other users.

- Create server-side rules that organize your e-mail folders by routing messages to specific folders.

How Outlook and Exchange Server work together

E-mail messages are sent and received through what is commonly referred to as a *client device*, such as a personal computer, workstation, or a mobile device, including mobile phones and Pocket PCs. The client typically connects to a network of centralized computer systems comprised of servers or mainframe computers where the e-mail mailboxes are stored. A computer running Exchange Server also stores Outlook data, including messages, calendars, contacts, and tasks. Storing data on a computer running Exchange Server allows you to access this data from any computer that has Outlook or Internet access by using an Exchange Server application called Microsoft Office Outlook Web Access. Outlook Web Access enables you to access Outlook or an Exchange personal e-mail account so that you can view your Inbox from any Web browser. The centralized e-mail servers connect to the Internet and to private networks where e-mail messages are sent to and received from other e-mail users.

How to Connect to Exchange Server Using Outlook

Access the E-mail Accounts dialog box to configure an Exchange Server e-mail account

E-mail Accounts

Exchange Server Settings
You can enter the required information to connect to your Exchange server.

Type the name of your Microsoft Exchange Server computer. For information, see your system administrator.

Microsoft Exchange Server:

☑ Use Cached Exchange Mode

Type the name of the mailbox set up for you by your administrator. The mailbox name is usually your user name.

User Name:

Check Name

More Settings ...

< Back   Next >   Cancel

Introduction

Configuring Outlook to use Exchange Server is a straightforward process. When a user calls with questions about how to configure Outlook to connect to a computer running Exchange Server, the method used is determined by whether the user has run Outlook since it was installed. This section explains the options for configuring Outlook to use Exchange Server and how to configure an Exchange Server account using an established Outlook profile.

Outlook configuration options

There are two options for configuring Outlook to use Exchange Server:

- If Outlook has not been run since it was installed, the Outlook Startup Wizard is used to add the Exchange Server account.

- If an Outlook account has been added, but an Exchange Server account has not been added, the Mail Setup tool in Control Panel is used to add the Exchange Server account.

How to configure an Exchange Server account

The following procedure explains how to configure an Exchange Server account using the Mail Setup tool. The process is nearly identical if you are using the Outlook Startup Wizard.

To configure an Exchange Server account using an established Outlook profile:

1. Click **Start**, and then click **Control Panel**.
2. Click **User Accounts**, and then click **Mail**.
3. In the **User Accounts** dialog box, click **Mail**.
4. In the **Mail Setup** dialog box, click **Show Profiles**.
5. On the **General** tab, click the profile that you want to use.
6. Click **Properties**.
7. In the **Mail Setup** dialog box, click **E-mail Accounts**.
8. In the **E-mail Accounts** dialog box, click **Add a new e-mail account**, and then click **Next**.

9. In the **E-mail Accounts** dialog box, click **Microsoft Exchange Server**, and then click **Next**.

10. In the **E-mail Accounts** dialog box, type the required information using the following guidelines:

- Microsoft Exchange Server: Type the Exchange Server name as provided by the system administrator.

- User Name: Type your name and click **Check Name**.

- Use Cached Exchange mode: Select this check box to enable Cached Exchange Mode. This option is selected by default.

11. Click **Next**, and then click **Finish**.

12. In the **Mail Setup** dialog box, click **Close**, and then click **OK**.

13. Close Control Panel.

Note   You cannot add an Exchange Server account while Outlook is running.

Note   Outlook can support only one Exchange Server account per profile. If you need to access multiple Exchange Server accounts, you must create a new profile in Outlook or configure your Exchange Server account to open additional mailboxes. For more information about creating profiles see the section titled "How to Create an Outlook Profile" in this module.

What Is RPC over HTTP?

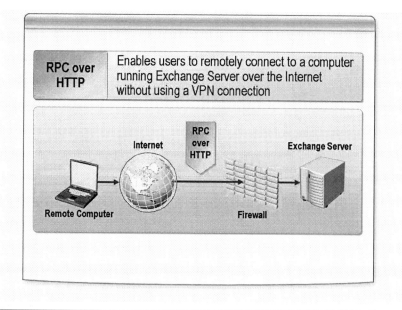

Introduction

In a local area network (LAN), Outlook communicates with computers running Exchange Server by using Transmission Control Protocol/Internet Protocol (TCP/IP). TCP/IP enables interconnected networks of computers with different hardware architectures and operating systems to communicate with each other. TCP/IP enables users who are directly logged on to a network to access a corporate network; however, it does not enable remote users to access a network. To access a corporate network, remote users typically require a virtual private network (VPN) connection to get past the corporate firewall and into the corporate network. Although a VPN connection is a reliable and secure method for network access, the VPN process is complex and it provides more network services than are required for simple e-mail access. RPC over HTTP enables users to remotely connect to a computer running Exchange Server over the Internet without using a VPN connection. This section describes the benefits of RPC over HTTP and briefly explains how the process works.

Benefits of RPC over HTTP

RPC over HTTP provides the following benefits:

■ Enables remote access to an Exchange Server account for users who are traveling or working outside the organization's firewall.

■ Provides a secure and reliable connection.

■ Does not require special connections or hardware, such as smart cards or security tokens.

■ Enables access to an Exchange Server account even if the server and the client computer are located on different networks.

How RPC over HTTP works

When Outlook 2003 is configured to use RPC over HTTP, it will, by default, first attempt to connect to its corporate Exchange mailbox server by means of RPC over TCP/IP, as it would in a corporate network setting. If the server is not located this way, Outlook 2003 attempts to connect to its corporate Exchange mailbox server by means of RPC over HTTP.

How to Remotely Connect to Exchange Server Using RPC over HTTP

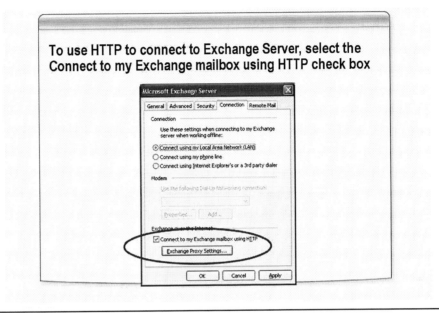

To use HTTP to connect to Exchange Server, select the Connect to my Exchange mailbox using HTTP check box

Introduction

This section describes how to remotely connect to a computer running Exchange Server by using RPC over HTTP.

RPC over HTTP requirements

The requirements for configuring Outlook to use RPC over HTTP include:

- Windows XP with Service Pack 1 (SP1) and the Q331320 hotfix (or a later service pack) installed on client computers

- Outlook 2003

- Exchange Server 2003 e-mail accounts

- Microsoft Windows Server™ 2003 (required for server components only)

Note To use RPC over HTTP, the computer running Exchange Server must be configured to permit connections by using HTTP.

How to connect to Exchange Server by using HTTP

To connect to a computer running Exchange Server by using HTTP:

1. In Outlook, on the **Tools** menu, click **E-mail Accounts**.

2. In the **E-mail Accounts** dialog box, click **View or change existing e-mail accounts**, and then click **Next**.

3. In the **E-mail Accounts** dialog box, in the **Outlook processes e-mail for these accounts in the following order** list, click **Microsoft Exchange Server**, and then click **Change**.

4. On the **Exchange Server Settings** page, click **More Settings**.

5. In the **Microsoft Exchange Server** dialog box, on the **Connection** tab, in the **Exchange over the Internet** area, select **Connect to my Exchange mailbox using HTTP**.

6. Click **Exchange proxy settings**.

7. Under **Connection settings**, in the **Use this URL to connect to my proxy server for Exchange box**, type the appropriate Internet address.

How to Create and Synchronize an .ost File

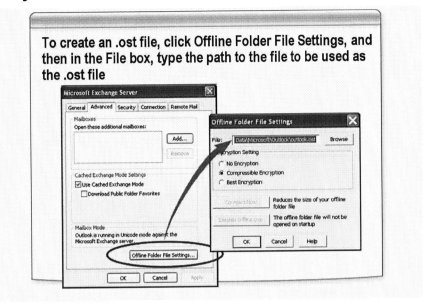

To create an .ost file, click Offline Folder File Settings, and then in the File box, type the path to the file to be used as the .ost file

Introduction

Sometimes remote users need to work on a local computer that is disconnected from the computer running Exchange Server. This may be necessary, for example, if the computer running Exchange Server is offline for maintenance, the user is out of the office and cannot connect to the computer running Exchange Server, or a slow connection to the server results in unacceptable performance.

What is an .ost file?

When you use Outlook and Exchange Server, you can work with folders "offline"; that is, you can use the contents of a folder without a network connection. You work with offline files the same way you work with files when you are connected to the network. When you reconnect to the network, any changes that you made to files while working offline are updated to the network by using synchronization.

Note When you work offline using Cached Exchange mode, by default Outlook will monitor the network connection to the computer running Exchange Server and reconnect when the server becomes available.

Note In Outlook, the Inbox, Outbox, Deleted Items, Sent Items, Calendar, Contacts, Tasks, Journal, Notes, and Drafts folders are automatically available offline when you set up offline folders.

Offline folders are stored in an offline folder (.ost) file; the default location for the .ost file is your current Windows folder. The difference between an .ost file and a set of personal folders (.pst files) is that an .ost file starts as a mirror image of your folders on the Exchange Server computer, and is updated by the server during synchronization. In contrast, a .pst file is simply a storage location on your hard disk or server other than the Exchange Server computer.

Note .pst files are discussed in more detail in the next lesson.

How to create an .ost file

To create an .ost file:

1. In Outlook, on the **Tools** menu, click **E-mail Accounts**.

2. In the **E-mail Accounts** dialog box, click **View or change existing e-mail accounts**, and then click **Next**.

3. In the **Outlook processes e-mail for these accounts in the following order** list, click **Microsoft Exchange Server**, and then click **Change**.

4. On the **Exchange Server Settings** page, click **More Settings**.

5. In the **Microsoft Exchange Server** dialog box, on the **Advanced** tab, click **Offline Folder File Settings**.

6. In the **Offline Folder File Settings** dialog box, in the **File** box, type the path to the file you want to use as the offline folder file.

Note The default file name of the newly created offline folder file is Outlook.ost. If this file name already exists, you are prompted to type a new name.

How to specify which folders are available offline

To specify which folders are available offline:

1. In Outlook, on the **Tools** menu, point to **Send/Receive**, point to **Send/Receive Settings**, and then click **Define Send/Receive Groups**.

2. In the **Send/Receive Groups** dialog box, in the **Group Name** list, click a Send/Receive group containing an Exchange Server account, and then click **Edit**.

3. In the **Send/Receive Settings – All Accounts** dialog box, under **Accounts**, select your Exchange Server account.

4. In the **Check folders from the selected account to include in send/receive** list, select the folders that you want to use offline in addition to your default folders.

5. If you want to download headers only, rather than full messages, click **Download Headers only** or click **Download complete item including attachments**. You can also configure **Send/Receive** settings to download headers for items larger than a specific size.

Note A *message header* is summary information about the message, such as who the message is from, the subject, the importance, the date received, and the size.

---

6. Click **OK**.

Note If you use the security feature for sealed messages while working offline, ensure that you download the Address Book along with full details of its information so that you can open sealed e-mail messages while you are offline.

What Is Cached Exchange Mode?

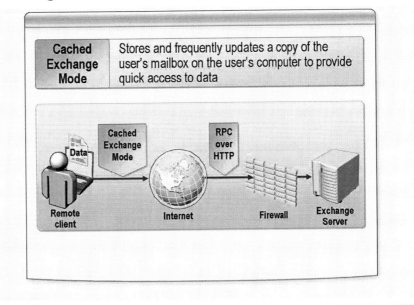

Cached Exchange Mode	Stores and frequently updates a copy of the user's mailbox on the user's computer to provide quick access to data

Introduction

When you run Outlook 2003 in *Cached Exchange Mode*, a copy of your mailbox is stored on your computer. This copy provides quick access to your data and is frequently updated with information from the mail server. If you work offline, whether by choice or because of a connection problem, your data is still available, regardless of your location. Any changes that you make while a connection to the server is not available are synchronized automatically the next time you log on to the network. You can continue to work while changes are synchronized.

Benefits of Cached Exchange Mode

The primary benefits of using Cached Exchange Mode include:

- Shields users from troublesome network and server connection issues. This means that users typically do not notice any difference in messaging performance when using Cached Exchange Mode, other than the lack of a slow network connection or poor server performance.

- Facilitates switching back and forth from online to offline for mobile users. Cached Exchange Mode also provides access to an Inbox over slow connections in which messages are slowly sent to and received from the computer running Exchange Server.

How Cached Exchange Mode works

Outlook 2003, using Cached Exchange Mode, connects to the computer running Exchange Server and automatically downloads all incoming content, such as e-mail, meeting requests, and tasks, to a dedicated .ost file, which serves as a local cache on the client computer. After the download is complete, the user can read, reply to, create, and delete e-mail as well as send tasks and meeting requests.

How to Configure Outlook to Use Cached Exchange Mode

Introduction	This section describes how to configure Outlook to use Cached Exchange Mode and how to adjust Cached Exchange Mode settings.

How to enable Cached Exchange Mode

To enable Cached Exchange Mode:

1. In Outlook, on the **Tools** menu, click **E-mail Accounts**.

2. In the **E-mail Accounts** dialog box, click **View or change existing e-mail accounts**, and then click **Next**.

3. In **E-mail Accounts** dialog box, in the **Outlook processes e-mail for these accounts in the following order** list, click **Microsoft Exchange Server**, and then click **Change**.

4. In the **E-mail Accounts** dialog box, under **Microsoft Exchange Server**, select the **Use Cached Exchange Mode** check box, click **Next**, and then click **Finish**.

5. Close and then restart Outlook.

How to adjust Cached Exchange Mode settings

If Outlook 2003 is connected to Exchange Server 2003, you can adjust the Cached Exchange Mode settings.

To adjust the Cached Exchange Mode settings:

1. In Outlook, on the **File** menu, click **Cached Exchange Mode**.

2. Select one of the following options:

    - **Download Headers and then Full Items**: When you select this option, Outlook downloads the e-mail message header first, and then downloads the full item (header, message body, and any attachments). Use this option when you do not have the time to download the full item and viewing the header is all that is needed. To download the full item, click the header.

    - **Download Full Items**: When you select this option, Outlook downloads headers, items, and any attachments at the same time. Use this option when you have a direct network connection or when you are using a dial-up connection.

    - **Download Headers**: When you select this option, Outlook downloads headers only. The full item is available on demand when you preview or open the item. Use this option when you want the amount of data transferred between Outlook and the computer running Exchange Server to be as small as possible.

3. Click **OK**.

Common Issues in Troubleshooting Exchange Server Configuration

✔ Incorrect Exchange Server account settings

✔ Connecting to Exchange Server using HTTP is unavailable

✔ The SSL certificate is not trusted

✔ HTTP as the default protocol

✔ Unable to activate Cached Exchange Mode

✔ Messages remain in the Outbox until synchronization

✔ Unable to download message headers

✔ Remote Mail cannot be used with Cached Exchange Mode

✔ Manual update of the OAB

Introduction

The process of troubleshooting connection issues to computers running Exchange Server is very much like the process of troubleshooting mailbox configuration issues. Most of these issues will relate to errors in account configuration. This section describes common issues related to connecting Outlook to the computer running Exchange Server, and the solutions to these issues.

How to view Exchange Server account settings

The **E-mail Accounts** dialog box in Outlook contains detailed information about your Exchange Server account settings. These settings can help you identify configuration problems.

To view details about Exchange Server account settings:

1. In Outlook, on the **Tools** menu, click **E-mail Accounts**.

2. In the **E-mail Accounts** dialog box, click **View or change existing e-mail accounts**, click **Next**, click **Microsoft Exchange Server**, and then click **Change**.

3. In the **Exchange Server Settings** dialog box, click **More Settings**.

4. In the **Microsoft Exchange Server** dialog box, on the **Connection** tab, in the **Exchange over the Internet** area, select the **Connect to my Exchange mailbox using HTTP** check box.

5. Click **Exchange Proxy settings**.

6. In the **Exchange Proxy Settings** dialog box, verify that the user entered the correct Web address, certificate principal name, and authentication type for the Exchange proxy server.

Connecting to Exchange Server using HTTP is unavailable

If the **Connect to my Exchange mailbox using HTTP** option in the **E-mail Accounts** dialog box is missing or not available, verify that the user is running Windows XP with SP1 and the Q331320 hotfix (or later). It is also possible that the network administrator did not configure this feature.

The SSL certificate is not trusted	If a user's computer does not trust the Secure Socket Layer (SSL) certificate on the server, browse to the address listed in the configuration page and add **/rpc** to the end. If you are prompted to trust a certificate, select **Yes** if you know that you are connecting to the correct server. For example, if your address was mail.example.msft, you would type **https://mail.example.mstf/rpc** into your browser. If you are using Microsoft Internet Explorer, you will be prompted to trust the certificate if it is not already trusted.
HTTP as the default protocol	If a user wants to connect to the computer running Exchange Server by using HTTP as the default protocol instead of TCP/IP, in the **Exchange Proxy Settings** dialog box, set the option to connect using HTTP first, and then connect using TCP/IP.
Unable to activate Cached Exchange Mode	You may be unable to activate Cached Exchange Mode if you do not have an Exchange e-mail account in the Outlook profile or if the Exchange Server administrator disabled Cached Exchange Mode.
Messages remain in the Outbox until synchronization	When you are using Cached Exchange Mode, a message may remain in the Outbox for up to one minute until the next synchronization with the computer running Exchange Server occurs. If you want to send the message immediately, in Outlook, on the **Tools** menu, point to **Send/Receive**, and then click **Send All**.
Unable to download message headers	The option to download headers is available only when you are using an Exchange Server 2003 e-mail account.
Remote Mail cannot be used with Cached Exchange Mode	You cannot use both Remote Mail and Cached Exchange Mode. Both Cached Exchange Mode and Remote Mail use the .ost file, but they use the file in different ways. Remote Mail is an Exchange Server feature that enables you to log on to a remote mail system by using a modem or LAN to view the mail on the server. You can then use Remote Mail to download the mail, download a copy of the mail, or delete the mail on the server.
Manual update of the OAB	The Offline Address Book (OAB) is automatically updated every 24 hours, unless Outlook is set to **Download Headers** or Outlook has detected a slow network connection and **On Slow Connections Download Headers Only** is selected. To update the Offline Address Book manually in Outlook, on the **Tools** menu, click **Send/Receive**, and then click **Download Address Book**.

Practice: Configuring Outlook for Exchange Server

In this practice, you will create a new profile in Outlook

Objective

In this practice, you will create a new profile in Outlook, configure Exchange Server e-mail service for this profile, and enable offline synchronization of your Outlook data.

Practice

▶ **Create a new profile in Outlook**

1. Start the 2262_London virtual machine.

2. After London displays the logon screen, start the 2262_Acapulco virtual machine.

3. Using Acapulco, log on to the domain as **AcapulcoUser** with the password **P@ssw0rd**

4. Click **Start**, and then click **E-mail**.

    The Windows Installer configures Office Professional 2003.

5. On the **Outlook 2003 Startup** page, click **Next**.

6. On the **E-mail Accounts** page, verify **Yes** is selected, and then click **Next**.

7. On the **Server Type** page, click **Microsoft Exchange Server**, and then click **Next**.

8. On the **Exchange Server Settings** page, in the **Microsoft Exchange Server** box, type **london**

9. In the **User Name** box, type **acapulcouser** and then click **Check Name**.

    London resolves to its fully qualified domain name (FQDN) and both the server and user entries are underlined.

10. On the **Exchange Server Settings** page, click **Next**, and then click **Finish**.

11. When prompted to enter your full name and initials, in the **User Name** dialog box, click **OK**.

12. Close all windows, log off, and pause Acapulco.

13. Pause London.

Lesson: Configuring Outlook Data

- What Are .pst Files?
- How to Create and Troubleshoot .pst Files
- How to Configure Junk-Mail Filters
- What Are Rules?
- How to Create Rules
- How to Archive Data
- How to Configure the Location for Storing Outlook Data
- How to Import and Export Outlook Data

Introduction

When you use Outlook on a daily basis, it is useful to send and receive e-mail by using multiple accounts. However, this creates a lot of contacts, notes, appointments, and tasks to manage, and it is easy to lose track of all of this information. Fortunately, Outlook includes several useful tools and features that can help you to organize and manage your data. This lesson describes some of these tools.

Lesson objectives

After completing this lesson, you will be able to:

- Explain the purpose and function of .pst files.
- Create and troubleshoot .pst files.
- Configure junk-mail filters.
- Explain the purpose and function of rules.
- Create rules.
- Archive Outlook data.
- Configure the location for storing Outlook data.
- Import and export Outlook data.

What Are .pst Files?

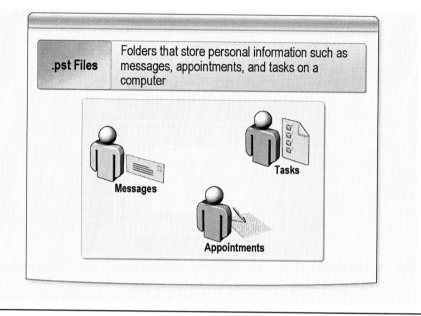

Introduction

A *personal folder (.pst) file* is a data file that stores personal information such as messages, appointments, tasks, and journal entries on your computer instead of on the computer running Exchange Server. You can assign a .pst file as the default delivery location for e-mail messages. You can also use a .pst file to organize and back up items for safekeeping.

Advantages and disadvantages of using .pst files

The following table lists some advantages and disadvantages of using a .pst file to store your Outlook data.

Advantages	Disadvantages
Data in .pst files is available at all times, whether you are working online or offline.	You cannot access data in .pst files if you are not using the computer on which the pst file is located.
You can copy .pst files to another computer and then open the file on that computer.	.pst files can grow very large in size and require a lot of hard-disk space.
You can archive older data that does not require regular access.	You must remember how to access archived data.

How to Create and Troubleshoot .pst Files

1 In Outlook, on the File menu, point to New, and then click Outlook Data File

2 In the New Outlook Data File dialog box, click OK

3 In the File name box, type a name for the file, and then click OK

4 In the Create or Open Outlook Data File dialog box, in the File name box, type a display name for the .pst file

5 Select any other appropriate options, and then click OK

Introduction

This section describes how to create and troubleshoot .pst files.

How to create a .pst file

To create a .pst file:

1. In Outlook, on the **File** menu, point to **New**, and then click **Outlook Data File**.

2. In the **New Outlook Data File** dialog box, click **OK**.

3. In the **File name** box, type a name for the file, and then click **OK**.

4. In the **Create or Open Outlook Data File** dialog box, in the **File name** box, type a display name for the .pst file.

5. Select any other options you prefer, and then click **OK**.

   The name of the folder that is associated with the data file appears in the **Folder** list.

The default location for .pst files is *x*:\Documents and Settings*user_name*\ Local Settings\Application Data\Microsoft\Outlook (where *x* is the letter of the drive on which Windows XP is installed).

Important You cannot automatically convert entire personal folders files created in previous versions of Outlook to an Outlook 2003 personal folders file (.pst) format. The best way to convert the files is to create a personal folders file in Outlook 2003 and then import items from the old data file to the new file.

Troubleshooting .pst files

There are two common issues that users sometimes have when working with .pst files:

- "I cannot open my .pst file."

    Remember the following key points about .pst files when troubleshooting this issue:

    - A .pst file can be accessed by only one user or program at a time. If you need to access a .pst file that is stored on a network share or on another computer, close any programs that might be using the .pst file and then try to open the file again.

    - A .pst file must have read/write permissions. A .pst data file that is stored on read-only media, such as a CD-ROM, cannot be opened. You can open a .pst file from a shared network folder, but you must have read/write permissions to do so. Also, the file cannot be set as read-only.

- "I get an error message stating that my .pst file is corrupt."

    When you receive this error message, you can use the Inbox Repair tool (scanpst.exe) to diagnose and repair errors in the .pst file. Scanpst.exe scans only .pst or .ost files to ensure that the file structure is intact. It does not scan your mailbox on the computer running Exchange Server.

How to Configure Junk-Mail Filters

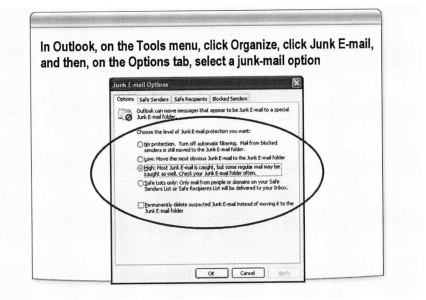

Introduction	Many users receive unsolicited advertisements in their e-mail Inboxes. This e-mail is called *junk mail*. If you do not want to receive junk mail, you can configure Outlook to automatically move this mail from your Inbox to your Deleted Items folder (or to any other folder that you specify), where you can review it before permanently deleting it. You can also configure Outlook to color-code junk mail in your Inbox so that you can easily identify it. You can also configure Outlook to move or delete all future messages from a particular sender. This section describes how to configure these junk-mail options.
How to configure junk-mail options	To view your junk-mail list, or to move, delete, or color-code all junk-mail messages in Office XP:

1. In Outlook, on the **Tools** menu, click **Organize**.
2. Click **Junk E-mail**.
3. Select the options that you want, and then click **Turn on** for each set of options that you choose.

How to add a name to the Add to Junk Senders list

To add a name to the **Add to Junk Senders** list:

1. In Outlook, in the Inbox, click a message from the sender whose messages you want to automatically delete.
2. On the **Actions** menu, point to **Junk E-mail**, and then click **Add Sender to Blocked Senders list**.

How to use Junk E-mail Filter

Outlook 2003 includes a new feature called Junk E-mail Filter, which helps users avoid reading junk-mail messages. The filter is on by default and the protection level is set to Low, which is designed to catch the most obvious junk-mail messages. The filter replaces the rules for processing junk-mail messages in previous versions of Outlook.

Note   To use the Junk E-mail Filter tool with an Exchange Server e-mail account, you must enable Cached Exchange Mode.

To use Junk E-mail Filter:

1. In Outlook, on the **Tools** menu, click **Options**.

2. On the **Preferences** tab, click **Junk E-mail**.

3. Select one of the following protection levels:

    No Automatic Filtering: Selecting this option turns the Junk E-mail Filter tool off; however, Outlook continues to move domain names and e-mail addresses that are on your **Blocked Senders** list to your Junk E-mail folder.

    Low: Select this option if you do not receive many junk-mail messages and want to see all but the most obvious junk messages.

    High: Select this option if you receive a large volume of junk-mail messages. If you select this option, you should periodically review the messages in your Junk E-mail folder because selecting this option can delete wanted messages as well.

    Safe Lists Only: Select this option if you want any e-mail message not on your **Safe Senders** list or your **Safe Recipients** list to be treated as junk mail.

4. Click **OK**.

5. Click **OK** to close **Options**.

6. Close all windows.

How to add a name to the Junk E-mail Options list

You can stop receiving e-mail from a particular source by adding the sender's e-mail address or domain name to the **Junk E-mail Options** list.

To add a name to the **Junk E-mail Options** list:

1. In Outlook, on the **Tools** menu, click **Options**, and then click **Junk E-mail**.

2. In the **Junk E-mail Options** dialog box, on the **Blocked Senders** tab, click **Add**.

3. In the **Enter an e-mail address or Internet domain name to be added to the list** box, type the name or e-mail address you want to add, and then click **OK**.

4. Repeat steps 2 and 3 for each name or e-mail address that you want to add.

5. Click **OK** to close the **Junk E-mail Options** dialog box.

6. Click **OK** to close **Options**.

7. Close all windows.

Key points

Consider the following points when determining how to filter junk mail:

- If you want all e-mail addresses listed in your Contacts folder to be considered trusted senders, in **Options**, on the **Preferences** tab, click **Junk E-Mail** and then on the **Safe Senders** tab, select the **Also trust e-mail from my Contacts** check box. When this option is selected, Junk E-mail Filter compares all incoming e-mail messages to the e-mail addresses in your Contacts folder.

- If you have existing lists of safe names and addresses, you can import the information into Outlook by saving the list into text or tab separated values (.txt) file format and then importing the list.

- To quickly add a sender, domain name, or mailing list name to the **Safe Senders**, **Safe Recipients**, or **Blocked Senders** list, right-click the message, point to **Junk E-mail** on the shortcut menu, and then click **Add Sender to Blocked Senders List**, **Add Sender to Safe Senders List**, or **Add Sender to Safe Recipients List**.

What Are Rules?

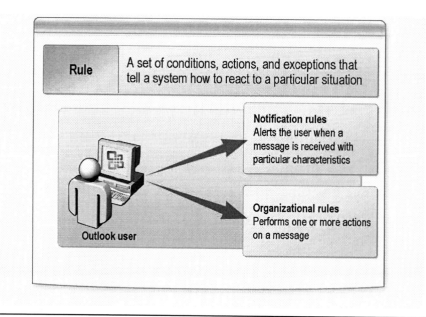

Introduction

A *rule* is a set of conditions, actions, and exceptions that tell a system how to react to a particular situation. In Outlook, rules help you manage your e-mail messages by performing actions on messages that match a specific set of conditions. After you create a rule, Outlook applies the rule to all your incoming or outgoing e-mail messages. For example, you could create a rule that:

- Forwards all messages that are sent by a specific person to another user.

- Assigns a category to all messages that you send that have a specific word in the **Subject** box.

- Highlights each meeting request or meeting update that you receive from a particular person.

Types of rules

There are two general categories of rules:

- *Notification rules.* Alert you when you receive a message with particular characteristics. For example, you could create a rule that automatically sends an e-mail message to your mobile telephone when you receive a message from a family member.

- *Organization rules.* Perform one or more actions on a message. For example, you could create a rule that automatically moves certain messages to a specific folder, or you could create a rule that automatically highlights meeting requests that you receive from specific senders.

Running rules manually

If you do not want Outlook to apply your rules automatically to every message, you can run one or more of your rules manually. Running rules manually allows you to selectively apply rules to messages in your Inbox or in another folder.

Creating exceptions to a rule

If you do not want Outlook to apply your rules all the time, you can create exceptions to a rule. If any of the exception conditions are met, the rule is not applied.

Important   Rules cannot be applied to HTTP e-mail accounts.

Server-based and client-only-based rules

If you have an e-mail account on a computer running Exchange Server, the server can apply rules to your messages even if you do not have Outlook running. These rules are called *server-based* rules. Server-based rules must be applied to messages when they are received in the Inbox on the server, and the rules must run to completion on the server. For example, a rule cannot be applied on the server if the rule specifies that a message is delivered to a folder that only exists on the client. If a rule cannot be applied on the server, it is applied when you start Outlook.

A rule that cannot be applied on the server has the words "client-only" added to the end of the rule's name. *Client-only-based rules* are applied after all other rules. If your list of rules contains rules that can be run on the server as well as those that cannot, the server-based rules are applied first, followed by the client-only-based rules.

How to Create Rules

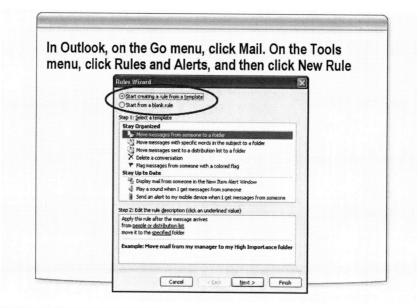

In Outlook, on the Go menu, click Mail. On the Tools menu, click Rules and Alerts, and then click New Rule

How to create a rule

To create a rule:

1. In Outlook, on the **Go** menu, click **Mail**.

2. On the **Tools** menu, click **Rules and Alerts**.

3. If you have more than one e-mail account, in the **Apply changes to this folder** list, click the **Inbox** you want.

4. Click **New Rule**.

5. You can now choose one of the following:

   a. Click **Start creating a rule from a template**.

   b. Under **Select the template**, select the template you want to use.

   −or−

   a. Click **Start from a blank rule**.

   b. Under **Select when messages should be checked**, select **Check messages when they arrive** or **Check messages after sending**, and then click **Next**.

6. Follow the remaining instructions in the Rules Wizard.

How to run a rules on an existing folder

To run a rule on an existing folder:

1. In Outlook, on the **Go** menu, click **Mail**.

2. On the **Tools** menu, click **Rules and Alerts**.

3. Click **Run Rules Now**.

4. In the **Run Rules Now** dialog box, select the rules you want to run.

5. In the **Run in folder** section, click **Browse**, select the folder in which you want to run the rule, and then click **OK**.

6. If you want the rule to run on all subfolders, select the **Include subfolders** check box.

7. In the **Apply rules to** section, select which messages you want the rule applied to. You can select **All Messages**, **Unread Messages**, or **Read Messages**.

8. Click **Run Now**.

9. When the rule finishes running, click **Close**.

How to Archive Data

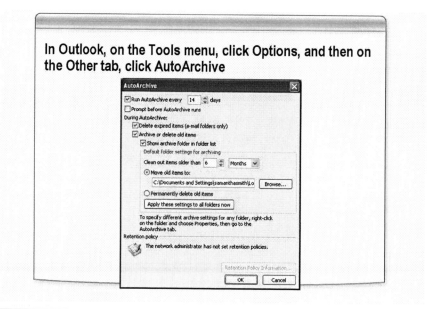

In Outlook, on the Tools menu, click Options, and then on the Other tab, click AutoArchive

Introduction

Because Outlook mailboxes grow with every item that is created or received, a method is needed for keeping mailboxes manageable. The Outlook AutoArchive feature allows you to store (or *archive*) old items that are important but not frequently used. AutoArchive is enabled by default and runs automatically at scheduled intervals, clearing out old and expired items from folders.

You can use AutoArchive to:

- Specify which items are archived.

- Specify how often items are archived.

- Automatically archive individual folders, groups of folders, or all Outlook folders.

- Permanently delete expired items.

- Delete or archive old items to an archive file.

Where archive files are stored

The first time that you run AutoArchive, Outlook creates the archive file automatically in the following location:

x:\Documents and Settings*UserName*\Local Settings\Application Data\ Microsoft\Outlook\Archive.pst, where *x* is the letter of the drive on which Windows XP is installed, and *UserName* is your user name.

Note   After Outlook archives items for the first time, you can access these items from Archive Folders in your Outlook Folder List.

How AutoArchive works

AutoArchive is a two-step process. First, you turn on AutoArchive. Second, you set the AutoArchive properties for each folder that you want archived. The AutoArchive properties of each folder are checked by date, and old items are moved to your archive file. Items in the Deleted Items folder are deleted.

How to turn on AutoArchive

To turn on AutoArchive:

1. In Outlook, on the **Tools** menu, click **Options**.

2. In the **Options** dialog box, on the **Other** tab, click **AutoArchive**.

3. In the **AutoArchive** dialog box, select the **Run AutoArchive Every** check box, and then specify how often the AutoArchive process will run by typing a number in the **days** box.

4. If you want to be notified before the items are archived, select the **Prompt before AutoArchive runs** check box.

5. In the **Move old items to:** box, type a file name for the archived items to be transferred to, or click **Browse** to select from a list.

6. Click **OK**, and then click **OK** again to close the **Options** dialog box.

How to set the AutoArchive properties

After you have turned on AutoArchive, you must set AutoArchive properties for each folder.

To set AutoArchive properties:

1. In Outlook, in the **Folder** list, right-click the folder that you want to AutoArchive, and then click **Properties**.

2. In the **Properties** dialog box, on the **AutoArchive** tab, to set AutoArchive for this folder, select **Archive this folder using these settings**.

3. To specify when items are automatically transferred to your archive file, type a number in the **Months** box.

4. To specify a folder for the archived items to be transferred to, click **Move old items to**.

5. In the **Move old items to** box, type a file name for the archived items, or click **Browse** to select from a list, and then click **OK**.

How to Configure the Location for Storing Outlook Data

Introduction

Outlook delivers e-mail messages to a location you specify. This section describes how to configure the location for storing Outlook data.

Where the default data store is located

The e-mail delivery location depends on the type of e-mail account:

- The default location, or data store, for POP3, IMAP, and HTTP e-mail accounts is a .pst file that is stored locally in the *x*:\Documents and Settings*user_name*\Local Settings\Application Data\Microsoft\Outlook folder (where *x* is the letter of the drive on which Windows XP is installed and *user_name* is your user name).

- The default data store for an Exchange Server e-mail account is typically on the server, unless you have Cached Exchange Mode enabled, in which case a local copy of your data is kept in an .ost file.

Advantages and disadvantages of configuring a .pst file as the default delivery location

If you use Outlook with an Exchange Server e-mail account, you can change the default delivery location, so that e-mail is sent to a .pst file instead of the default data store. The following table lists the advantages and disadvantages of configuring a .pst file as the default delivery location.

Advantage	Disadvantage
E-mail is available when the user is offline.	Advanced workgroup information sharing is only available when the default delivery location is an Exchange Server mailbox. For example, rules that direct mail to a folder exist as a client-based rule rather than a server-based rule.
User can save, copy, and move a .pst file to another location on the hard drive, floppy disk, or a server.	Outlook Web Access cannot be used to read old e-mail messages—it can only be used to receive new e-mail messages.

Note   You cannot change the default delivery location for HTTP and Simple Mail Transfer Protocol (SMTP) e-mail accounts.

How to configure a new e-mail delivery location

To configure a new e-mail delivery location:

1. In Outlook, on the **Tools** menu, click **E-mail Accounts**.

2. In the **E-mail Accounts** dialog box, click **View or change existing e-mail accounts**, and then click **Next**.

3. In the **E-mail Accounts** dialog box, in the **Deliver new e-mail to the following location** list, select where you want to the new messages to be delivered.

4. Click **Finish**.

   The new settings will take effect the next time you start Outlook.

How to Import and Export Outlook Data

Access the Import and Export Wizard to import files into Outlook and export files from Outlook

Import a File

Select file type to import from:

ACT! 3.x, 4.x, 2000 Contact Manager for Windows
Comma Separated Values (DOS)
Comma Separated Values (Windows)
Lotus Organizer 4.x
Lotus Organizer 5.x
Microsoft Access
Microsoft Excel
Personal Address Book

< Back   Next >   Cancel

Introduction

Outlook provides a tool called the Import and Export Wizard to help you import data from other programs into Outlook and export Outlook data to other programs.

Importing data into Outlook

Outlook allows you to copy data from many programs so that you can use that data in Outlook. For example, you might want to import existing information such as names and addresses from other programs, such as Microsoft Mail or Microsoft Schedule+, so that you do not have to manually reenter the same data in Outlook.

Exporting data from Outlook

Outlook also allows you to copy data, such as names and addresses, to several other programs, including dBase, Microsoft Office Access, Microsoft Office Excel, Microsoft Office Word, and Microsoft Office PowerPoint®. For example, you might want to export your contacts to Excel so that you can use a worksheet to sort names and addresses.

How to import files into Outlook

To import a file by using the Import and Export Wizard:

1. In Outlook, on the **File** menu, click **Import and Export**.

2. In the **Import and Export Wizard** dialog box, click **Import from another program or file**, and then click **Next**.

3. In the **Import a File** dialog box, select the type of file to import, and then click **Next**.

4. Click **Browse**, select the file you want to import, and then choose one of the following options:

   - **Replace duplicates with items imported**. When this option is chosen, existing data is overwritten with the information in the imported file.

   - **Allow duplicates to be created**. When this option is chosen, existing data is not overwritten, and duplicate information in the file is added to the current Outlook folder.

   - **Do not import duplicate items**. When this option is chosen, existing data is kept, and the duplicate information in the file is not added to the current Outlook folder.

5. Click **Next**.

6. Select the folder you want to import data into, and then click **Next**.

7. If necessary, map fields from the file you are importing to the Outlook fields, and then click **Next**.

8. Click **OK**.

How to export files from Outlook

To export a file by using the Import and Export Wizard:

1. In Outlook, on the **File** menu, click **Import and Export**.

2. In the **Import and Export Wizard** dialog box, click **Export to a file**, and then click **Next**.

3. In the **Export to a File** dialog box, in the list, click the file type you want to export to, and then click **Next**.

4. If you want to export to a file for use in Word or PowerPoint, choose either **Tab Separated Values** or **Comma Separated Values**.

5. Follow the remaining instructions in the Import and Export Wizard.

Note   Folder properties, such as permissions, rules, descriptions, forms, and views, are not saved when you export to a .pst file—only the actual content is exported.

Outlook-compatible file formats

Outlook is compatible with the following file formats:

File Type	Compatibility
Personal Folders file (.pst)	Outlook can import and export all types of data from and to a .pst file. The .pst files are used in archiving and as default data stores.
Personal Address Book (.pab)	Outlook can import a Microsoft Exchange Personal Address Book. The data is imported to the Outlook Contacts. You can also configure the Personal Address Book as another Address Book in Outlook.
Act! 3.0, 4.0, or 2000 Contact Manager for Windows (.dbf)	Outlook can import Contact data from this format.
iCalendar (.ics), vCalendar (.vcs)	Outlook can import calendar data from this format, and you can save calendar data in this format by clicking the **File** menu, and then clicking **Save As**.
Virtual Business Card vCard (.vcf)	Outlook can import contact data from this format, and you can save contacts in this format by clicking the **File** menu, and then clicking **Save As**.
Microsoft Schedule+ 7x and Interchange (.scd, .sc2)	Outlook can import calendar data from Schedule+ calendars.
Microsoft Access (.mdb), Microsoft Excel (.xls)	Outlook can import and export all types of data from and to an Access database or an Excel spreadsheet. The field or column data can be matched to Outlook's field.
Text Files (.csv and .txt)	Outlook can import and export all types of data from and to Comma Separated Value and Tab Separated value text files. The field or column data can be matched to Outlook's field.

Practice: Managing Outlook Data

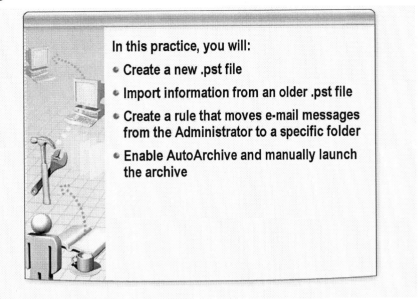

In this practice, you will:

* Create a new .pst file

* Import information from an older .pst file

* Create a rule that moves e-mail messages from the Administrator to a specific folder

* Enable AutoArchive and manually launch the archive

Objective

In this practice, you will create a new personal folders (.pst) file, import information from an older .pst file, create a rule that moves e-mail messages from the Administrator to a specific folder, enable AutoArchive, and manually launch the archive.

Practice

▶ **To create a new .pst file**

1. Resume London.

2. Resume Acapulco.

3. Using Acapulco, log on to the domain as **Administrator** with the password **P@ssw0rd**.

4. Click **Start**, and then click **E-mail**.

   After you click **E-mail**, a dialog box may appear stating installation steps are being performed.

5. In Outlook, on the **File** menu, point to **New**, and then click **Outlook Data File**.

6. In the **New Outlook Data File** dialog box, verify **Office Outlook Personal Folders File (.pst)** is selected and then click **OK**.

7. In the **Create or Open Outlook Data File** dialog box, click **My Documents**, then in the **File name** box, type **Administrator.pst** and then click **OK**.

8. In the **Create Microsoft Personal Folders** dialog box, click **OK** to accept the default folder name.

► **Import information from an older .pst file**

1. In Outlook, click **File**, and then click **Import and Export**.

2. In the **Import and Export Wizard** dialog box, verify **Import from another program or file** is selected, and then click **Next**.

3. On the **Import a File** page, select **Personal Folder File (.pst)**, and then click **Next**.

4. On the **Import Personal Folders** page, click **Browse**.

5. In the Open Personal Folders window, in the **File name** box, type **C:\Program Files\Microsoft Learning\2262\Practices\Mod04\ Outlook_2002_Personal_Folders** and then click **Open**.

6. On the **Import Personal Folders** page, click **Next**.

7. On the **Import Personal Folders** page, select **Import items into the same folder in**, select **Mailbox – Administrator** from the list, and then click **Finish**.

8. In the **Folder** list, under **Mailbox – Administrator**, you should now see several folders in the Personal Folders window.

9. Close Outlook.

► **Create a rule that moves e-mail messages from the Administrator to a specific folder**

1. Start Outlook.

2. In the **Microsoft Exchange Server** dialog box, click **Connect**.

3. In the folder list, under **Mailbox – Administrator**, click **Inbox**.

4. On the **Tools** menu, click **Rules and Alerts**.

5. In the **Rules and Alerts** dialog box, on the **E-mail Rules** tab, click **New Rule**.

6. In the Rules Wizard, under **Stay Organized**, click **Move messages from someone to a folder**.

7. Under **Step 2**, click **people or distribution list**.

8. In the **Rule Address** dialog box, in the **Name** list, click **Administrator**, click **From**, and then click **OK**.

9. Under **Step 2**, click the **specified** link.

10. In the **Rules and Alerts** dialog box, click **New**.

11. In the **Create New Folder** dialog box, in the **Name** box, type **E-mail from Administrator** and then click **OK** twice.

12. In the Rules Wizard, click **Finish**.

13. In the **Rules and Alerts** dialog box, click **OK**.

14. Send a message to yourself (Administrator) to test the rule.

▶ **Enable AutoArchive and manually launch the archive**

1. On the **Tools** menu, click **Options**.

2. In the Options window, on the **Other** tab, click **AutoArchive**.

3. In the AutoArchive window, in the **Run AutoArchive every** box, select **2 days**.

4. In the **Default folder settings for archiving** box, in the **Clean out items older than** box, select **1 days**, and then click **OK**.

5. In the Options window, click **OK**.

6. On the **Tools** menu, click **Mailbox Cleanup**.

7. In the Mailbox Cleanup window, click **AutoArchive**.

   What happened when you enabled AutoArchive?

   _____

   _____

   _____

   _____

8. Close all windows, log off, and pause Acapulco.

9. Pause London.

Lesson: Configuring Outlook for Internet E-Mail

* How to Create an Outlook Profile
* How to Configure POP3, IMAP, and HTTP for E-Mail Services
* Common Issues in Troubleshooting Mailbox Configuration

Introduction

This lesson explains how to create an Outlook profile and how to configure e-mail accounts that belong to that profile. You must understand how to perform these tasks so that you can assist users in troubleshooting Outlook configuration issues.

Objectives

After completing this lesson, you will be able to:

- Create Outlook profiles.
- Configure POP3, IMAP, and HTTP for e-mail services.
- Troubleshoot common issues in mailbox configuration.

How to Create an Outlook Profile

1	Click Start, and then click Control Panel
2	In Control Panel, click User Accounts, and then click Mail
3	In the Mail Setup dialog box, click Show Profiles
4	On the General tab, select Prompt for a profile to be used, and then click OK
5	In the Profile Name field, type a descriptive name, and click OK
6	Click Add a new e-mail account, and then click Next
7	Select the server type, and then click Next
8	Type required information, click Next, and then click Finish
9	Click OK

Definition

A *profile* is a group of e-mail accounts, address books, and personal folders. A user can create any number of profiles. Multiple profiles are useful if more than one person uses the computer.

How to create a new profile with an e-mail account

To create a new profile with an e-mail account:

1. Click **Start**, and then click **Control Panel**.

2. In Control Panel, click **User Accounts**, and then click **Mail**.

3. In the **Mail Setup** dialog box, click **Show Profiles**.

4. In the **Mail** dialog box, on the **General** tab, select **Prompt for a profile to be used**, and then click **Add**.

5. In the **New Profile** dialog box, in the **Profile Name** field, type a descriptive name for the new profile, and then click **OK**.

6. In the **E-mail Accounts** dialog box, click **Add a new e-mail account**, and then click **Next**.

7. Select the appropriate server type for your new e-mail account, and then click **Next**.

8. Type in the appropriate information as prompted, click **Next**, and then click **Finish**.

9. Click **OK**.

Note The OAB and .pst files are automatically added to each new profile, except in Exchange Server.

Note For more information about how to create a new e-mail profile in Outlook, see Microsoft Knowledge Base (KB) article 287072.

How to Configure POP3, IMAP, and HTTP for E-Mail Services

Introduction

Before users can receive e-mail in Outlook, they need to properly configure an e-mail service with which to send and receive messages. Post Office Protocol 3 (POP3) and Internet Message Access Protocol (IMAP) are used for receiving mail messages; Hypertext Transfer Protocol (HTTP) is used to send messages from a Web server to the browser used to view a Web page. This section describes how to configure POP3, IMAP, and HTTP for e-mail services.

Using POP3 to receive messages

As a DST, it is essential that you understand how to configure POP3 because it is the protocol most commonly used by Internet service providers (ISPs) for enabling users to receive e-mail. When a user cannot access her e-mail, you may need to troubleshoot her e-mail service.

Using IMAP to receive messages

IMAP is similar to POP3 but it supports some additional features. For example, IMAP enables a user to access and view an e-mail message header and the message sender while the message is still on the Mail server. This way, the user can determine which messages to download to her computer. Users can create and manipulate folders or mailboxes on the server, delete messages, or search for certain parts or entire messages. Because e-mail messages are maintained on the server using IMAP, users can access e-mail messages from more than one computer. If an e-mail is deleted on a computer, it is still located on the server and can be accessed by using computer.

Using HTTP to send messages

When you configure a mailbox for HTTP, Outlook immediately downloads the headers of the e-mail messages that are stored on the Web server. To view the entire message, double-click the message header.

How to configure POP3, IMAP, or HTTP for e-mail services

The procedure for configuring POP3, IMAP, or HTTP for e-mail services is exactly the same except for steps 3 and 4. When configuring POP3, IMAP, or HTTP for e-mail services, use the following procedure, but note the specific information in steps 3 and 4 for POP3, IMAP, and HTTP.

To configure POP3, IMAP, or HTTP e-mail services:

1. In Outlook, on the **Tools** menu, click **E-mail Accounts**.

2. In the **E-mail Accounts** dialog box, click **Add a new e-mail account**, and then click **Next**.

3. In the **E-mail Accounts** dialog box, under **Server Type**, click **POP3**, and then click **Next**.

Note   For IMAP, in step 3, in the **E-mail Accounts** dialog box, under **Server Type**, click **IMAP**, and then click **Next**.

For HTTP, in step 3, in the **E-mail Accounts** dialog box, under **Server Type**, click **HTTP**, and then click **Next**.

---

4. In the **E-mail Accounts** dialog box, type the required information according to the following guidelines:

    a. **User Information**

      • Your Name: This should be your full name.

      • E-mail: Type your e-mail address.

    b. **Logon Information**

      • User Name: This is the part of your e-mail address to the left of the @ sign.

      • Password: Create a password that is easy to remember but is not obvious to other users.

      • Remember Password: Select this check box if you want Outlook to remember your e-mail account password so that you do not have to reenter it every time you access your e-mail.

Warning   It is recommended that you do not select the **Remember Password** check box because doing so can jeopardize the security of your Outlook data.

---

    c. **Server Information**

      For POP3:

      • *Incoming e-mail server (POP3):* This is the name of the POP3 server that holds your messages before you download them onto your computer. Enter the server name in lowercase. The name may be in the form of *mail.myisp.net*, or in the form of an Internet Protocol (IP) address such as 192.168.255.255.

- *Outgoing e-mail server (SMTP):* This is the name of the Outgoing e-mail server. Enter the server name in lowercase. The name may be in the form of mail.myisp.net, or in the form of an IP address such as 192.168.0.0.

  To test the account, click **Test Account Settings**. This feature verifies that your system is connected to the Internet, that you are logged on to the SMTP server, and that you are logged on to the POP3 server. If Test Account Settings determines that you need to log on to the POP3 server before the SMTP server, Outlook automatically remembers to log on to the POP3 server before messages are sent in the future. Test Account Settings also sends a test message. This message contains details about any changes that Outlook made to your initial setup.

  For IMAP:

- *Incoming e-mail server (IMAP):* This is the name of the IMAP server that holds your messages before you download them onto your computer. Enter the server name in lowercase. The name may be in the form of mail.myisp.net, or in the form of an IP address.

- *Outgoing e-mail server (SMTP):* This is the name of the outgoing e-mail server. Enter the server name in lowercase. The name may be in the form of mail.myisp.net, or in the form of an IP address.

  For HTTP:

  HTTP Mail Service Provider: This menu lists all of the Web e-mail providers that are enabled. Microsoft Hotmail® is available on this list. If you click **Other**, the **Server URL** text box is available. You can enter the URL location of your HTTP e-mail service here.

5. Click **Next**, and then click **Finish**.

How use to POP3

Because POP3 does not store e-mail messages on the server, if you want to access your e-mail from more than one computer, you can configure your Outlook account to leave copies of your e-mail on the e-mail server. Leaving copies of your e-mail on the server ensures that you can access this information from multiple locations.

To leave copies of e-mail on the server:

1. In Outlook, on the **Tools** menu, click **E-mail Accounts**.

2. In the **E-mail Accounts** dialog box, click **View or change existing E-mail Accounts**, and then click **Next**.

3. In the **E-mail Accounts** dialog box, select your POP3 e-mail account, and then click **Change**.

4. In the **E-mail Accounts** dialog box, click **More Settings**.

5. In the **Internet E-mail Settings** dialog box, on the **Advanced** tab, select **Leave a copy of messages on the server**.

6. Click **OK**.

7. Click **Next**, and then click **Finish**.

Note For more information about configuring Internet e-mail accounts, see KB article 287532.

Note For more information on configuring Outlook to receive messages from an IMAP server, see KB article 286197.

Note For more information on how to configure Outlook with Hotmail, see KB article 287424.

Common Issues in Troubleshooting Mailbox Configuration

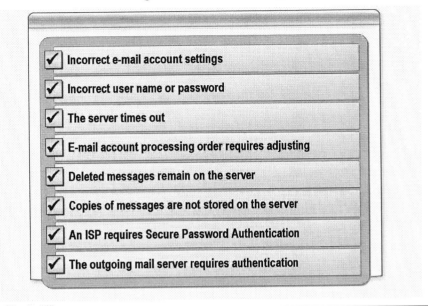

Introduction	This section describes common issues related to mailbox configuration and the resolutions to these issues.
Incorrect e-mail account settings	Most issues with POP3, IMAP, and HTTP e-mail accounts in Outlook are related to errors in e-mail account configuration. If an e-mail account is not configured correctly, users may receive a variety of error messages, such as Send/Receive Error, or Invalid Username and Password. The first place to look when you troubleshoot mailbox configuration issues is the **E-mail Accounts** dialog box. The **E-mail Accounts** dialog box in Outlook displays detailed information about the current account configuration. It also allows you to modify existing accounts, add new accounts, and remove accounts.
Incorrect user name or password	The password and user name may be case-sensitive, depending upon the specifications of your ISP. Ensure that you entered the correct user name and password, or e-mail server name, in the **E-mail Accounts** dialog box.
The server times out	If the server times out, you need to make the e-mail server timeout setting longer. You can adjust these settings in the **E-mail Accounts** dialog box.
E-mail account processing order requires adjusting	To change the order in which e-mail accounts are processed, adjust the order in which the accounts are listed in the **E-mail Accounts** dialog box.
Deleted messages remain on the server	If deleted messages remain on the server, you may have set an option to keep a copy of your messages on the POP3 e-mail server. If you delete a message that was delivered to a local file, the copy stored on the Internet e-mail server is not affected.

Copies of messages are not stored on the server

When copies of messages are not stored on the server, there are two possible solutions:

- You may have set an option to delete copies of your messages from the POP3 e-mail server after a specified number of days. When you set this option, messages left on the Internet e-mail server are removed after five days unless you specify otherwise.

- You may be using a different computer than the one you used to set the option to keep a copy of messages on the server. If you did not select the **Leave a copy of messages on the server** check box in the **E-mail Accounts** dialog box on this additional computer, your messages will be downloaded to it and deleted from the server.

An ISP requires Secure Password Authentication

If an ISP requires Secure Password Authentication (SPA), in the **E-mail Accounts** dialog box, select the **Log on using Secure Password Authentication (SPA)** check box.

The outgoing mail server requires authentication

If the outgoing mail server requires authentication, in the **E-mail Accounts** dialog box, click **More Settings**. On the **Outgoing Server** tab, enter the required authentication information.

Practice: Configuring Outlook for Internet E-Mail

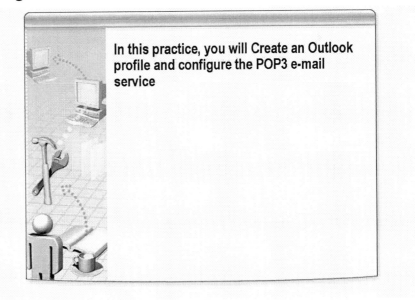

In this practice, you will Create an Outlook profile and configure the POP3 e-mail service

Objective

In this practice, you will examine features of Outlook and Outlook Express and then create a new Outlook profile and configure the profile with POP3 e-mail service.

▶ **Create an Outlook profile and configure the POP3 e-mail service**

1. Resume London and Acapulco.

2. Using Acapulco, log on to the domain as **AcapulcoUser** with the password **P@ssw0rd**.

3. Click **Start**, right-click **E-mail**, and then click **Properties**.

4. In the **Mail Setup – Outlook** dialog box, click **Show Profiles**.

5. In the **Mail** dialog box, click **Prompt for a profile to be used**, and then click **Add**.

6. In the **New Profile** dialog box, in the **Profile Name** box, type **Internet E-mail** and then click **OK**.

   The E-mail Accounts Wizard is displayed.

7. On the **E-mail Accounts** page, verify that **Add a new e-mail account** is selected, and then click **Next**.

8. On the **Server Type** page, click **POP3**, and then click **Next**.

9. On the **Internet E-mail Settings (POP3)** page, enter the following information:

   - Your Name: **AcapulcoUser**

   - E-mail Address: **AcapulcoUser@nwtraders.msft**

   - Incoming mail server: (POP3): **London.nwtraders.msft**

   - Outgoing mail server (SMTP): **London.nwtraders.msft**

   - User Name: **AcapulcoUser**

   - Password: **P@ssw0rd**

10. On the **Internet E-mail Settings (POP3)** page, click **Test Account Settings**.

11. In the Test Account Settings window, click **Close**.

12. On the **Internet E-mail Settings (POP3)** page, click **Next**.

13. On the **E-mail Accounts** page, click **Finish**.

14. Close all windows, log off, and pause Acapulco.

Lesson: Troubleshooting Outlook

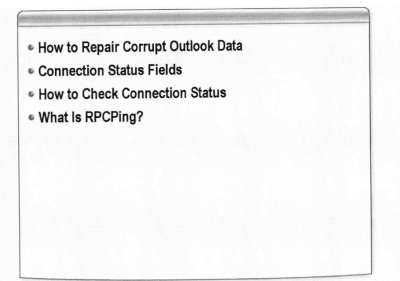

- How to Repair Corrupt Outlook Data
- Connection Status Fields
- How to Check Connection Status
- What Is RPCPing?

Introduction

Outlook includes a tool called the Inbox Repair Tool that enables you to fix corrupt data in .pst and .ost files. Two other tools, the Exchange Server Connection Status window and the **RPCPing** command, allow you to view the status of connections between Outlook and the computers running Exchange Server. This lesson describes how to troubleshoot Outlook by using these tools.

Lesson objectives

After completing this lesson, you will be able to:

- Repair corrupt Outlook data.
- Describe the Connection Status fields.
- Check connection status.
- Explain the purpose and function of RPCPing.

How to Repair Corrupt Outlook Data

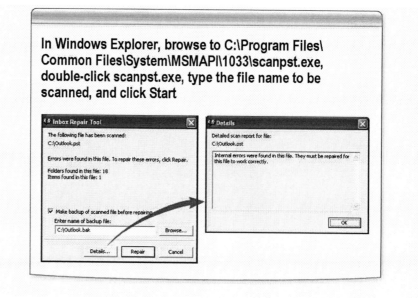

In Windows Explorer, browse to C:\Program Files\
Common Files\System\MSMAPI\1033\scanpst.exe,
double-click scanpst.exe, type the file name to be
scanned, and click Start

Introduction

As a DST, you may receive calls from users who are having issues viewing or working with their Outlook information. If you suspect that .pst or .ost data files are corrupt, you can use the *Inbox Repair Tool* to diagnose and repair errors in the files.

About the Inbox Repair Tool

The Inbox Repair Tool, or Scanpst.exe, is included with Microsoft Office, and installs automatically during setup. Scanpst.exe is usually located in the following folder:

C:\Program Files\Common Files\System\MSMAPI\1033\Scanpst.exe

How the Inbox Repair Tool works

The Inbox Repair Tool scans .pst and .ost files to verify that the file structure is intact. If it discovers a problem, it attempts to recover and repair the corrupt item.

Note The Inbox Repair Tool only scans .pst and .ost files—it does not scan mailboxes on Exchange Server.

How to use the Inbox Repair Tool

To use the Inbox Repair Tool to scan a .pst or .ost file:

1. In Outlook, on the **File** menu, click **Exit**.

2. In Windows Explorer, browse to the following file: C:\Program Files\
   Common Files\System\MSMAPI\1033\scanpst.exe.

   Note If you cannot find the Inbox Repair Tool (Scanpst.exe) in either of these locations, search for the file in Windows Explorer. (Click **Start**, point to **Search**, and then in the **Search for files or folders named** box, type **scanpst.exe**)

3. Double-click **scanpst.exe**.

4. In the **Enter the name of the file you want to scan** box, type the name of the .pst or .ost file that you want to check, or click **Browse** to look for the .pst or .ost file.

5. To specify scan log options, click **Options**, and then select specific options.

6. Click **Start**.

   The Inbox Repair Tool starts scanning your Inbox.

7. When the scanning is complete—and if errors are found—you are prompted to start the repair process.

   To change the name or location of the backup file created during the repair process, in the **Enter name of backup file** box, type a new file name, or click **Browse** to look for the file.

8. Click **Repair**.

How to view repaired items

To view repaired items:

1. In Outlook, ensure that you use the profile that contains the .pst file that you tried to repair.

2. In Outlook, on the **Go** menu, click **Folder List**.

   If the Inbox Repair Tool was able to repair any items, you will see a Recovered Personal Folders folder in the Folder List. If the repair was not able to repair any items, you will not see a Recovered Personal Folders folder.

3. Click **Recovered Personal Folders**, and then click the **Lost and Found** folder.

   The Lost and Found folder contains folders and items that the Inbox Repair tool recovered. Items that are not recovered to the Lost and Found folder cannot be repaired.

How to move repaired items to a new .pst file

After you have used the Inbox Repair Tool to repair items, you may want to create a new .pst file. You can move items that were recovered from the repair process into this new file.

To move repaired items into a new .pst file:

1. Create a new .pst file.

2. In the Lost and Found folder, press and hold the CTRL key, click each item that you want to move, and drag these items into the new .pst file.

When you have finished moving all items into the new .pst file, you can delete the recovered Personal Folders (.pst) file, including the Lost and Found folder, from your profile.

Note For more information about using the Inbox Repair Tool to recover messages, see KB article 287497.

Connection Status Fields

Field	Describes
Server Name	The server to which Outlook is connected
Type	The server type, such as Directory or Mail Server
Interface	The network connection used to connect to the computers running Exchange Server
Conn	The type of connection
Status	The connection status
Req/Fail	The number of successful or failed RPC requests
Avg Resp	The time it takes for the server to respond
Version	The Exchange Server version number

Introduction

If your Outlook 2003 e-mail account is set up to use a computer running Exchange Server, you can view detailed information about the connection between Outlook and Exchange Server in the Exchange Server Connection Status window. You can use this information to identify how Outlook is connecting to the computer running Exchange Server and to troubleshoot connection issues.

Connection status fields

The following table describes each of the fields in the Exchange Server Connection Status window.

Field	Describes
Server Name	The server to which Outlook is connected
Type	The server type, such as Directory or Mail Server
Interface	The network connection used to connect to the computers running Exchange Server
Conn	The type of connection, such as TCP/IP or RCP over HTTP
Status	The connection status, such as Established, Connecting, Disconnecting, or Disconnected
Req/Fail	The number of successful or failed RPC requests
Avg Resp	The time (in milliseconds) it takes for the server to respond to requests
Version	The Exchange Server version number

How to Check Connection Status

Access the Exchange Server Connection Status window
to view detailed information about the status of an
Outlook and Exchange Server connection

**How to view the
Exchange Server
Connection Status
window**

To view the Exchange Server Connection Status window in Outlook 2003:

1. Press and hold the CTRL key and right-click the **Microsoft Outlook** icon in
    the system tray.

2. Click **Connection Status**.

    The Exchange Server Connection Status window appears.

**Reconnecting to
Exchange Server**

If you lose your connection to the computer running Exchange Server or you
want to reset your connection, in the Exchange Server Connection Status
window, click **Reconnect**. This restores connectivity to the computer running
Exchange Server.

What Is RPCPing?

Introduction

RPCPing is used to confirm the RPC connectivity between the computer running Exchange Server and any of the supported Exchange Server client computers on the network. If you cannot connect to the computer running Exchange Server, use this tool to see if you have RPC connectivity.

Where to locate RPCPing

Rpcping.exe is included with the Windows Server 2003 Resource Kit tools. To download the resource kit tools, visit the following Microsoft Web site: http://www.microsoft.com/downloads/details.aspx?FamilyID=9d467a69-57ff-4ae7-96ee-b18c4790cffd&DisplayLang=en.

How RPCPing works

RPCPing is a utility that determines whether a specific IP address is accessible by sending packets to the specific address and then waiting for a reply. RPCPing works much like the PING utility for TCP/IP connections, except that it tests RPC connectivity instead of IP connectivity. Because many services in Windows Server 2003 use RPCs to communicate with clients, RPC information can help you troubleshoot a server that has a successful ping, but has some unresponsive services.

Because RPCPing is only checking for connectivity, it does not attempt to interpret the response that is received from the server. Any response from the server means that there is RPC connectivity between the computers.

RPCPing works much like the PING utility in that you only need to provide an IP address to test basic connectivity. Using only the /s parameter and no others, RPCPing assumes a TCP/IP connection and does not authenticate with the server.

Using RPCPing

To use RPCPing, open a command prompt and type: **rpcping /s** *Exchange_Server_name* and then press ENTER.

Analyzing RPCPing output

If the RPCPing is successful, you will see the following type of output:

```
Completed 1 calls in 1 ms
1000 T/S or 1.000 ms/T
```

If the RPCPing is not successful, you will see the following type of output:

```
Exception 1722 (0x000006BA)
Number of records is: 2
ProcessID is 2956
System Time is: 2/26/2003 21:28:48:130
Generating component is 8
Status is 1722
Detection location is 322
Flags is 0
NumberOfParameters is 0
ProcessID is 2956
System Time is: 2/26/2003 21:28:48:130
Generating component is 8
Status is 11001
Detection location is 320
Flags is 0
NumberOfParameters is 1
Unicode string: server1
```

Note For information about using RPCPing in Microsoft Windows NT®, see KB article 167260.

Practice: Troubleshooting Outlook

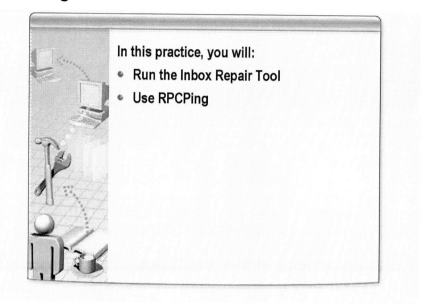

In this practice, you will:
- Run the Inbox Repair Tool
- Use RPCPing

Objective

In this practice, you will run the Inbox Repair Tool and use RPCPing.

▶ **Run the Inbox Repair Tool**

1. Resume Acapulco.

2. Using Acapulco, log on to the domain as **Administrator** with the password **P@ssw0rd**.

3. Click **Start**, and then click **Run**.

4. In the **Run** box, type **C:\Program Files\Common Files\System\ MSMAPI\1033\scanpst.exe** and then click **OK**.

5. In the **Inbox Repair Tool** dialog box, click **Browse**.

6. In the **Select File to Scan** dialog box, browse to C:\Program Files\Microsoft Learning\2262\Practices\Mod04\Outlook_2002_Personal_Folders, and then click **Open**.

7. In the **Inbox Repair Tool** dialog box, click **Start**.

   When the scanning is completed, you will be prompted to start the repair process if errors were found.

8. Click **Repair**, and then click **OK**.

▶ **Use RPCPing**

1. Click **Start**, and then click **Run**.

2. In the **Run** box, type **cmd** and then click **OK**.

3. At the command prompt, type **cd c:\program files\microsoft learning\ 2262\practices\mod04** and then press ENTER.

4. At the command prompt, type **rpcping /s london** and then press ENTER.
   Was the RPCPing test successful?

   _____

5. For both London and Acapulco, turn off and delete changes.

Lab: Troubleshooting Issues Related to Outlook

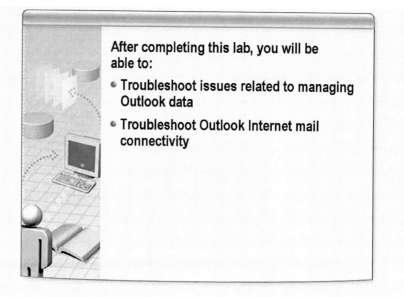

After completing this lab, you will be able to:

- Troubleshoot issues related to managing Outlook data
- Troubleshoot Outlook Internet mail connectivity

Objectives

After completing this lab, you will be able to:

- Troubleshoot issues related to managing Outlook data.
- Troubleshoot Outlook Internet mail connectivity.

Prerequisites

Before working on this lab, you must have an understanding of how to use Microsoft Virtual PC.

Before You Begin

For each exercise in this lab, use the password **P@ssw0rd**.

In Virtual PC, <right>ALT+DEL is the equivalent of CTRL+ALT+DEL.

Estimated time to complete this lab: 30 minutes

Exercise 1
Troubleshooting Issues Related to Managing Outlook Data

In this exercise, you will troubleshoot issues related to managing Outlook Data.

Scenario

A user calls and says the computer running Exchange Server must be down because he is not getting any mail. He also informs you that he recently set up filters to organize his incoming mail and enabled the Junk-Mail Filter feature to filter out unwanted e-mail. Since then he has not received any e-mail. You contact the Exchange Server administrator who confirms the server is up and functioning properly.

Tasks	Guidance for completing the task
1. Start the London and Acapulco virtual machines and, using Acapulco, log on as **NWTRADERS\Max**.	▪ Use the Virtual PC console.
2. Using Acapulco, use Outlook Web Access, log on as **Administrator**, and send Max two test messages.	▪ Use Microsoft Internet Explorer to browse to http://london/exchange/administrator.
3. Open Outlook to view the messages sent from the Administrator.	
❷ Did Max receive either of the messages you sent from the Administrator's mail account?	
4. Resolve the Outlook data-management issue.	▪ Refer to the Managing Outlook Data lesson.
5. Using Acapulco, close all windows and log off.	

Exercise 2
Troubleshooting Outlook Internet Mail Connectivity

In this exercise, you will troubleshoot issues related to Outlook Internet mail connectivity.

Scenario

A user calls and says e-mail is disappearing from her inbox. She retrieves e-mail both from home and from work. At work she uses Outlook 2003; at home she uses Outlook Express. She says that she eventually finds the e-mail on one computer or the other, but occasionally she receives few if any e-mail messages at work even though at the same time her computer at home receives e-mail all day.

Tasks	Guidance for completing the task
1. Using Acapulco, log on to the domain as **Samantha** with the password **P@ssw0rd** and then start Outlook 2003.	
2. Using Acapulco, start Outlook Express.	<ul><li>You are starting two applications to simulate Samantha receiving mail at home (Outlook Express) and at work (Outlook 2003).</li><li>Do not make Outlook Express your default mail client.</li><li>Configure Outlook Express with the following values:<ul><li>Display name: **Samantha Smith**</li><li>Email address: **Samantha@nwtraders.msft**</li><li>Incoming/Outgoing mail server: **london.nwtraders.msft**</li><li>Account name: **Samantha**</li><li>Password: **P@ssw0rd**</li></ul></li></ul>
3. Using Acapulco, use Outlook Web Access to send a message from the Administrator to Samantha Smith.	<ul><li>Use Internet Explorer to browse to http://london/exchange/ administrator.</li></ul>
4. Starting with Outlook, check mail on both applications.	<ul><li>In Outlook 2003 and Outlook Express, press F5.</li></ul>

(*continued*)

Tasks	Guidance for completing the task
❓ Did both e-mail applications receive the e-mail sent from the Administrator?	
5. Resolve the Outlook Internet mail connectivity issue.	▪ Refer to the Common Issues in Troubleshooting Mail Configuration topic.
6. On both London and Acapulco, close and delete changes.	

Lab Discussion

After you have completed the exercises in this lab, take a moment to answer the following questions. When the entire class has finished the lab, the instructor will facilitate a lab discussion based on students' answers to these questions.

1. How did you determine the cause(s) of the issue(s)?

2. How did you resolve the issue(s)?

3. What are some other ways the issue(s) could have been resolved?

Course Evaluation

Your evaluation of this course will help Microsoft understand the quality of your learning experience.

At a convenient time before the end of the course, please complete a course evaluation, which is available at http://www.CourseSurvey.com.

Microsoft will keep your evaluation strictly confidential and will use your responses to improve your future learning experience.

Module 5:
Troubleshooting Issues
Related to Office

Contents

Overview

- Configuring and Troubleshooting an Office Installation
- Configuring Office Security
- Configuring Office Recoverability
- Configuring Office Language Features

Introduction

Many of the calls that you receive from users as a desktop support technician (DST) will relate to one or more of the Microsoft® Office applications. Your familiarity with each of these applications, as well as your understanding of how to perform critical tasks such as installing the software and managing its security, will greatly assist you in the troubleshooting process.

Objectives

After completing this module, you will be able to:

- Configure and troubleshoot an Office installation.
- Configure Office security.
- Configure Office recoverability.
- Configure Office language features.

Lesson: Configuring and Troubleshooting an Office Installation

- Types of Office Installations
- Methods, Sources, and Tools for Installing Office
- Office Integration with Other Applications
- Office Customization Options and Log Files
- The Office Upgrade Process
- How to Activate Office
- Guidelines for Troubleshooting an Office Installation or Upgrade

Introduction

Because there are a variety of types of Office installations, users sometimes require assistance in choosing an option. Other users need assistance in determining which method, source, or tool to use when installing Office. This lesson describes the process of installing and upgrading Office 2003. It also discusses how to activate Office after it is installed. Finally, this lesson provides guidelines for troubleshooting Office installations and upgrades. Your understanding of how the installation process works and your ability to identify key points in this process will enable you to assist your users as they install Office on computers running Microsoft Windows® XP Professional or Windows XP Home Edition.

Objectives

After completing this lesson, you will be able to:

- Describe the types of Office installations.
- Explain the methods, sources, and tools for installing Office.
- Describe the integration of Office with other applications.
- Describe the Office customization options and log files.
- Describe the Office upgrade process.
- Activate Office by using the Microsoft Office Activation Wizard.
- Apply guidelines for troubleshooting an Office installation or upgrade.

Types of Office Installations

Type	Disk space	Description
Typical Install	331 MB	Installs the most commonly used components
Complete Install	577 MB	Installs all components
Minimal Install	251 MB	Installs the minimum required components
Custom Install	Based on selected features	Enables the user to select the features that are installed
Upgrade	Based on previous installation options	Installs the current configuration and removes previous versions

Introduction

During an Office installation, the Setup program allows you to specify the type of installation that you want to perform. This decision should be made based on your available disk space and the files that you want to install. The following table describes the types of installations that are available and the disk space required to perform each installation type in Office.

Type	Disk space required	Description
Typical Install	331 MB	Installs the most commonly used components of Office. Additional features may be installed on first use, or added later through Add or Remove Programs in Control Panel.
Complete Install	577 MB	Installs all of Office on the computer, including all optional components and tools.
Minimal Install	251 MB	Installs Office with only the minimal required components. Recommended for low-disk space installation.
Custom Install	Based on selected features	Enables the user to select the features of Office that are installed on the computer, and whether to keep or remove previous versions of Office. Recommended for advanced users.
Upgrade	Based on previous installation options	Installs Office based on the current Office configuration, and removes previous versions of Office from your computer.

Methods, Sources, and Tools for Installing Office

	Type
Method	• Manual installation • Automated installation • Upgrade installation
Source	• CD • Network location
Tool	• Group Policy • System Management Server

Introduction

You may receive calls from users who are attempting to install Office and are not sure which method or source to use. This section describes the Office installation methods, sources, and tools for installing Office.

Office installation methods

The Office Setup program uses Windows Installer technology. There are three ways to install Office in Microsoft Windows XP:

- *Manual installation.* The user begins the installation process and follows the on-screen prompts to complete the installation. This method enables users to specify the files that are installed and to configure advanced settings for the Office applications.

- *Automated installation.* The installation proceeds according to an installation script that was created specifically for the computer or network. All installation options are pre-selected.

- *Upgrade installation.* You have a previous version of Office installed and you want to install a new version, or you want to update a specific component of the current version.

Sources for installing Office

Your users may be installing Office from the following sources:

- *CD.* Place a CD into the CD drive and run the setup routine.

- *Network location.* You can configure a network to support a software deployment. For example, when users start their computers or log on to the network, the installation process begins. You can also place an icon on users' desktops or notification areas that allows them to launch the installation process. Or you can allow users to select components to install from Add or Remove Programs.

Tools for deploying multiple Office installations

When companies deploy software packages such as Office, they must have a centralized, organized, and secure method of successfully supporting multiple installations. The following two tools are used for deploying Office company-wide:

- *Group Policy*. This tool enables administrators to install and maintain Office for all users or on all computers in a designated group. In a small or medium-sized organization, Group Policy is the preferred tool for managing software deployment, particularly if the Active Directory® directory service is deployed and all clients have consistent software and hardware configurations.

- *Systems Management Server (SMS)*. This tool enables administrators to manage large numbers of clients in a complex and rapidly changing business environment. SMS is designed for medium-sized and large organizations. Unlike Group Policy, SMS does not require Active Directory, and SMS can be used to deploy software applications to a variety of Windows clients.

Office Integration with Other Applications

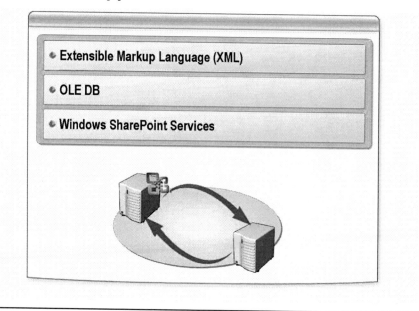

Introduction	Office 2003 includes tools that enhance its capabilities of integration with other applications and systems. With the new functionality of Office 2003, systems speak the same language; users have access to current data at all times, and can retrieve it from almost any source; and teams can collaborate and coordinate with one another no matter where they are.
XML	Microsoft has built the *Extensible Markup Language* (XML) into the heart of Office 2003 applications. XML is a data description language standard used throughout the world to share business information on the Web without worrying about incompatible programs, computer networks, data structures, and operating systems.
Benefits of XML	The benefits of XML include:

- *Easy exchange of data.* XML allows data to be retrieved and used from disparate and otherwise incompatible systems.

- *Simple reuse of data.* Reuse of information through XML eliminates the need to rekey or recode, and thereby reduces the time required and errors generated in repurposing information.

- *Easily searchable information.* XML helps give structure and meaning to electronic information, so that information becomes much easier to search and organize.

- *Different views of the same data.* Because XML separates content from its presentation, the same information can be used in different environments, formats, applications, and devices, depending on the needs of the user.

- *Rapid solution development.* Business applications can be written from the ground up by developers, or even generated by experienced users, more quickly and easily by using the XML data format to structure information.

Windows SharePoint Services

Office 2003 is closely integrated with Windows SharePoint® Services. Windows SharePoint Services is a platform that enables teams to create Web sites for information sharing and document collaboration. You can use many of the menu commands and task panes in Office 2003 applications to take advantage of the document storage and management features of Windows SharePoint Services, create SharePoint sites, import and export lists on SharePoint sites, and link list data from SharePoint sites to your databases. Using shared workspaces, you can collaborate, plan, schedule, and interact with other users in real time.

For more information about the integration of Office 2003 and Windows SharePoint Services, go to http://www.microsoft.com/office/sharepoint/ prodinfo/relationship.mspx.

Case study: How users can benefit from Office integration features

The following example illustrates how a company can benefit from the integration of XML and Office 2003 features:

A financial equity research company exposes data from public and private companies to their analysts through a solution that uses a standard XML schema for financial reporting and a Microsoft Office Excel 2003–based smart client solution. Cells in the Excel spreadsheet are mapped to various elements of the XML document. The spreadsheet imports a list of companies into the Excel task pane, and automatically enters individual or combined results into the spreadsheet as the analyst selects the companies. After analysis, a task pane in Office Word 2003 exposes the XML data for preparation of a dynamic, user-ready report. Because the solution relies on XML, both the Excel spreadsheet and the Word document are constantly up-to-date with changes in both the spreadsheet and the format of the incoming data. And when data changes, the analysts need only to refresh either file to immediately update the information in the appropriate places within the report.

Office Customization Options and Log Files

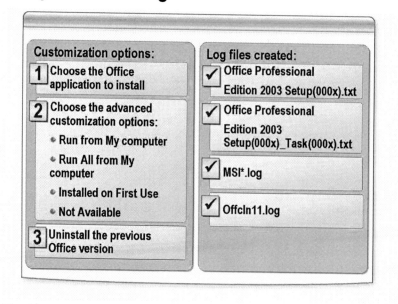

Customization options:	Log files created:
1 Choose the Office application to install	✓ Office Professional Edition 2003 Setup(000x).txt
2 Choose the advanced customization options:	✓ Office Professional Edition 2003 Setup(000x)_Task(000x).txt
• Run from My computer	✓ MSI*.log
• Run All from My computer	✓ Offcln11.log
• Installed on First Use	
• Not Available	
3 Uninstall the previous Office version	

Introduction

When your users call with installation issues, one of the first questions you should ask is, "What type of installation are you trying to perform?" The Office installation process varies slightly depending on the type of installation and the installation source that is used. For example, the procedure for performing an automated installation is different than the procedure for installing Office from a CD. This topic describes the general process of performing Office installations from a CD. The actual steps vary depending on the type of installation that is chosen, such as typical, minimal, complete, or custom installation.

Customization options

Performing a customized Office installation is similar to the installation-from-CD procedure except that the user must select specific features and components of Office to install on the computer. A customized installation requires the user to make the following choices:

- To choose the Office applications to install, in the **Custom Setup** dialog box, select the specific applications to install.

- To choose the Office application features and tools to install, click **Choose Advanced Customization of Applications**, and then select the specific application features and tools to install. The advanced customization options are:

  - **Run from My Computer**. Run the component from the local computer.

  - **Run All from My Computer**. Install the component plus all components lower down in the hierarchy.

  - **Installed on First Use**. Office prompts you to install the component the first time you attempt to use it.

  - **Not Available**. Omit installing the component.

  If you have a previous version of Office on your computer, you can select how much of that previous version to uninstall.

Note Keep in mind that the set of Office 2003 components that you choose is not final. You can later rerun Office Setup to add or remove components. Setup remembers and displays the exact set of applications, tools, and features that were previously installed. You can then adjust that set, adding or removing specific features.

Log files created during installation

When Office is installed, several log files are created in the temporary directory of the user's computer. As a DST, you can use these files to troubleshoot a user's installation issues. The following log files contain detailed information about the Office installation:

- Office Professional Edition 2003 Setup(000x).txt
- Office Professional Edition 2003 Setup(000x)_Task(000x).txt
- MSI*.log
- offcln11.log (present only if you've uninstalled Office 2003 previously)

Note For information about the individual applications that are available in each edition of Office 2003, refer to http://www.microsoft.com/office/Preview/choosing/default.asp.

The Office Upgrade Process

To upgrade to Office 2003 from a CD:

1 Insert the Office CD in the CD-ROM drive

2 Complete the steps and type the product key

3 Select Upgrade as the installation type

4 Setup displays a list of applications that will be installed

5 Click Install and Setup completes the installation and removes the old version of Office

---

Introduction

The term *upgrading* describes a process of installing a more recent version of currently existing software on your computer. Upgrading from a previous version of Office is very similar to installing Office for the first time.

Overview of the upgrade process

To upgrade to Office 2003 from a CD:

1. Insert the Office CD in the CD-ROM drive to launch the Office Setup program. If Setup does not run automatically, you can manually run the Setup.exe program in the root folder of the Office CD.

2. Provide the information required by the first three **Setup** dialog boxes, and in the **Product Key** dialog box, type the product key displayed on the label on the Office CD container.

3. Select **Upgrade** as the installation type.

4. Setup displays a list of applications that will be installed. Click **Install** to complete the installation.

   After you click **Install**, Setup completes the installation of Office and removes your old version.

How to Activate Office

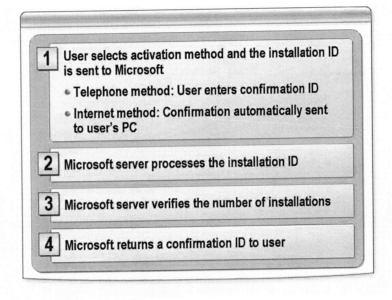

Introduction	After Office is installed or updated, it must be *activated*. Microsoft Product Activation is an anti-piracy technology designed to verify that software products are legitimately licensed.
How activation works	Product Activation works by verifying that a software program's product key, which you must use to install the product, has not been used on more personal computers than permitted by the program's license. Office 2003 includes the Microsoft Office Activation Wizard that enables you to provide your product ID to Microsoft either through an encrypted transfer over the Internet or by telephone. The installation ID is sent back to your computer to activate your product.
How to activate Office	Each time you start an Office application, the Activation Wizard automatically starts until the product is activated.

Note If the Activation Wizard does not start automatically, you can start the activation process manually. On the **Start** menu, point to **Programs** (or **All Programs**, depending on the version of Windows), point to **Office Tools**, and then click **Activate Product**.

There are two methods for activating Office:

- *Internet activation.* If you choose to activate your product over the Internet, the Activation Wizard automatically detects your Internet connection, and then connects to an internal Microsoft server to transfer your installation ID to Microsoft. (An *installation ID* includes an encrypted form of the product key and a hardware identifier that contains information about your current hardware configuration. The hardware identifier does not include any personal data.) The only user information required is the name of the country in which the product is installed, although you may opt to provide personal information for registration purposes. A confirmation ID is sent to your personal computer, which automatically activates Office. This process normally takes just a few seconds to complete.

- *Telephone activation.* To activate a product over the telephone, you can simply call the toll-free telephone number displayed on your monitor during the activation process. You are asked for the installation ID number displayed on the screen, the number is entered into a database, and you are sent a confirmation ID. After you type the confirmation ID, Office is activated.

Note If you overhaul your personal computer by replacing a substantial number of hardware components, you may have to reactivate Office. If this occurs you can call the telephone number displayed on the activation screen to reactivate the software.

Consequences of not activating Office

You have 50 grace launches before you must activate Office. If you do not activate within 50 launches, Office goes into reduced-functionality mode. At this point, you cannot edit documents or create new ones; however, you can view and print existing documents. When Office is in reduced-functionality mode, you can activate it at any time to enable its full functionality.

Optional product registration

As part of the activation process, you can register your product, which enables you to receive information about product updates and special offers directly from Microsoft. This is a completely voluntary part of the activation process and does require sharing some personal information, such as a valid e-mail address. Any registration information provided is stored separately from any activation information, on a guarded, internal server at Microsoft. No information is ever lent or sold to third parties.

Note For more information about Office XP Product Activation, go to http://www.microsoft.com/office/editions/prodinfo/activation.mspx. For additional information about deploying, maintaining, and supporting Office, go to http://www.microsoft.com/technet/prodtechnol/office/office2003/default.mspx.

Guidelines for Troubleshooting an Office Installation or Upgrade

> ✓ Check for operating system updates
>
> ✓ Verify a qualifying product
>
> ✓ Close other running programs
>
> ✓ Record Setup errors

Introduction

There are a number of problems that can occur when installing and upgrading to Office 2003. Refer to the following best practices when troubleshooting installation and upgrade issues.

Check for operating system updates

To ensure that Office installs properly, verify that the operating system is up-to-date. Verify that the user has installed all the latest updates. Also, verify that the user has installed the most current device drivers.

Check the Web site of the program's manufacturer to see if an update or patch is available. Check the Microsoft Windows Update Web site at http://office.microsoft.com/en-us/officeupdate/default.aspx to see if an update is available for the program.

Verify a qualifying product

If a user receives a "No Qualifying Product" error, the user may have purchased the incorrect version of Office. Office 2003 is available as a non-upgrade version (full version) and as an upgrade version. To install the upgrade version, one of the following requirements must be met:

- A valid qualifying product, such as Office XP, Office 2000, or Office 97, is installed on the computer.

  - or -

- The installation media of the valid, qualifying product is available.

  When Office 2003 Setup is run, it attempts to detect the qualifying product on the computer. If Setup cannot detect the qualifying program, an error message is displayed. If the user does not have a valid qualifying product, the Office 2003 upgrade version should be returned, and a full retail version of Office 2003 should be purchased.

Close other running programs

Advise users to close other applications that are currently running before they begin the installation process. If they are running an antivirus program, ask them to exit this program.

Record Setup errors

Recommend that your users write down any errors (and each error's associated error number) that occur during the Setup process. Most errors are documented in the Microsoft Knowledge Base (KB) or on the Internet.

Practice: Determining an Office Installation Methodology

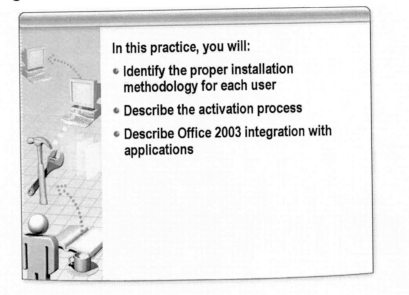

In this practice, you will:

- Identify the proper installation methodology for each user
- Describe the activation process
- Describe Office 2003 integration with applications

Objective

In this practice, you will read scenarios and provide a response to each question. You will recommend a method of installing Office 2003, describe the activation process, and explain how Office 2003 is integrated with other applications.

Practice

▶ **Identify the proper installation methodology for each user**

Scenario

You receive a call from a user who recently purchased Office 2003 from a local retailer. The user asks you for advice on how to install it.

How should you respond?

_____

_____

_____

_____

Scenario

You receive a call from a systems administrator at a small company that just bought Office 2003. The administrator asks you for information on the installation methods that are available for her to deploy Office 2003 company-wide. She tells you that her network has deployed Active Directory.

How should you respond?

_____

_____

_____

_____

▶ **Describe the activation process**

Scenario

You receive a call from a user who did not activate Office, and now he is running the Office programs in reduced-functionality mode. The user does not want to activate Office because he is worried that his personal information will be made available to other vendors.

How should you respond?

_____

_____

_____

_____

▶ **Describe Office 2003 integration with applications**

Name three databases that Office 2003 can connect to:

_____

_____

_____

Lesson: Configuring Office Security

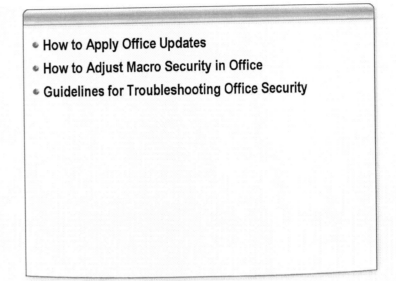

- How to Apply Office Updates
- How to Adjust Macro Security in Office
- Guidelines for Troubleshooting Office Security

Introduction

This lesson describes tools that are available in Office to help you ensure that your users' Office applications are up-to-date and secure.

Objectives

After completing this lesson, you will be able to:

- Apply Office updates.
- Adjust macro security in Office.
- Apply guidelines for troubleshooting issues related to Office security.

How to Apply Office Updates

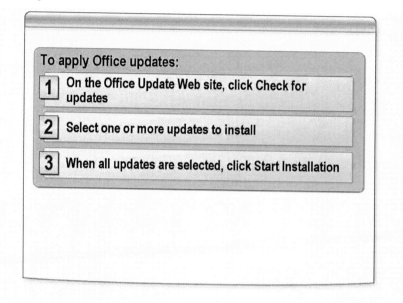

To apply Office updates:

1 On the Office Update Web site, click Check for updates

2 Select one or more updates to install

3 When all updates are selected, click Start Installation

Office Update Web site

The Microsoft Office Update Web site is an online extension of Office that helps users keep their applications up-to-date. Because new content is added to the site regularly, users can always get the most recent updates and fixes to protect Office and keep it running smoothly. The Office Update Web site can be accessed at http://office.microsoft.com/en-us/officeupdate/default.aspx.

How Office Update works

Office Update scans your computer and provides you with a tailored selection of updates that apply only to the items on your computer. This list appears on the Office Update screen.

Critical Updates

Any update that is considered critical to the operation of computer is called a *Critical Update* and is automatically selected for installation during the scan. These updates are provided to help resolve known issues, and to protect computers from known product vulnerabilities. Critical updates that apply to a specific operating system, software programs, or hardware are listed in the Critical Updates category on the Web site.

Procedure

Advise your users to check the Office Update site regularly by performing the following steps:

1. When you enter the Office Update Web site, click **Check for updates**.

2. Select one or more updates to install. You can read a full description of each item by clicking the **More information** link.

3. When you have selected all the updates you want, click **Start Installation**.

Note   Some updates may require that you restart your computer. Save your work and close any open programs before beginning the installation process.

How to Adjust Macro Security in Office

The Security dialog box:

The Macro Security dialog box:

Introduction	Many applications are associated with a macro language, such as Microsoft Visual Basic® for Applications. Often, these macro languages have extraordinarily powerful command sets available that enable them to manipulate the system in ways that are dangerous from a security standpoint.
What are macro viruses?	A *macro virus* is a type of computer virus that is stored in a macro within a file, template, or add-in. For the best protection against macro viruses, you should purchase and install specialized antivirus software.

Important   To further reduce the risk of macro infection in Office files, set the macro security level to High or Medium and use digital signatures.

What are digitally signed macros?	A *digital signature* confirms that the macro originated from the developer who signed it and that the macro has not been altered. When a file is opened or an add-in is loaded that contains a digitally signed macro, the digital signature appears on the computer as a certificate. The certificate names the macro's source, including any additional information about the identity and integrity of the source. Because a digital signature does not necessarily guarantee the safety of a macro, you must decide whether you trust a digitally signed macro.

For example, you might trust macros signed by someone you know or by a well-established company. If you are unsure about a file or add-in that contains digitally signed macros, carefully examine the certificate before enabling macros or, to be even safer, disable the macros. If you know you can always trust macros from a particular source, you can add that macro developer to the list of trusted sources when you open the file or load the add-in.

Macro security levels

The following information summarizes how macro virus protection works under each setting on the **Security Level** tab in the **Macro Security** dialog box (**Tools** menu, **Options** submenu, **Security** tab). Under all settings, if antivirus software that works with Office 2003 is installed, it scans files for known viruses before you open them.

The following table describes the function of each security level.

Security level	Function
High	You can run only macros that have been digitally signed and that you confirm are from a trusted source. Before trusting a source, you should confirm that the source is responsible and uses a virus scanner before signing macros. Unsigned macros are automatically disabled, and the file is opened without any warning.
Medium	A warning is displayed whenever a macro is encountered from a source that is not on your list of trusted sources (described later). You can choose whether to enable or disable the macros when you open a file. If the file could contain a virus, you should choose to disable macros.
Low	If you are sure that all the files and add-ins you open are safe, you can select this option—it turns off macro virus protection. At this security level, macros are always enabled when you open files.

By default, the security level is set to High. If the security level is set to Medium or High, you can maintain a list of trusted macro sources. When you open a file or load an add-in that contains macros developed by any of these sources, the macros are automatically enabled.

When to trust a source

When you open a file that includes signed macros, you are prompted to indicate whether you want to trust all macros originating from that source. If you select this option, you add the certificate's owner to your list of trusted sources. Before you decide to do this, you should review the details of the digital certificate. For example, look at the **Issued to** and **Issued by** fields to determine whether you trust its source, and look at the **Valid from** field to determine if the certificate is current. The certificate may also include details such as the e-mail address, name, or Web site of the person who obtained the certificate.

After you add a person (or corporation) to your list of trusted sources, Office will enable macros signed by this trusted source without showing you a security warning. However, it is possible to remove entries from the list of trusted sources.

Guidelines for Troubleshooting Office Security

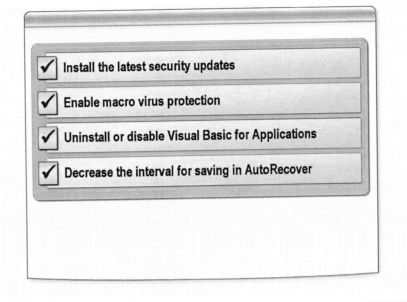

✔	Install the latest security updates
✔	Enable macro virus protection
✔	Uninstall or disable Visual Basic for Applications
✔	Decrease the interval for saving in AutoRecover

Introduction

There are a number of issues related to Office security that you need to be aware of as a DST. Refer to the following best practices when troubleshooting installation and upgrade issues:

Install the latest security update

Always make sure that the latest security updates are installed.

Enable macro virus protection

To enable macro virus protection in Office applications:

1. On the **Tools** menu, click **Options**.

2. In the **Options** dialog box, on the **Security** tab, click **Macro Security**, and then select the level of macro protection.

3. Repeat steps 1 and 2 for each additional Office 2003 application.

After you turn on macro virus protection, you are prompted to enable or disable macros whenever you open a file that contains a Microsoft Visual Basic for Applications macro.

Note Turning on macro virus protection does not protect your computer from macro viruses written in the Excel 4.0 macro language.

Uninstalling Visual Basic for Applications

Uninstalling Visual Basic for Applications is the best way to ensure that Visual Basic for Applications macros cannot run in Office applications. To uninstall Visual Basic for Applications, use the Office 2003 Setup program.

Decrease the interval for saving in AutoRecover

The amount of new information that the recovered file contains depends on how frequently an Office program saves the recovery file. For example, if the recovery file is saved only every 15 minutes, your recovery file will be missing up to 15 minutes of work that was done before the power failure or similar problem occurred, assuming that a manual save within that time interval was not performed. To change the AutoRecover save interval, on the **Tools** menu, click **Options** and then click the **Save** tab. Then enter a number in the **minutes** box.

When you restart an Office program after a power failure or similar problem, the program automatically opens any recovered files.

If for some reason the recovery file does not open, you can open it yourself. To open the recovery file:

1. On the **Standard** toolbar, click **Open**.

2. In the folder list, locate and double-click the folder in which recovered files are stored.

    Recovered files are usually stored in C:\documents and settings\ *username*\Application Data\Microsoft*program name*.

3. In the **Files of type** box, click **All Files**.

    Each recovered file is named "AutoRecover Save of *file name*" and has the program's default file name extension.

4. Click the name of the file you want to recover, and then click **Open**.

5. On the **Standard** toolbar, click **Save**.

6. In the **File name** box, enter the name of the existing file.

7. When you see a message asking whether or not you want to replace the existing file, click **Yes**.

Practice: Troubleshooting Office Security

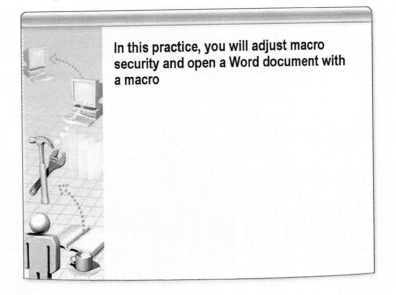

In this practice, you will adjust macro security and open a Word document with a macro

Objective

In this practice, you will adjust security and open a Word document with a macro.

Practice

▶ **Adjust macro security and open a Word document with a macro**

1. Using Acapulco, log on locally as Administrator with a password of **P@ssw0rd**.

2. On the **Start** menu, point to **All Programs**, point to **Office**, and then click **Office Word 2003**.

3. In Word, on the **File** menu, click **Open**.

4. In the **Open** dialog box, in the **File name** box, type **c:\program files\ microsoft learning\2262\practices\mod05\macro_doc.doc** and then click **Open**.

5. In the **Security warning** box, click **Disable Macros**.

6. On the **Tools** menu, point to **Macro**, and then click **Macros**.

7. In the **Macros** dialog box, click **Macro1**, and then click **Run**.

   What happened when you ran the macro?

   _____

   _____

8. On the **Tools** menu, point to **Macro**, and then click **Security**.

9. In the **Security** dialog box, on the **Security Level** tab, click **Low**, and then click **OK**.

10. Close Word.

11. On the **Start** menu, point to **All Programs**, point to **Microsoft Office**, and then click **Microsoft Office Word 2003**.

12. In Word, on the **File** menu, click **Open**.

13. In the **Open** dialog box, in the **File name** box, type **C:\Program Files\ Microsoft Learning\2262\practices\Mod05\Macro_Doc.doc** and then click **Open**.

    What happened when you opened the document?

    _____

    _____

14. Close all windows, log off, and then pause the 2262_Acapulco virtual machine.

Lesson: Configuring Office Recoverability

- How to Add and Remove Office Components
- How to Repair Office Applications
- How to Recover Office Application Files
- What Is AutoRecover?
- How to Recover Office Application Files by Using AutoRecover
- How to Prevent Data Loss by Using Shadow Copy

Introduction

This lesson describes how to repair an Office application and Office application files that are corrupt or are not working properly. It also explains how to help your users recover lost data.

Objectives

After completing this lesson, you will be able to:

- Add and remove Office components after installation.
- Repair Office applications.
- Recover Office application files.
- Describe the configuration options of AutoRecover.
- Recover Office application files by using AutoRecover.
- Prevent data loss by using Shadow Copy.

How to Add and Remove Office Components

Adding components to an existing installation of Office

Introduction

If your users are having problems with one or more Office components or features and you suspect that program files or registry settings are corrupt, you can suggest that they rerun Office Setup at any time to add or remove specific features or components. Setup remembers and displays the exact set of applications, tools, and features that were previously installed. You can then guide your users through the process of adjusting that set by adding or removing specific features.

Procedure

To add or remove components of Office, you need to rerun Office Setup in maintenance mode.

To add or remove Office components:

1. On the **Start** menu, click **Control Panel**, and then click **Add or Remove Programs**.

2. Select the Office program from the program list, and then click **Change**.

3. On the **Maintenance Mode Options** page, click **Add or Remove Features**, and then click **Next**.

   Setup will display the same installation options that you selected when you most recently ran Setup. You need to change only the installation options for features you want to add or remove; the rest of your installation will not be disturbed.

4. Select the individual components that you want to install and then click **Install**.

How to Repair Office Applications

Detect and Repair from the Microsoft Office 2003 Setup
Application and from the Application's Help Menu:

Introduction

Office 2003 takes full advantage of the self-repairing features that are offered by the *Microsoft Windows Installer*. Windows Installer is a component of the Windows XP operating system that simplifies the process of installing and configuring products and applications. If a resource that is required to start an Office program is missing, such as a file or registry key, Windows Installer detects the missing resource and repairs the program.

Note For more information about the Windows Installer, refer to http://msdn.microsoft.com/library/default.asp?url=/library/en-us/msi/setup/overview_of_windows_installer.asp.

How to reinstall or repair Office applications

If your users are having issues with an Office application, you can recommend that they attempt to reinstall or repair the application.

To reinstall Office or repair problems associated with Office:

1. On the **Start** menu, click **Control Panel**, and then click **Add or Remove Programs**.

2. Select the **Office** program from the program list, and then click **Change**.

3. On the **Maintenance Mode Options** page, click **Reinstall or Repair**, and then click **Next**.

    On the **Reinstall or Repair Office** page, you can select one of the following options:

    -   **Reinstall Office**. Instructs Setup to reinstall all Office files and reset all registry settings, whether or not they appear to be defective.

    -   **Detect and Repair errors in my Office installation**. Instructs Setup to detect defective files or settings and make just the repairs that are necessary. If you have changed or deleted any of the default shortcuts that Office Setup adds to your Windows Start menu and you want to restore the original shortcuts, select the **Restore my Start Menu Shortcuts** check box.

Tip If your users are not sure if they should reinstall Office or repair Office, recommend that they try to repair it first. If the problem persists, advise them to reinstall.

How to detect and repair Office applications from the Help menu

In Office 2003, you can use the **Detect and Repair** command from the **Help** menu of any of the major Office applications to have Office detect and repair errors in the application. This command provides an additional option that discards your customized settings and restores all defaults.

To detect and repair Office applications from the **Help** menu:

1. On the **Help** menu in any Office 2003 program, click **Detect and Repair**.

2. In the **Detect and Repair** dialog box, select any of the following:

   - If you want to keep your custom Office shortcuts, select the **Restore my shortcuts while repairing** check box. By default, this check box is selected. If you clear this check box, Detect and Repair will remove your custom Office shortcuts.

   - If you want your settings to return to the state they were in when you first installed Office, before you performed any customization, select the **Discard my customized settings and restore default settings** check box.

   The following default settings will be restored:

   - The Assistant character selection.

   - The most-recently-used entries on the **File** menu will be removed.

   - The size of the program window for all programs.

   - Menu and toolbar position and any customizations.

   - The security level for each program.

   - View settings in the program, such as the Calendar view in Microsoft Outlook®.

   You must re-enter your user name and initials when you restart your Office programs.

3. Click **Start**.

4. Click **Ignore** if the **Close Office Programs** dialog box displays the following message (where *program* is any Office 2003 program that is currently running):

   To correctly pick up or restore your settings, the following programs must be closed:

   Microsoft *program*

5. After the repair process has been completed, click **OK** to respond to the following message (where *edition* is the version of Office 2003 that you have installed):

   Office *edition* 2003 Setup completed successfully.

Note For more information on the Detect and Repair feature of Office 2003, refer to KB article 822238.

How to Recover Office Application Files

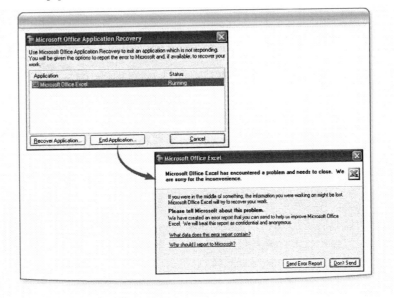

Introduction

The Office Application Recovery tool provides a method of recovering data from an Office 2003 application that stops responding due to the operating system crashing or a power failure. When this occurs, you can use the Office Application Recovery tool to recover your documents and restart your application.

To use the Office Application Recovery tool:

1. On the **Start** menu, point to **All Programs**, point to **Microsoft Office**, point to **Microsoft Office Tools**, and then click **Microsoft Office Application Recovery**.

   The **Microsoft Office Application Recovery** dialog box lists all of the Office applications that are currently running and displays status information for each.

2. Select the name of the application that you want to recover, and then click **Recover Application**.

Recovering the application terminates the application and it attempts to save any unsaved changes.

Warning   Clicking **End Application** in the Microsoft Office Application Recovery tool causes the specified application to terminate without attempting to save your data.

What Is AutoRecover?

AutoRecover options for Word

```
☐ Make local copy of files stored on network or removable drives
☑ Save AutoRecover info every:        [10  ▲▼] minutes
☑ Embed smart tags
☐ Save smart tags as XML properties in Web pages

Default format
Save Word files as:    [Word Document (*.doc)          ▼]
☐ Disable features introduced after:  [Microsoft Word 97  ▼]
```

Introduction

AutoRecover is an Office 2003 feature that recovers data in Office application files that are corrupt. Recovery is facilitated by the application saving open files at a specific interval to avoid loss of large amounts of work in the event of a catastrophe that causes it to close prematurely. Specifically, events such as power outages are targeted by the AutoRecover functionality.

Customized functionality

You can change the automatic save location on a global basis and disable AutoRecover for specific files.

What triggers AutoRecover to save?

Under normal operation, the AutoRecover feature saves any modified open file at the interval specified. For example, when an existing file is opened and AutoRecover is enabled, AutoRecover does not save the file until the first change is made to the file and the AutoRecover save time interval passes. After AutoRecover saves the file, the file is saved at subsequent save intervals only if further changes are made. If you perform a manual **Save** or **Save As**, the AutoRecover file is deleted.

When AutoRecover files are deleted

The AutoRecover file is also deleted under the following circumstances:

- You rename the file using **Save As**.

- You close the file.

- You exit the application (you are prompted at that time to save any modified files, so you make the decision).

- You disable AutoRecover for the current file.

- You disable AutoRecover globally.

How to Recover Office Application Files by Using AutoRecover

To recover a deleted file:

1. Open the Office application

2. In the Document Recovery task pane, review the files

3. Click the arrow next to the file's name, and then click Open or Save As

4. Click Close

Introduction

This topic looks at the mechanics of document recovery from within the Office 2003 applications.

Crash Recovery

Applications constantly track which files are open, their full paths, and the full path to each file's AutoRecover location. When you start an Office application, it checks for evidence in the registry that files may have not been saved when it was last run. If such evidence is found, the application implements Crash Recovery, and it displays a recovery interface.

File formats covered by AutoRecover

AutoRecover saves all file formats that can be opened in Office 2003 at the assigned interval. However, in order to maintain speed and simplicity, AutoRecover saves all files in the current application default file format, regardless of the original file format opened. The file is saved as a hidden file with an arbitrary filename. When you attempt to save a recovered file upon reopening the application after some catastrophe, the original file format and name is suggested as the Save file type.

Possible support issues with AutoRecover

When an Office application stops responding and new files are open, but not saved, AutoRecover cannot reestablish the links to the unsaved file. This occurs because AutoRecover saves unsaved files using the application's default file name extension (.xls, .doc, .ppt, and so on) even though the extension is not added to the file until it is saved for the first time. This means that when an unsaved file is opened during recovery, it has a different file name (such as *filename*.xls) than the link in the destination file specifies (such as *filename*Sheet1!A1). Any unsaved file must be saved to its intended location after recovery. After this is done, you can use **Change Source** in the **Edit Links** dialog box to fix the link in the destination file.

Procedure

To recover files by using AutoRecover:

1. Open the Office application.

2. Review the files listed in the Document Recovery task pane, and decide which to keep.

   - If a file has **[Recovered]** in the title it is usually a file that contains more recent changes than a file with **[Original]** in the title.

   - If you want to view what repairs were made to a file, point to the file in the Document Recovery task pane, click the arrow next to the file's name, and then click **Show Repairs**.

   - If you want to review the versions that were recovered, open all of the versions and save the best one.

3. For each file you want to keep, point to the file in the Document Recovery task pane, click the arrow next to the file's name, and then do one of the following:

   - To work with the file, click **Open**.

   - To save the file, click **Save As**, and then enter a name for the file. By default, the file is saved in the same folder as the original file. If you use the same name as the original file, the original is overwritten. When you see a message asking whether you want to replace the existing file (with the changes you made up to the last time you saved the file), click **Yes**.

4. When you have opened or saved all of the files you want to keep, in the Document Recovery task pane, click **Close**.

Additional file security

Files can be further protected by using the AutoRecover feature to periodically save a temporary copy of an open file. To recover work, the AutoRecover feature must be activated before the problem occurs. You can set the AutoRecover save interval to less than 10 minutes (its default setting). For example, if you set AutoRecover to save every 5 minutes, you generally recover more information than if you set it to save every 10 minutes if you made changes to the file or if you did not manually save the file during the time interval.

How to Prevent Data Loss by Using Shadow Copy

> **Right-click the folder that contains the file to be recovered, click Properties, and then on the Previous Versions tab, click Copy or Restore**
>
> Important.doc Properties
>
> General | Security | Summary | Previous Versions
>
> To view a previous version of a file, select the version from the following list and then click View. You can also save a file to a different location or restore a previous version of a file.
>
> File versions:
>
> | Name | Time |
> | --- | --- |
> | Important.doc | Tuesday, September 07, 2004, 3:00 PM |
>
> View | Copy... | Restore
>
> OK | Cancel | Apply | Help

Introduction

Shadow Copy is a Microsoft Windows Server™ 2003 technology that tracks the history of documents located on the server and allows users to roll back changes made to these files or to restore files if they are accidentally deleted.

To use the Shadow Copy features in Windows XP, the Shadow Copy client software package must be installed. This package installs a **Previous Versions** tab in the **Properties** dialog box of files and folders located on shared network folders and drives.

How to recover a deleted file

To use Shadow Copy to recover a deleted file:

1. Navigate to the folder that contained the deleted file.
2. Position the cursor over a blank space in the folder, right-click, and then click **Properties**.
3. In the **Properties** dialog box, on the **Previous Versions** tab, select the version of the folder that contained the file that was deleted, and then click **View**.
4. In the folder, select the file to be recovered.
5. Drag the shadow copy to the desktop or folder on the end user's local computer, or use a cut-and-paste operation to move the file.

How to recover an overwritten or corrupt file

To use Shadow Copy to recover an overwritten or corrupt file:

1. Right-click the overwritten or corrupt file and then click **Properties**.
2. Select **Previous Versions**.
3. If you want to view the old version, click **View**. To copy the old version to another location, click **Copy**. To replace the current version with the older version, click **Restore**.

How to recover a deleted folder

To use Shadow Copy to recover a folder:

1. Position the cursor so that it is over a blank space in the folder that will be recovered. If the cursor hovers over a file, that file will be selected.

2. Right-click and select **Properties** from the menu. Click the **Previous Versions** tab.

3. Select **Copy** or **Restore**.

   Selecting **Restore** enables the user to recover everything in that folder in addition to all subfolders. Selecting **Restore** will not delete any files.

Practice: Troubleshooting Office Recoverability

In this practice, you will run an Office repair

Objective

In this practice, you will run an Office repair.

Practice

▶ **Run an Office repair**

1. Start 2262_Acapulco and log on locally as **Administrator** with a password of **P@ssw0rd**.

2. In the **Add or Remove Programs** dialog box, click **Microsoft Office Professional Edition 2003**, and then click **Change**.

3. On the **Maintenance Mode Options** page, click **Reinstall or Repair**, and then click **Next**.

4. On the **Reinstall or Repair Office** page, click **Detect and Repair errors in my Office installation**, and then click **Install**.

5. In the **Reinstalling Office progress** dialog box, click **Cancel**.

6. In the **Office 2003 Setup** box, click **Yes**, and then click **OK**.

7. Close all dialog boxes.

Lesson: Configuring Office Language Features

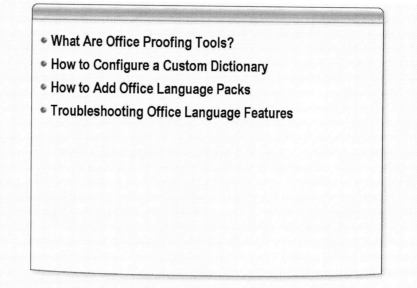

- What Are Office Proofing Tools?
- How to Configure a Custom Dictionary
- How to Add Office Language Packs
- Troubleshooting Office Language Features

Introduction

This lesson describes the language features and capabilities that are available in Office 2003, such as custom dictionaries, proofing tools, language packs, and the **Language** toolbar. These features allow users to work more efficiently with data files, regardless of the language in which they were created.

Objectives

After completing this lesson, you will be able to:

- Describe the proofing tools available in Office 2003.
- Configure a custom dictionary.
- Add Office language packs to an existing installation.
- Troubleshoot common issues with Office language features.

What Are Office Proofing Tools?

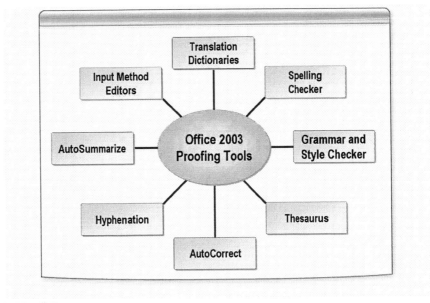

Introduction	Office provides an add-in feature called *Proofing Tools*, which is a collection of editing technologies that enable users to proof Office documents in multiple languages. These tools include spelling and grammar checkers, AutoCorrect lists, AutoSummarize capabilities for Word, Input Method Editors (IMEs) for East Asian languages, and more. The Proofing Tools for Office 2003 are located on a single CD and can be added on to any Office 2003 suite or individual program.
Installation requirements	Proofing Tools are installed by using the Proofing Tools CD, or by using the Custom Installation Wizard to create a custom transform if it was not created during an automated installation. Hard disk space requirements vary by language. German language Proofing Tools, for example, require 48 megabytes (MB) of hard disk space, while Simplified Chinese Proofing Tools require 365 MB of hard disk space. Asian languages require as much as 120 MB of hard disk space to include the necessary fonts and IMEs.
Translation dictionaries	Translation dictionaries are used to look up words in a different language. If the translation dictionary does not list the word you need, or if you need to translate a longer piece of text, you can connect to translation services on the Web.
Spelling checker	The spelling checker identifies possible misspellings in a text file by comparing the contents of the file with a database of accepted spellings. The spelling checker is one of the most frequently used features of Word. Spelling checkers can also perform more sophisticated tasks. For some languages, inflectional information (that is, variations of a word) is introduced in algorithms to fine-tune the output. This is the case for highly inflectional languages such as Swedish and Romanian.
Grammar and style checker	The grammar and style checker corrects sentences using a system of rules that defines the grammatical structure of a language. Word integrates this tool and it runs in the background, making corrections automatically.

Thesaurus

The thesaurus enables users to look up synonyms for a particular word. However, the thesauri in Proofing Tools perform more sophisticated tasks than simply retrieving direct synonyms for a given term from a database. Special algorithms in thesauri extract inflectional information from a stem word (that is, base word) to provide a series of synonyms with the same inflection. For example, looking up the word "running" would yield the possible synonym "jogging."

AutoCorrect

AutoCorrect automatically detects and corrects typos, misspelled words, grammatical errors, and incorrect capitalization. For example, if you type "teh" plus a space, AutoCorrect replaces the text with "the." You can also use AutoCorrect to quickly insert text, graphics, or symbols. For example, type (c) to insert ©, or type "aw" to insert "Adventure Works."

Hyphenation

The hyphenation tool enables users to connect or divide words with a hyphen. Using hyphens helps eliminate gaps in text that is aligned on both the right and left and helps to maintain even line lengths in narrow columns. Languages vary in their flexibility on hyphenation rules.

AutoSummarize

AutoSummarize identifies the key points in a document by analyzing a document and then assigning a score to each sentence. Sentences that contain frequently used words are given a higher score. The user then chooses the highest-scoring sentences to display in the summary. AutoSummarize is most useful on highly structured documents such as reports, articles, and scientific papers.

IME

An IME works with the operating system to allow users to enter Asian text in Windows and enabled applications—including Office 2003—by converting keystrokes into Asian characters. Often the only visual indication that an IME is installed on a computer is a floating toolbar for controlling the conversions, and an indicator on the Windows taskbar. Different Asian languages require different IMEs—for example, to type Japanese text, use the Japanese IME.

How to Configure a Custom Dictionary

Adding, Creating, or Modifying a Custom Dictionary in Word

Adding Words to a Custom Dictionary in Word

Introduction

A *custom dictionary* is a list of words that you create. These words may not be listed in the standard dictionary, but you want spelling checker to accept them as correct. All Office 2003 applications have access to these files. Although every Office application can create and modify a custom dictionary, each application uses a different method to achieve this.

Important The following procedures use Microsoft Word. While each Office application has the same functionality, the user interface (UI) may differ.

How to create a custom dictionary

To create a custom dictionary:

1. On the **Tools** menu, click **Options** and then click the **Spelling and Grammar** tab.
2. Click **Custom Dictionaries** and then click **New**.

How to add, delete, or edit words in a custom dictionary

To add, delete, or edit words in a custom dictionary:

1. On the **Tools** menu, click **Options**, and then click the **Spelling & Grammar** tab.
2. In the **Office Word** warning box, click **Yes**.
3. Click **Custom Dictionaries**.
4. Select the dictionary you want to edit, but do not clear its check box.
5. Click **Modify**, and then do one of the following:
   - To add a word, type it in the **Word** box, and then click **Add**.
   - To delete a word, select it in the **Dictionary** box, and then click **Delete**.
   - To edit a word, delete it and then add it with the spelling you want.

How to add words to a custom dictionary during a spell check

To add words to a custom dictionary during a spell check:

1. On the **Tools** menu, click **Spelling and Grammar**.

2. In the **Not in Dictionary** box, make sure you see the word you want to add to a custom dictionary.

3. To select the custom dictionary you want to add words to, click **Options**, select **Custom Dictionary**, click a dictionary in the **Custom Dictionaries** box, click **OK**, and then click **OK** again.

4. Click **Add to Dictionary**.

How to change the language associated with a custom dictionary

By default, when you create a new custom dictionary, Word sets the dictionary to All Languages, meaning that the dictionary is used when you check the spelling of text in any language. However, you can associate a custom dictionary with a particular language so that Word uses that dictionary when you check spelling of text only in a particular language.

To change the language associated with a user dictionary:

1. On the **Tools** menu, click **Options**, and then click the **Spelling & Grammar** tab.

2. Click **Custom Dictionaries**.

3. In the **Dictionary** box, click the dictionary you want to configure.

4. Click **Modify**.

5. In the **Language** box, click the language you want for the dictionary.

How to change the default custom dictionary

You can change the custom dictionary that Word uses by default to check spelling, either for all languages or for a particular language.

To change the default custom dictionary:

1. On the **Tools** menu, click **Options**, and then click the **Spelling & Grammar** tab.

2. Click **Custom Dictionaries**.

3. In the **Dictionary list** box, select the dictionary you want to have as the default.

   If the **Dictionary list** box contains any dictionaries that are associated with a particular language, then dictionary names appear under the appropriate language heading, or under **All languages**.

   • To change the default dictionary for all languages, click the dictionary name under **All languages**.

   • To change the default dictionary for a particular language, click the dictionary name under that language heading.

4. Click **Change Default**.

   The next time you check spelling, Word uses the default custom dictionary you selected.

Note   Each dictionary language grouping, including All languages, has a default custom dictionary.

How to Add Office Language Packs

To add an MUI Pack:

1. Create an administrative installation point for Office 2003

2. Create an administrative installation point for the MUI pack files

3. Customize the MUI Pack installation

4. Deploy Office with the selected MUI Packs

5. Install one or more MUI Packs by using a customized Setup.ini file or by allowing users to choose MUI Packs

Introduction

Office 2003 Multilingual User Interface (MUI) Pack provides multilingual capabilities by translating text in the UI, Help, wizards, and templates in Office applications. When users use the MUI Pack, they may be working in the English version of Office, but they can also view commands, dialog box options, Help topics, wizards, and templates in another language as well.

How to install MUI Packs with an Office installation

If you know the language requirements of your organization at the time that you deploy Office, you can choose to install Office and the MUI Packs at the same time.

To install MUI Packs with an Office installation:

1. Create an administrative installation point for Office 2003.

2. Create an administrative installation point for the MUI Pack files you want to deploy.

   You can use the Office administrative installation point or a separate server share.

3. Customize your MUI Pack installation.

   Use the Custom Installation Wizard to create a transform for Office, for individual MUI Packs, or both. For an Office transform, you can store language settings with other Office settings in an Office profile settings file (.ops file), or set language settings in the Custom Installation Wizard.

4. Deploy Office with selected MUI Packs to your users.

   Office is typically installed on users' computers before the MUI Pack files are, but you can circumvent this default process by using the Setup property CHECKINSTALORDER. You set this option when you cannot otherwise ensure the deployment order for the components being installed—for example, if you are deploying by using Group Policy technologies for software installation.

5. Install one or more MUI Packs by using a separate customized Setup settings file (Setup.ini) or by allowing users to choose MUI Packs with the MUI Pack Wizard.

MUI Pack components

The components in an MUI Pack enable you to create customized multilingual deployment. The following table lists the MUI Pack components in Office 2003:

Component	Description
MUI Packs (Lpk.msi files)	There is one package (MSI file) per language.
Multilingual User Interface Pack Wizard (Lpkwiz.msi)	Used by Multilingual User Interface Pack Setup, this wizard file allows users to choose languages from the administrative installation point to install on their computers.
System Files Update (Osp.msi)	This component contains required Office 2003 system and shared files for different languages.

Note In some deployment scenarios, you must know the locale identifier (LCID) for a language to install the correct MUI Pack. A table with this information can be found at http://www.microsoft.com/resources/documentation/office/2003/all/reskit/en-us/oe_inta03.mspx.

Troubleshooting Office Language Features

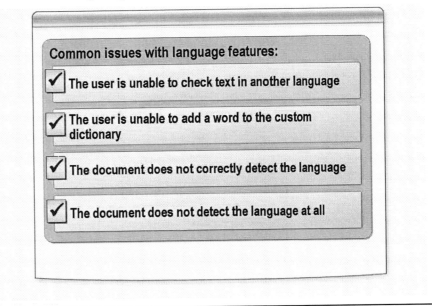

Common issues with language features:

✔ The user is unable to check text in another language

✔ The user is unable to add a word to the custom dictionary

✔ The document does not correctly detect the language

✔ The document does not detect the language at all

Introduction	As a DST, you may receive calls from users who are having issues with the language features available in Office.
	Many of the common issues and resolutions follow.
Check text in another language	"How do I check the text in Hindi?"
	If you want to check text in another language, you need to install the spelling and grammar tools for that language, and make sure that language is enabled for editing. Thereafter, Word will automatically detect the language in your documents and use the correct spelling and grammar tools.
Custom dictionaries	"I can't add a word to the custom dictionary."

- Make sure that the word contains 64 characters or fewer, and that it doesn't contain spaces.

- Make sure that the number of words in the custom dictionary does not exceed 5,000, and that its file size does not exceed 64 kilobytes (KB).

- Custom dictionaries are American National Standards Institute (ANSI) text files, so you cannot add characters that don't conform to that encoding standard.

- Before you can use a custom dictionary to check spelling, you must activate it by selecting the check box next to its name in the **Custom Dictionaries** dialog box. In addition, if you add a word to the custom dictionary while another program is running, the addition does not appear until you restart Microsoft Word.

- Word has simplified its methods for working with custom dictionaries so that you no longer need to use a separate text editor to work with the content of your custom dictionary. Notepad is no longer the recommended tool.

Automatic language detection

"Word doesn't correctly detect my language."

- Make sure you have enabled the language for editing by using the Office Language Settings tool.

- Type at least one sentence that contains five or more words in the language. The more you type, the higher the accuracy of the detection.

- The language Word detected may be only subtly different from another language (for example, Norwegian and Danish, or Spanish and Portuguese). When languages have subtle differences in spelling, Word may not be able to identify the correct language, especially if there are only a few words in the sentence.

- If you have two similar languages enabled for editing and you write in only one of these languages, try to disable the language you do not use.

- The text may contain a mixture of languages. Word evaluates text sentence-by-sentence to determine its language. If a sentence contains words from more than one language, or many scientific or other special terms, Word may apply the default language for the document or it may apply the language of the preceding sentence. If a word has a wavy underline because it is in a different language, you can apply the correct language. Right-click the word, point to **Language** on the shortcut menu, and then click the language you want.

"Word doesn't detect my language at all."

- The language may not be supported by Word.

- Make sure you have enabled the language for editing by using the Office Language Settings tool.

Practice: Troubleshooting Office Language Features

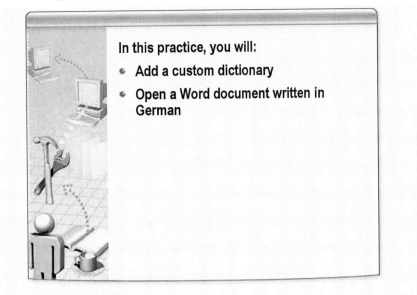

In this practice, you will:

• Add a custom dictionary

• Open a Word document written in German

Objective

In this practice, you will add a custom dictionary and open a Word document written in another language.

Practice

▶ **Add a custom dictionary**

1. Resume the 2262_Acapulco virtual machine.

2. Using Acapulco, log on locally as **Samantha Smith** with the password **P@ssw0rd**.

3. On the **Start** menu, point to **All Programs**, point to **Microsoft Office**, and then click **Microsoft Office Word 2003**.

4. In the **User Name** dialog box, click **OK**.

5. In Word, on the **Tools** menu, click **Options**, and then click the **Spelling and Grammar** tab.

6. Click **Custom Dictionaries**.

7. In the **Custom Dictionaries** dialog box, click **Add**.

8. In the **Add Custom Dictionary** box, in the **File name** box, type **c:\program files\microsoft learning\2262\practices\mod05\2262_Dic.dic** and then click **OK**.

9. In the **Custom Dictionaries** dialog box, click **OK**.

10. In the **Options** dialog box, click **OK**.

▶ **Open a Word document written in German**

1. In Word, on the **File** menu, click **Open**.

2. In the **Open** box, in the **File name** box, type **c:\program files\microsoft learning\2262\practices\mod05\german.doc** and then click **Open**.

3. On the **Tools** menu, click **Language**, and then click **Set Language**.

   Word 2003 automatically detects the language in which documents are written. What language did Word detect for this document?

   _____

4. Shut down the 2262_Acapulco virtual machine and delete changes.

Lab: Troubleshooting Issues Related to Office

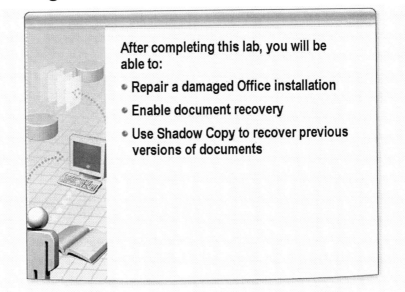

After completing this lab, you will be able to:

• Repair a damaged Office installation

• Enable document recovery

• Use Shadow Copy to recover previous versions of documents

Objectives

After completing this lab, you will be able to:

■ Repair a damaged Office installation.

■ Enable document recovery.

■ Use Shadow Copy to recover previous versions of documents.

Prerequisites

Before working on this lab, you must have an understanding of how to use Microsoft Virtual PC.

Before you begin

For each exercise in this lab, use the password **P@ssw0rd**.

In Virtual PC, RIGHT ALT+DEL is the equivalent of CTRL+ALT+DEL.

Estimated time to complete this lab: 30 minutes

Exercise 1
Repairing a Damaged Office installation

In this exercise, you will troubleshoot issues related to a damaged Office installation.

Scenario

A user calls and says that he accidentally deleted a system file used by Microsoft PowerPoint® and is not sure what to do. He does not know which file was deleted and does not have a backup of his drive. He needs to use PowerPoint to create a presentation for his boss and has asked you what he should do.

Tasks	Guidance for completing the task
1. Start the Acapulco virtual machine, and then log on locally as **Administrator**.	▪ Use the Virtual PC console.
2. Start PowerPoint.	
❓ Did PowerPoint start normally?	
3. Quit PowerPoint.	
4. Using Acapulco, browse to **C:\Program Files\ Microsoft Learning\2262 \Labfiles\Lab05** and run 2262_Lab05_Ex01.	▪ This step simulates the user deleting a PowerPoint system file.
5. Start PowerPoint.	
❓ Did PowerPoint start normally?	
❓ What should the user do to resolve the problem?	
6. Close all windows and log off Acapulco.	

Exercise 2
Enabling Document Recovery

In this exercise, you will use AutoRecover to recover a document in Word.

Scenario

A user calls and says that the building in which she works has frequent power outages and she often loses her work despite the fact that she frequently saves her changes. She would like you to help her minimize the amount data she loses when the power is lost and she is working in Word.

Tasks	Guidance for completing the task
1. Using Acapulco, log on locally as **Samantha Smith**.	▪ Use the Virtual PC console.
2. Resolve the issue by using AutoRecover.	▪ Configure a one-minute interval.
3. Test your solution by running Bad Macro.doc.	▪ Create a document, type some text, wait two minutes, and then without saving the document, open C:\Program Files\Microsoft Learning\ 2262\Labfiles\Lab02\Bad Macro. ▪ Enable the macro to run, and then click inside the document. Word stops responding. ▪ To end the Winword.exe process, press CTRL+ALT+DEL, click **Task Manager**, and then on the **Processes** tab, click **Winword.exe**, and click **End Process**.
❓ Were you able to recover the document? _____ _____	
4. Close all windows and log off Acapulco.	

Exercise 3
Using Shadow Copy

In this exercise, you will use Shadow Copy to recover a previous version of a document.

Scenario

A user calls and says that he often loses the changes he has made to documents that are located on the server. Usually this occurs because he inadvertently saves over existing documents. He asks you if there is a way to recover previous versions of a document located on a server share. Recently, the user accidentally deleted most of the content of a file and then saved the changes. Now he would like to access the most recent version of the document. The file is located on \\London\RAHelp, and the user wants to know if you can restore it from backup.

Tasks	Guidance for completing the task
1. Start the 2262_London virtual machine and resume the 2262_Acapulco virtual machine.	▪ Use the Virtual PC console. ▪ Wait for London to display the log in window before starting Acapulco.
2. Using Acapulco, log on to the domain as **Administrator**.	
3. Resolve the user issue by recovering the most recent version of \\london\RAHelp\ Important.doc.	▪ This issue is successfully resolved when the recovered Important.doc file displays "Congratulations! You have recovered the user's document."
4. Turn off the 2262 London virtual machine and delete changes. Pause the Acapulco virtual machine.	

Lab Discussion

After you have completed the exercises in this lab, take a moment to answer the following questions. When the entire class has finished the lab, the instructor will facilitate a lab discussion based on how you resolved the issues.

1. How did you diagnose the cause(s) of the issue(s)?

2. How did you resolve the issue(s)?

3. What are other ways the issue(s) could have been resolved?

Module 6: Troubleshooting Issues Related to Outlook Express

Contents

Overview

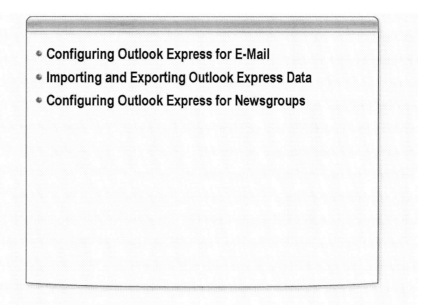

* Configuring Outlook Express for E-Mail
* Importing and Exporting Outlook Express Data
* Configuring Outlook Express for Newsgroups

Introduction

Microsoft® Outlook® Express is a messaging tool used for e-mail transactions and newsgroup communications. It is the e-mail client that is included with Microsoft Internet Explorer and the Microsoft Windows® operating systems. As a desktop support technician (DST), you will need to assist users with basic tasks such as creating, testing, and troubleshooting e-mail accounts or creating identities that enable users to receive mail from multiple e-mail accounts. You will also need to assist users with more complex tasks such as using the Outlook Express migration tools to export and import existing mail settings, Address Book entries, and e-mail messages. Understanding how to perform and troubleshoot these tasks is a vital aspect of the DST role.

Objectives

After completing this module, you will be able to:

■ Configure Outlook Express for e-mail.

■ Import and export Outlook Express data.

■ Configure Outlook Express for newsgroups.

Lesson: Configuring Outlook Express for E-Mail

- E-Mail Protocols Supported by Outlook Express
- Information Required to Create an E-Mail Account
- How to Create, Test, and Troubleshoot an Account
- Where Outlook Express Stores Data
- How to Repair a Damaged Default Mail Folder
- How to Back Up and Restore Default Settings
- File Formats Supported by Outlook Express
- How to Create, Delete, and Modify an Identity
- Guidelines for Troubleshooting E-Mail Issues

Introduction

This lesson introduces you to Outlook Express and describes the most common tasks you will be asked to perform as a DST. Although using Outlook Express is similar to using Outlook, the processes are not exactly the same for both. As a DST, you must support both Outlook (commonly used in corporations, companies, and small businesses) and Outlook Express (commonly used by home users and small home-based businesses). In this lesson, you will learn the most basic Outlook Express tasks, such as creating a POP3 or IMAP account for a home user, testing and troubleshooting that account, and creating identities.

Objectives

After completing this lesson, you will be able to:

- Describe the e-mail protocols supported by Outlook Express.
- Describe the information required to create an e-mail account.
- Create, test, and troubleshoot an e-mail account.
- Explain where Outlook Express stores data.
- Repair a damaged default mail folder.
- Back up and restore default settings.
- Describe the file formats used by Outlook Express.
- Create, delete, and modify an identity.
- Apply guidelines for troubleshooting e-mail issues.

E-Mail Protocols Supported by Outlook Express

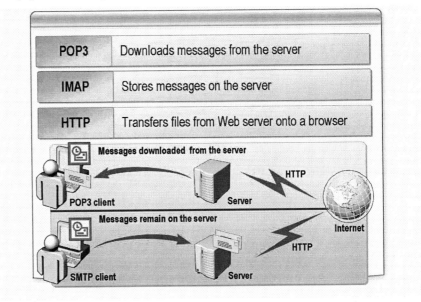

POP3	Downloads messages from the server
IMAP	Stores messages on the server
HTTP	Transfers files from Web server onto a browser

Introduction

Storing messages on a server is useful for users who need to read their e-mail from more than one computer. When a user logs on to his or her account from a different computer, Outlook Express downloads e-mail messages according to the options that the user set. POP3, IMAP, and HTTP are Internet protocols that enable users to gain access to messages that are stored on a server from any computer with an Internet connection. As a DST in a tier 1 position, you will be called on to set up POP3, IMAP, and HTTP e-mail accounts in Outlook Express. This section discusses these protocols.

POP3

POP3 is by far the most commonly used protocol for retrieving messages. With a POP3 e-mail account, messages are received and held on a mail server (either on a local network or at an Internet Service Provider [ISP]). The user's client software accesses the server and downloads those messages at the user's convenience. The client software deletes the messages from the server after they are downloaded.

IMAP

IMAP, an extension of POP3, is similar to POP3 except that instead of the messages being downloaded from the server, they are stored on the server and the user works with them there. Because IMAP stores messages on the server, users can access their e-mail from any computer with an Internet connection.

HTTP

HTTP is an Internet protocol for transferring files from a Web server onto a browser so that a user can view a Web page that is on the Internet. HTTP only transfers the contents of a Web page into a browser for viewing—it does not download files. For example, Web-based e-mail services, such as MSN® Hotmail®, use HTTP to enable users to access their e-mail account by using a Web browser.

Information Required to Create an E-Mail Account

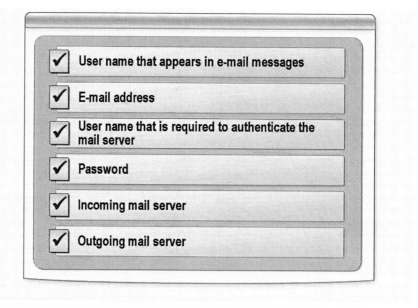

Introduction

Before you can create an e-mail account in Outlook Express, you must have the following information from an ISP or LAN administrator:

- *User name that appears in e-mail messages*. The user's name as it should appear in the From line of e-mail messages that are sent from the user.

- *E-mail address*. The user's full e-mail address, including the suffix (that is, *user@domainname*.com).

- *User name that is required to authenticate the mail server*. This can be a name or the e-mail address. If you are setting up an account for a user with an ISP, the ISP should have provided the information to the user.

- *Password*. The password that is required to authenticate to the mail server.

- *Incoming mail server*. The name of the incoming mail server. The names of incoming and outgoing servers should also have been provided by the user's ISP (if you are setting up an ISP account). If the user cannot find this information, it is often available on the ISP's Web site.

- *Outgoing mail server*. The name of the outgoing mail server.

Note   Users typically obtain this information from their Internet service provider (ISP) or local area network (LAN) administrator.

How to Create, Test, and Troubleshoot an Account

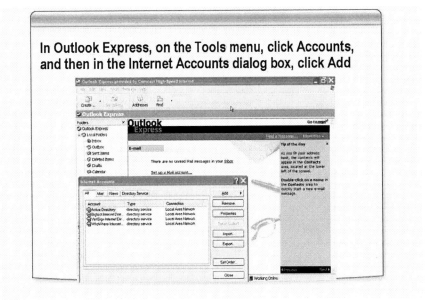

In Outlook Express, on the Tools menu, click Accounts, and then in the Internet Accounts dialog box, click Add

Introduction

To create, test, and troubleshoot e-mail accounts in Outlook Express, you use the Internet Accounts dialog box. The options in this dialog box enable you to add accounts, view properties, and make changes to existing e-mail accounts. This section describes how to create an account, how to test the account to ensure that mail can be sent and received, and how to troubleshoot the account if a problem occurs.

How to create an account

To create a POP3, IMAP, or HTTP e-mail account:

1. In Outlook Express, on the **Tools** menu, click **Accounts**.

2. In the **Internet Accounts** dialog box, click **Add**, and then click **Mail**.

   The Internet Connection Wizard starts.

3. In the **Internet Connection Wizard** dialog box, on the **Your Name** page, type the name of the user, and then click **Next**.

4. On the **Internet E-Mail Address** page, type the e-mail address, and then click **Next**.

5. On the **E-Mail Server Names** page, in the **My incoming mail server is a** *InternetProtocol* **server** box, click **POP3, IMAP, or HTTP**.

6. In the **Incoming mail (POP3, IMAP, or HTTP) server** box, type the name of the incoming mail server.

7. In the **Outgoing mail (SMTP) server** box, type the name of the outgoing mail server, and then click **Next**.

8. On the **Internet Mail Logon** page, type the account name and password and then click **Next**.

9. Click **Finish**, and then in the **Internet Accounts** dialog box, click **Close**.

How to test a new account

After you create an account, you must test it to ensure that mail can be sent and received.

To test a new account:

1. In Outlook Express, click **Create Mail**.

2. In the **To** box, type the address of the e-mail account you created in the previous section. (This is user's account.)

3. In the **Subject** box, type **Test** and then click **Send**.

4. Click **Send/Recv**.

5. Verify that the e-mail was sent and received.

How to troubleshoot a new account

The following procedure describes the steps you can perform to troubleshoot issues with sending and receiving mail.

To troubleshoot a new account:

1. In Outlook Express, on the **Tools** menu, click **Accounts**.

2. In the **Internet Accounts** dialog box, on the **Mail** tab, select the account that is not working, and then click **Properties**.

3. In the *account name* **Properties** dialog box, on the **General** tab, verify that the user information (including the name and e-mail address) is correct. If any information is incorrect, make the appropriate corrections.

4. In the **Properties** dialog box, on the **Servers** tab, verify that the server information (including incoming server name, incoming and outgoing mail servers, account name, password, and authentication settings) is correct. If any information is incorrect, make the appropriate corrections.

Note If you are unsure of some of the server settings, contact the ISP to verify the settings.

---

5. Click **OK**, and then click **Close**.

6. Send another test e-mail.

7. If the e-mail still fails, verify the following:

   • Verify that the user is connected to the Internet.

   • Verify with the ISP that the e-mail address is correct.

   • Verify the names of the mail servers.

Where Outlook Express Stores Data

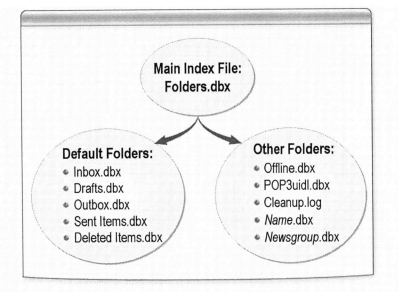

Main Index File:
Folders.dbx

Default Folders:
* Inbox.dbx
* Drafts.dbx
* Outbox.dbx
* Sent Items.dbx
* Deleted Items.dbx

Other Folders:
* Offline.dbx
* POP3uidl.dbx
* Cleanup.log
* *Name*.dbx
* *Newsgroup*.dbx

Introduction

All Outlook Express data is stored in a database called the *Store root folder*. (The Store root folder is also referred to as the Store root or the Store folder.) The Store root folder consists of a series of database index (.dbx) files that are stored in the C:\Documents and Settings*User*\Local Settings\Application Data\Identities*GUID*\Microsoft\Outlook Express folder.

Note   GUID is a unique personal identifier; no two are alike.

The Folders.dbx file is the main index of the Store root folder. If this index is not found, it is created automatically by Outlook Express. If it becomes damaged, you should delete it and recreate the remainder of the files. The Folder.dbx file contains all default files as well as other files that are created as a result of user actions. This section describes these files.

Default mail files

Many of Folder.dbx files are default files that are created automatically. If Outlook Express does not find these files, Outlook Express creates them. The files are:

■   Inbox.dbx. This file is the default message delivery location.

■   Drafts.dbx. This file contains saved unsent messages.

■   Outbox.dbx. This file contains messages to be sent.

■   Sent Items.dbx. This file is where all sent messages are stored.

■   Deleted Items.dbx. This file is created when an item is deleted. It contains the deleted messages from other files.

Other mail files

- Offline.dbx. This file stores IMAP and Hotmail actions that are carried out offline. This file is created only if an IMAP or Hotmail account exists.

- POP3uidl.dbx. This file tracks messages left on a POP3 mail server. This file is created automatically if the user has created a POP3 account.

- Cleanup.log. This file condenses files when Outlook Express is idle. The log is created when *automatic maintenance* is enabled. To disable this feature:

  a. On the **Tools** menu, click **Options**.

  b. On the **Maintenance** tab, clear the **Compact messages in the background** check box.

- *Name*.dbx. This is a user-created file that can be used to organize and store e-mail. You can have as many of these files as your available hard disk space can support.

Important   If the *Name*.dbx files exceed 1 MB, you may experience various problems with Outlook Express retrieving e-mail from other files.

- *Newsgroup*.dbx. This newsgroup file is used to keep track of the newsgroups to which a user is subscribed.

How to Repair a Damaged Default Mail Folder

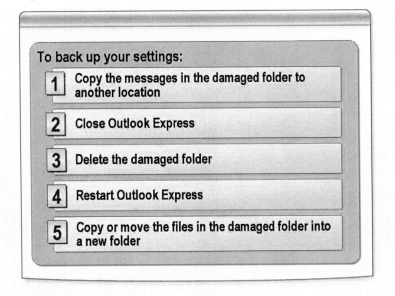

To back up your settings:

1 Copy the messages in the damaged folder to another location

2 Close Outlook Express

3 Delete the damaged folder

4 Restart Outlook Express

5 Copy or move the files in the damaged folder into a new folder

Procedure

If one of the default mail folders becomes damaged, you can recover it. To recover a damaged folder:

1. Copy all of the messages in the damaged folder to another location for safe keeping.

2. Close Outlook Express.

3. Delete the damaged folder (for example, delete the Inbox.dbx file).

4. Restart Outlook Express.

   Outlook Express will search for the default folder, find that it is not there, and then create an empty folder of the same name in its place.

5. Copy or move the files that were in the damaged folder into the new folder.

How to Back Up and Restore Default Settings

To back up settings:

1. On the Tools menu, click Accounts

2. On the All tab, select an account, and then click Export

3. Select the destination, type the file name, and then click Save

4. Click Close

To restore settings:

1. On the Tools menu, click Accounts

2. On the All tab, click Import

3. Select the .iaf file, and then click Open

4. Click OK

Introduction

Outlook Express can be used to create an Internet Accounts file (.iaf file) to back up and store information about the mail folders and mail and news account settings for a single Outlook Express identity. Backing up this information makes it easy to restore, if necessary, following a computer crash or in the event a new computer is obtained or purchased. These .iaf files will not store subscribed newsgroup information, message rules, or blocked senders, and they will not retain information about custom toolbars, but they offer a quick and easy way to back up and restore settings.

How to back up settings

To back up your settings:

1. In Outlook Express, on the **Tools** menu, click **Accounts**.

2. In the **Internet Accounts** dialog box, on the **All** tab, select an account, and then click **Export**.

3. In the **Export Internet Account** dialog box, browse to a location to save the file or accept the default, type a file name, and then click **Save**.

4. In the **Internet Accounts** dialog box, click **Close**.

Note   Outlook Express creates an .iaf file.

How to restore settings

To restore your settings:

1. In Outlook Express, on the **Tools** menu, click **Accounts**.

2. In the **Internet Accounts** dialog box, on the **All** tab, click **Import**.

3. In the **Import Internet Accounts** dialog box, select the .iaf file that contains the settings for that account, and then click **Open**.

4. Click **OK**.

File Formats Supported by Outlook Express

Introduction

Outlook Express uses several file formats for contacts and messages. For both functions, the files are readable in other applications.

Contacts formats

You can export your Address Book contacts to:

- Windows Address Book (.wab) files.
- Microsoft Exchange Personal Address Book (.pab) files.
- Any comma separated values (.csv) files.

Message formats

Outlook Express can save e-mail messages in the following formats:

- Mail (*.eml) files. This is the default format.
- Text (*.txt) files. Text files are readable by numerous applications.
- HTML (*.htm, *.html) files. This format can be read by any Web browser and by any other application that reads HTML files.

How to Create, Delete, and Modify an Identity

In Outlook Express, on the File menu, click Identities, and then click Add New Identity

Introduction

Each Outlook Express user has a unique *identity* that contains information particular to that user. Multiple identities can be created so that each user can log on to the same computer with a separate account. For example, you and a family member could share a computer. If you each create an identity, you would each see your own mail and your own contacts when you log on under your identity. After creating the identities, you can switch among them without having to shut down your computer or close your Internet connection.

How to create a new identity

To create a new identity:

1. In Outlook Express, on the **File** menu, click **Identities**, and then click **Add New Identity**.

2. In the **New Identity** dialog box, type the name of the new user.

3. If you want to include a password for this identity, select the **Require a password** check box, and then type a password.

4. Click **OK**.

   Outlook Express asks you if you want to log on as the new user. If you answer **Yes**, you are prompted for information about your Internet connection. If you answer **No**, the current user remains logged on.

Note   Identities are usually created in Outlook Express; however, you can also create identities directly from your Address Book when you open your Address Book from the **Start** menu. To open the Address Book from the **Start** menu, click **All Programs**, click **Accessories**, and then click **Address Book**.

How to delete an identity

To delete an identity:

1. In Outlook Express, on the **File** menu, click **Identities**, and then click **Manage Identities**.

2. In the **Manage Identities** dialog box, select an identity, and then click **Remove**.

Note   You cannot delete an identity you are currently using. When you delete an identity, the corresponding settings are deleted, but the data is not deleted.

---

3. Click **Close**.

How to modify an identity

To modify the current identity's settings:

1. In Outlook Express, on the **File** menu, click **Identities**, and then click **Manage Identities**.

2. In the **Manage Identities** dialog box, change any of the following settings:

   • To change the identity name or password, select an identity name, click **Properties**, type the appropriate name or password information, and then click **OK**.

   • To change the identity that opens on startup, select the appropriate identity and ensure that the **Use this identity when starting a program** check box is selected. (When the **Use this identity when starting a program** check box is cleared, the user is prompted for an identity each time the user opens an identity-aware program.)

   • To change the identity to use when starting a program, select the appropriate identity from the list.

3. Click **Close**.

Guidelines for Troubleshooting E-Mail Issues

Common Issues:

- ✓ Sent e-mail never leaves the outbox
- ✓ SMTP errors

Guidelines:

- ✓ Create a new identity
- ✓ Create a new account
- ✓ Rename and repair damaged files

Introduction

Troubleshooting Outlook Express settings can be a challenge because there are many factors that can contribute to an issue. This topic provides guidelines for troubleshooting various issues customers may have in Outlook Express.

Common issues

There are two common issues you may encounter in using Outlook Express:

- *Sent e-mail never leaves the Outbox.* When you try to send an e-mail message, the e-mail message moves to the Outbox, but the message is not sent. Some of the common causes of this are:

  - The e-mail message was opened in the Outbox before the e-mail message was sent.

  - The user is working offline.

  - The user's sending options are not set to send e-mail messages immediately by using the correct connection.

  - The mail folders or e-mail messages within the folders are damaged.

  Note   For information on resolving this problem, see KB article 873022 or 821403.

- *SMTP error.* When using SMTP to send an e-mail message, you get an error.

  To begin troubleshooting this problem, you can create the Smtp.log file. This log documents what occurs when the protocol is accessed and should provide information on where the error is occurring.

Guidelines

You can resolve many common issues by performing the following procedures:

- Create a new identity.
- Create a new account with the Internet Connection Wizard.
- Rename and repair damaged files.

  The files that you need to rename depend on the error message that you receive and the files that are associated with the function that you are trying to perform.

Practice: Configuring Outlook Express for E-Mail

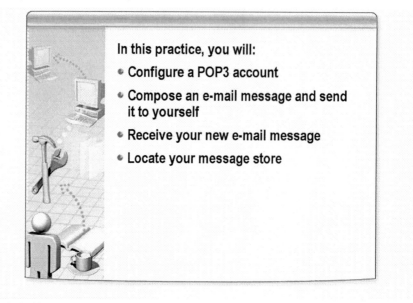

In this practice, you will:

• Configure a POP3 account

• Compose an e-mail message and send it to yourself

• Receive your new e-mail message

• Locate your message store

Objective

In this practice, you will configure a POP3 account in Outlook Express. You will send an e-mail message to yourself, and then connect to the server and download the message. You will also locate your default message store.

Scenario

You receive a call from a user who wants to configure Outlook Express. She plans to use Outlook Express as her primary e-mail client and she would like to learn how to configure the settings to use POP3.

Practice

▶ **Configure a POP3 account**

1. Start the 2262_London virtual machine.

2. Start the 2262_Acapulco virtual machine.

3. Using Acapulco, log on to the NWTRADERS domain as **Samantha** with the password **P@ssw0rd**.

4. Click **Start**, point to **All Programs**, and then click **Outlook Express**.

5. In the **Outlook Express** dialog box asking to make Outlook Express the default mail client, clear the **Always perform this check when starting Outlook Express** checkbox, and then click **No**.

6. On the **Your Name** page, in the **Display name** box, type **Samantha Smith** and then click **Next**.

7. On the **Internet E-mail Address** page, in the **E-mail address:** box, type **Samantha@nwtraders.msft** and then click **Next**.

8. On the **E-mail Server Names** page, in the **Incoming mail (POP3, IMAP or HTP) server** box, type **london.nwtraders.msft**

9. On the **E-mail Server Names** page, in the **Outgoing mail server** box, type **london.nwtraders.msft** and then click **Next**.

10. On the **Internet Mail Logon** page, in the **Account name** box, verify that **Samantha** is displayed.

11. On the **Internet Mail Logon** page, in the **Password** box, in the **password** field, type **P@ssw0rd** and then click **Next**.

12. On the **Congratulations** page, click **Finish**.

▶ **Compose an e-mail message and send it to yourself**

1. In Outlook Express, on the toolbar, click **Create Mail**.

2. In the New Message window, in the **To** box, type **samantha@nwtraders.msft**

3. In the **Subject** field, type **Test E-Mail**

4. In the text body, type **Testing POP3 e-mail using Outlook Express**

5. Click **Send**.

▶ **Receive your new e-mail message**

1. In Outlook Express, in the **Folders** list, click **Inbox**.

2. If the message you sent is not already in the Inbox folder, on the toolbar, click **Send/Recv**.

3. Open the e-mail message with Test E-Mail in the Subject line by double-clicking that message.

4. In the Test E-mail window, on the **File** menu, click **Close**.

▶ **Locate your message store**

1. In Outlook Express, on the **Tools** menu, click **Options**.

2. In the **Options** dialog box, on the **Maintenance** tab, click **Store Folder**.

3. In the **Store Location** dialog box, in the **Your personal message store is located in the following folder** box, select then right-click the path that is listed, and then click **Copy**.

4. In the **Store Location** dialog box, click **OK**.

5. In the **Options** dialog box, click **Cancel**.

6. On the **File** menu, click **Exit**.

7. Click **Start** and then click **Run**.

8. In the **Run** dialog box, right-click inside the **Open** box, click **Paste**, and then click **OK**.

9. After reviewing the files, close the Outlook Express window.

   What would happen if the files in this window were deleted?

   _____

   _____

10. Using Acapulco, close all windows, log off, and pause the virtual machine.

11. Pause London.

Lesson: Importing and Exporting Outlook Express Data

* Types of Data That Outlook Express Can Import and Export
* How to Export Outlook Express Data
* How to Import Outlook Express Data
* Guidelines for Troubleshooting Issues with Importing and Exporting Data

Introduction

After you successfully create an e-mail account in Outlook Express, you can import a user's Address Book and existing messages into Outlook Express. There are multiple ways to import an Address Book; however, when configuring a new account for a home user, the easiest way to import an Address Book is to have previously exported it as a .csv text file. Working with an Address Book using this technique works in almost any situation, including moving Address Books between computers (such as from a home computer to a laptop or from an old computer to a new one) and moving an existing Address Book from an old e-mail account configuration to a new one on the same or on different computers. It also provides an excellent way to back up the Address Book; teaching the end user to do this is a good idea. This section discusses how to first export an existing Address Book as a .csv text file and then how to import it into the new account.

Objectives

After completing this lesson, you will be able to:

* Explain the types of data that Outlook Express can import and export.
* Export Outlook Express data.
* Import Outlook Express data.
* Apply guidelines for troubleshooting issues with importing and exporting data.

Types of Data That Outlook Express Can Import and Export

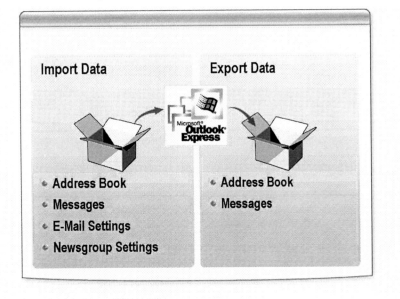

Introduction	This topic examines the various types of data that Outlook Express can import and export.
Data that can be imported	You can easily import items from other programs into Outlook Express. The following table lists many of these items.

Item	Notes
Address books from Microsoft and other products	You can import Address Book data that uses the comma separated values (CSV) format
Messages from other e-mail programs	You can import messages from Microsoft Outlook and older versions of Outlook Express
E-mail account settings	When you import your e-mail account settings, your Outlook Express account will have many, if not all, of the customization and information details from your previous account
Newsgroup account settings	When you import your newsgroup account settings into Outlook Express, your subscription records and other data are placed into your Outlook Express newsgroup account

Data that can be exported	You can also export items from Outlook Express to use in other programs. The following table lists the items you can export from Outlook Express.

Item	Notes
Address Book	You can export the Address Book from Outlook Express so that it can be used in Outlook
Messages	You can export messages from one or more of your folders

How to Export Outlook Express Data

In Outlook Express, on the File menu, click Export

Introduction

This section describes how to export an Address Book and messages.

How to export an existing Address Book

To export an existing Address Book:

1. In Outlook Express on the old computer, laptop, or existing computer, on the **File** menu, click **Export**, and then click **Address Book**.

2. In the **Address Book Export Tool** dialog box, click **Text File (Comma Separated Values)** and click **Export**.

3. In the **CSV Export** dialog box, click **Browse**.

4. In the **Save As** dialog box, choose a location to save the file, name the file, and then click **Save**.

5. In the second **CSV Export** dialog box, select the fields to export, and then click **Finish**.

   Note   When selecting the fields to export, be sure to select the **First Name**, **Last Name**, and **E-Mail Address** fields.

6. When the export process is complete, click **OK**, and then close the **Address Book Export Tool** dialog box.

How to manually export messages

To manually export messages:

1. On the desktop, create a new folder named Exported Mail.

Tip To create this folder, right-click on an empty space of the desktop, click **New**, click **Folder**, and then type the name for the folder.

---

2. In Outlook Express, if necessary, resize the Outlook Express window so that the desktop is visible.

3. Click the folder that contains the messages that you want to export (for example, the Inbox folder).

4. Select the messages that you want to export by holding down the SHIFT key and then clicking each message that you want to export.

Tip To select all messages in a folder, click one message, and then, on the **Edit** menu, click **Select All**.

---

5. Drag the selected messages from the Outlook Express window into the Exported Mail folder that you created in step 1.

6. Close Outlook Express.

How to Import Outlook Express Data

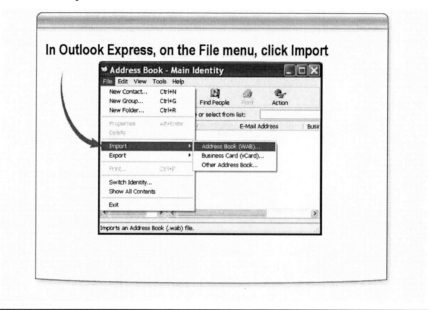

Introduction

After you have exported the existing Address Book and messages, you are ready to import the data into the new account. This section describes these procedures.

How to import an Address Book

To import an existing Address Book into a new account:

1. In Outlook Express, on the **File** menu, click **Import**, and then click **Other Address Book**.

2. In the **Address Book Import Tool** dialog box, select **Text File (Comma Separated Values)**, and then click **Import**.

3. In the **CSV Import** dialog box, click **Browse**.

4. In the **Open** dialog box, locate the exported Address Book, and then click **Open**.

5. In the **CSV Import** dialog box, click **Next**.

6. In the second **CSV Import** dialog box, select the fields to import, and then click **Finish**.

   Note   When selecting the fields to import, be sure to select the **First Name**, **Last Name**, and **E-Mail Address** fields.

7. When the import process is complete, click **OK**, and then close the **Address Book Import Tool** dialog box.

How to import messages

To import messages:

1. In Outlook Express, on the **File** menu, click **Import**, and then click **Messages**.

2. In the **Outlook Express Import** dialog box, in the **Select an e-mail program to import from** box, click **Microsoft Outlook Express 6**, and then click **Next**.

3. In the **Import From OE6** dialog box, select the appropriate identity, and then click **Next**.

4. In the **Location of Messages** dialog box, accept the defaults, and then click **Next**.

   Note   Accept the defaults unless the mail folder has been moved. If the mail folder has been moved, you must click **Browse** to locate the folder before you can click **Next**.

5. In the **Select Folders** dialog box, click **All Folders** or **Selected Folders**.

   Note   If you click **Selected Folders**, you must select the folders to import. To select more than one folder, hold down the CTRL key, and then click **Next**.

6. After all the messages are successfully imported, click **Finish**.

How to manually import messages

To manually import messages:

1. Open the version of Outlook Express into which you want to import the messages.

   Warning   You cannot run two instances of Outlook Express concurrently.

2. If necessary, resize the window so that the desktop is visible.

3. Open the Exported Messages folder that you created in step 1 in the procedure titled "How to manually export messages."

4. Select the messages that you want to import.

5. Drag the messages from the Exported Messages window into the appropriate folder in the Outlook Express window.

6. Close the Exported Messages window.

Guidelines for Troubleshooting Issues with Importing and Exporting Data

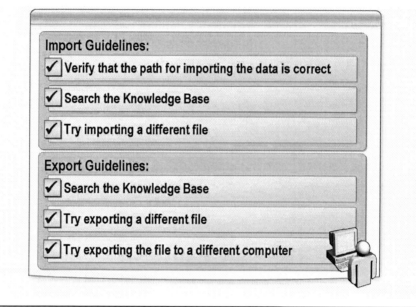

Introduction

Troubleshooting Outlook Express data issues generally falls into two well-defined categories: importing Address Book data or message data, and exporting Address Book data or message data.

Import guidelines

To troubleshoot issues related to importing data:

- Verify that you have the correct path for the data you are trying to import.
- If you are receiving an error message, search the Knowledge Base for information pertaining to that message.
- Try importing a different file to pinpoint whether the problem is with the file you are trying to import, or with Outlook Express.

Export guidelines

To troubleshoot issues related to exporting data:

- If you are receiving an error message, search the Knowledge Base for information pertaining to that message.
- Try exporting a different file to pinpoint whether the problem is with the file you are trying to export, or with Outlook Express.
- If you have access to another computer, try exporting to it to see if the problem is possibly on the receiving computer.

Practice: Importing and Exporting Outlook Express Data

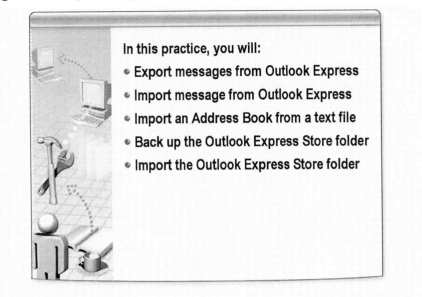

In this practice, you will:
- Export messages from Outlook Express
- Import message from Outlook Express
- Import an Address Book from a text file
- Back up the Outlook Express Store folder
- Import the Outlook Express Store folder

Objective

In this practice, you will import and export messages and Address Books between Outlook and Outlook Express. You will also back up and restore your default message store. Each practice is preceded by a situation demonstrating when you would choose to perform the following procedures.

Practice 1

You receive a call from an Outlook Express user who wants to archive some messages. You need to take the user step-by-step through copying messages from Outlook Express to a temporary folder on the desktop. After you have done this, you need to verify that the user can copy the messages back to Outlook Express, which creates a duplicate copy of the original message.

▶ **Export messages from Outlook Express**

1. Resume the 2262_London virtual machine.

2. Resume the 2262_Acapulco virtual machine.

3. Using Acapulco, log on to the domain as **Samantha** with the password **P@ssw0rd**.

4. Right-click on an empty space of the Desktop, point to **New**, click **Folder**, and name it **Exported Mail**.

5. Click **Start**, point to **All Programs**, and then click **Outlook Express**.

6. If necessary, resize the Outlook Express window so that the portion of the desktop that shows the Exported Mail folder is still visible.

7. In Outlook Express, in the **Folder** list, click **Inbox**.

8. Click the message with the subject **Test E-Mail**.

9. Drag and drop the selected messages from the Outlook Express window to the **Exported Mail** folder on your desktop.

▶ **Import messages from Outlook Express**

1. On the desktop, double-click **Exported Mail**.

2. Select the **Test E-Mail** message that you want to import.

3. Drag the messages from the Exported Mail window into the Inbox folder in the Outlook Express window.

4. Close all windows, log off, and pause the 2262_Acapulco virtual machine.

Practice 2

You receive a call from an Outlook Express user who received an Address Book from a work associate. You need to show the user how to import the Address Book.

▶ **Import an Address Book from a text file (.csv file)**

1. In Outlook Express, on the **File** menu, click **Import**, and then click **Other Address Book**.

2. In the **Address Book Import Tool** dialog box, click **Text File (Comma Separated Values)**, and then click **Import**.

3. In the **CSV Import** dialog box, in the **Choose a file to import** box, click **Browse**.

4. In the **File name** box, type **C:\Program Files\Microsoft Learning\2262\ Practices\Mod06\OE_Practice_Addresses.CSV** and then click **Open**.

5. In the **CSV Import** dialog box, click **Next**.

6. Click **Finish**.

7. In the **Address Book** dialog box, click **OK**.

8. In the **Address Book Import Tool** dialog box, click **Close**.

9. In **Outlook Express**, on the toolbar, click **Addresses**.

10. In the **Address Book – Mail Identity** dialog box, scroll through the list of addresses and verify that they were imported correctly, and then close the Address Book.

Practice 3

Before troubleshooting Outlook Express, you decide to backup the user's Outlook Express data.

▶ **Back up the Outlook Express Store folder**

1. In Outlook Express, on the **Tools** menu, click **Options**.

2. In the **Options** dialog box, on the **Maintenance** tab, click **Store Folder**.

3. In the **Store Location** dialog box, in the **Your personal message store is located in the following folder** box, right-click the path that is listed, click **Copy**, and then click **OK**.

4. In the Options window, click **OK**.

5. Close Outlook Express.

6. Click **Start**, and then click **Run**.

7. In the **Run** box, right-click inside the **Open** box, click **Paste**, and then click **OK**.

8. In the Outlook Express window, on the **Edit** menu, click **Select All**.

9. On the **File** menu, click **Send to**, and then click **My Documents**.

10. Open **My Documents** to verify the files were copied.

11. Close all windows.

Practice 4

After you have found the cause of the user's problem, you need to import the user's messages back to Outlook Express.

▶ **Import the Outlook Express Store folder**

1. Click **Start**, point to **All Programs**, and then click **Outlook Express**.

2. In Outlook Express, in the Folder list, click **Inbox**.

3. Select all the messages in Outlook Express, and then on the toolbar, click **Delete**.

4. On the **File** menu, point to **Import**, and then click **Messages**.

5. In the **Outlook Express Import** dialog box, in the **Select an e-mail program to import from** box, click **Microsoft Outlook Express 6**, and then click **Next**.

6. In the **Import From OE6** dialog box, click **Import mail from OE6 store directory**, and then click **OK**.

7. In the **Outlook Express Import** dialog box, in the **It was determined that your messages are stored in the following location. If this is not the correct location or you would like to import from a different location, please select a new folder** box, click **Browse**.

8. In the **Browse for Folder** dialog box, click **My Documents**, click **OK**, and then click **Next**.

9. On the **Select Folders** page, verify **All folders** is selected, click **Next**, and then click **Finish**.

    The user's e-mail messages are restored.

10. Close all windows, log off, and pause Acapulco.

11. Pause London.

Lesson: Configuring Outlook Express for Newsgroups

- What Are Newsgroups?
- How to Create a Newsgroup Account
- How to Subscribe to a Private Newsgroup
- How to Configure Outlook Express as the Default Newsgroup Reader
- Guidelines for Troubleshooting Newsgroup Issues

Introduction

Because newsgroups can be an invaluable source of information, end users often have questions about these groups. As a DST, you will need to explain to users the purpose and function of these groups, how to locate newsgroups, how to create a newsgroup account, and so on. This lesson describes how to accomplish these tasks as well as how to subscribe to a private newsgroup and how to configure Outlook Express as the default newsgroup reader. Finally, this lesson provides guidelines for troubleshooting common newsgroup issues.

Lesson objectives

After completing this lesson, you will be able to:

- Explain the purpose and function of newsgroups.
- Create a newsgroup account.
- Subscribe to a private newsgroup.
- Configure Outlook Express as the default newsgroup reader.
- Apply guidelines for troubleshooting newsgroup issues.

What Are Newsgroups?

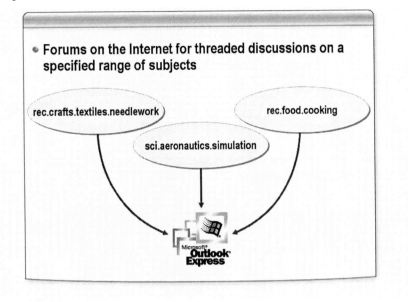

Definition

A *newsgroup* is a forum on the Internet for threaded discussions on a specified range of subjects. A newsgroup consists of articles and follow-up posts. An article with all of its follow-up posts, which are supposed to be related to the specific subject named in the original article's subject line, constitutes a *thread*.

Newsgroup naming

Each newsgroup has a name that consists of a series of words, separated by periods, indicating the newsgroup's subject in terms of increasingly narrow categories, such as rec.crafts.textiles.needlework, sci.aeronautics.simulation, and rec.food.cooking. Some newsgroups can be posted to and read only on one site; others, such as those in the seven Usenet hierarchies or those in ClariNet, circulate throughout the Internet.

Using Outlook Express with newsgroups

Outlook Express can be configured to act as a newsgroup reader. To use newsgroups in Outlook Express, your ISP must offer links to one or more news servers. After you set up an account for each server you want in Outlook Express, you can use Outlook Express to read and post messages in any of the newsgroups stored on that news server.

When you find a newsgroup you like, you can subscribe to it so that it is displayed in your Outlook Express Folders list. Subscribing provides easy access to your favorite newsgroups, eliminating the need to scroll through the long list on the server each time you want to visit a favorite newsgroup.

Newsgroups can contain thousands of messages, and sorting through them can be a time-consuming process. Outlook Express has a variety of features that make it easier to find the information you want in newsgroups.

How to Create a Newsgroup Account

Introduction

To read newsgroup messages, you must create an account and configure it properly.

Important   Before you can create a newsgroup account in Outlook Express, you must have the same information described earlier for creating an e-mail account (user name, e-mail address, password, and incoming and outgoing mail server) including the name of NNTP server.

How to create a mail or newsgroup account

To create a mail or newsgroup account:

1. In Outlook Express, on the **Tools** menu, click **Accounts**.

2. In the **Internet Accounts** dialog box, click **Add**, and then click **News**.

3. In the **Internet Connection Wizard** dialog box, in the **Display name** box, type a display name, and then click **Next**.

4. In **E-mail address** box, type the e-mail address, and then click **Next**.

5. In the **News (NNTP) server** box, type the name of the NNTP news server.

6. Click **Finish**.

How to Subscribe to a Private Newsgroup

To subscribe to a private newsgroup you must provide a:

* User name
* Password

Internet Connection Wizard

Internet News Server Logon

Type the account name and password your Internet service provider has given you.

Account name: [ ]

Password: [ ]

☐ Remember password

If your Internet service provider requires you to use Secure Password Authentication (SPA) to access your news account, select the 'Log On Using Secure Password Authentication (SPA)' check box.

☐ Log on using Secure Password Authentication (SPA)

‹ Back   Next ›   Cancel

Definition

Private newsgroups are newsgroups that are carried and distributed by a private or corporate news server. They are viewable only by members of the organization or those who are specifically given access.

About private newsgroups

Most newsgroups that you access are *public* or anonymous newsgroups. These newsgroups do not require a user to log on to access the group. *Private* newsgroups, on the other hand, require you to physically log on to have access to the newsgroup. Outlook Express can be configured to access both public and private newsgroups. This is done by entering a user name and password when subscribing to the NNTP server. After configuring a subscription, you can also configure Outlook Express to make messages available offline.

How to subscribe to a private newsgroup

To subscribe to a private newsgroup:

1. In Outlook Express, on the **Tools** menu, click **Accounts**.

2. In the **Internet Accounts** dialog box, click **Add**, and then click **News**.

3. In the **Internet Connection Wizard** dialog box, type a display name, and then click **Next**.

4. Type your e-mail address, and then click **Next**.

5. Type the name of the NNTP news server, select the **My news server requires me to log on** check box, and then click **Next**.

6. Type your name and password, if appropriate, select the **secure password authentication** check box, and then click **Next**.

7. Click **Finish**.

How to make a newsgroup available offline

To make a newsgroup available offline:

1. In Outlook Express, in the Folder list, right-click the newsgroup you want to be available offline and then click **Properties**.

2. In the **Newsgroup Properties** dialog box, on the **Synchronize** tab, click **When synchronizing this newsgroup, download**, and then select one of the following options:

   - **New headers**

   - **New messages (headers and bodies)**

   - **All messages (headers and bodies)**

3. Click **OK**.

How to Configure Outlook Express as the Default Newsgroup Reader

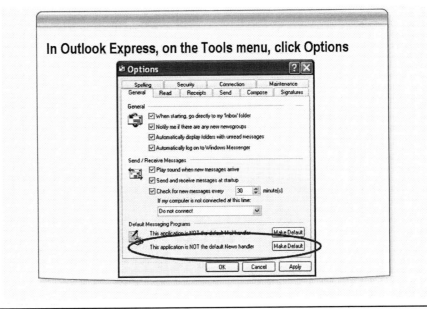

Introduction

You can configure Outlook Express to act as your default reader when connecting to newsgroups on the Web. After doing so, Outlook Express opens whenever you click a newsgroup link on a Web page or choose the newsreader command in your Web browser.

Procedure

To set Outlook Express as your default newsreader:

1. In Outlook Express, on the **Tools** menu, click **Options**.

2. In the **Options** dialog box, on the **General** tab, in the **Default Messaging Programs** area, next to **This application is NOT the default News handler**, click **Make Default**.

3. Click **OK**.

Guidelines for Troubleshooting Newsgroup Issues

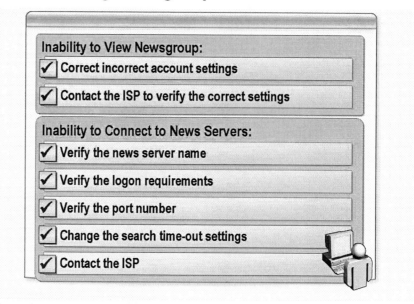

Introduction

There are basically two types of issues that a DST will encounter when troubleshooting newsgroup issues:

- The inability to view newsgroups
- The inability to connect to news servers

Inability to view newsgroups

If you can connect to your ISP, but cannot view any newsgroups, compare the settings to those given to you by your ISP by applying the following guidelines:

- If the settings do not match, correct the settings on the appropriate tab, and attempt to access the newsgroups again.
- If the settings match, contact your ISP to verify that you have the correct settings and that the ISP servers are operating correctly.

Inability to connect to news servers

If you receive a news connection error message on a specific server and cannot connect to one or more news servers, there might be a problem with one or more of the settings for the news servers to which you are attempting to connect. When this occurs, apply the following guidelines:

- Make sure the news server name matches the name given to you by your ISP.
- If your ISP requires a logon account name and password, be sure you have them.

Note   If you are required to log on to this news server, check that the account name and password you have entered match those given to you by your ISP. If you are not required to log on to this news server, clear the **This server requires me to log on** check box.

- Confirm that the port number matches the number given to you by your ISP. Most ISPs use port 119.

- Make sure that the search time-out is set to **Short**. Some servers might take longer to make a connection. To allow more time for your computer to make the connection, move the slider toward **Long**.

- Contact the ISP.

Practice: Configuring Outlook Express for Newsgroups

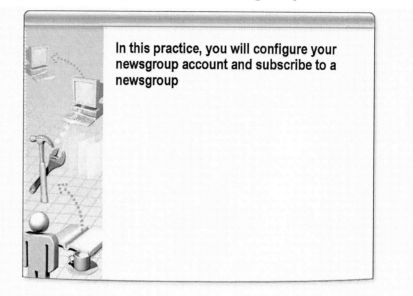

In this practice, you will configure your newsgroup account and subscribe to a newsgroup

Objective

In this practice, you will configure a newsgroup account in Outlook Express. You will also learn how to find and subscribe to a newsgroup.

Scenario

You receive a call from a user who wants to know if he can access newsgroups from Outlook Express. You need to walk him through the process of configuring a newsgroup account in Outlook Express.

Practice

▶ **Configure your newsgroup account and subscribe to a newsgroup**

1. Resume the 2262_London and 2262_Acapulco virtual machines.

2. Using Acapulco, log on to the domain as **Samantha** with a password of **P@ssw0rd**

3. Click **Start**, point to **All Programs**, and then click **Outlook Express**.

4. In Outlook Express, on the **Tools** menu, click **Accounts**.

5. In the **Internet Accounts** dialog box, click **Add**, and then click **News**.

6. On the **Your Name** page, in the **Display name** box, verify **Samantha Smith** is displayed and then click **Next**.

7. On the **Internet News E-mail Address** page, in the **E-mail address** box, verify **Samantha@nwtraders.msft** is displayed, and then click **Next**.

8. On the **Internet News Server Name** page, in the **News (NNTP) server** box, type **london.nwtraders.msft**, select the **My news server requires me to log on** check box, and then click **Next**.

9. On the **Internet News Server Logon** page, in the **Account name** box, verify **samantha** is displayed, in the **Password** box, type **P@ssw0rd** and then click **Next**.

10. On the **Congratulations** page, click **Finish**.

11. In the **Internet Accounts** dialog box, click **Close**.

12. In the **Would you like to download newsgroups from the news account you added?** warning box, click **Yes**.

13. In the **Newsgroup Subscriptions** dialog box, select **nwtradersnews**, click **Subscribe**, and then click **OK**.

14. In the Folder list, click **nwtradersnews**.

15. In **Outlook Express**, click **New Post**.

16. In the **New Message** dialog box, in the **Subject** box, type **Test From Samantha** and then in the message body, type **This is a Test from Samantha** and then click **Send**.

17. In the **Post News** dialog box, click **OK**.

18. In Outlook Express, on the **Tools** menu, click **Synchronize Newsgroup**.

19. In the **Synchronize Newsgroup** box, select the **Get the following items** checkbox, click **All messages**, and then click **OK**.

    Your post is displayed.

20. For both London and Acapulco, close the virtual machines and delete changes.

Lab: Troubleshooting Issues Related to Outlook Express

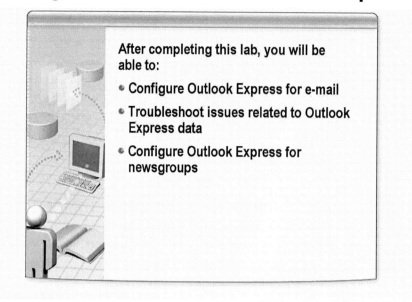

After completing this lab, you will be able to:

* Configure Outlook Express for e-mail
* Troubleshoot issues related to Outlook Express data
* Configure Outlook Express for newsgroups

Objective

After completing this lab, you will be able to:

- Configure Outlook Express for e-mail.
- Troubleshoot issues related to Outlook Express data.
- Configure Outlook Express for newsgroups.

Scenario

In this lab, you are a DST working for a large ISP. You answer phone calls from customers who are having trouble with their e-mail and newsgroups. The following scenarios are typical situations you might encounter during any given shift. Use your available resources to resolve these customers' issues.

For more information

Use the following resources to complete this lab:

- The information in this module
- Help and Support on your classroom computer
- The Microsoft Knowledge Base
- Other online resources

Estimated time to complete this lab: 30 minutes

Exercise 1
Configuring Outlook Express for E-Mail

In this exercise, you will troubleshoot a problem accessing a POP3 account using Outlook Express.

Scenario

A user calls stating that he is not getting his e-mail. He is using Outlook Express to connect to his company's Exchange Server. When he clicks Send/Recv on the Outlook Express toolbar, he receives an error message stating that his server cannot be found. Your job is to enable the user to successfully connect to the Exchange Server using Outlook Express and to verify that the user is able to send and receive e-mail.

Tasks	Guidance for completing the task
1. Start the London and Acapulco virtual machines, and using Acapulco, log on to the NWTRADERS domain as **Max** with a password of **P@ssw0rd**.	<ul><li>Use the Virtual PC console.</li><li>Wait for London to display the log on screen before starting Acapulco.</li></ul>
2. Using Acapulco, reproduce the user's problem.	<ul><li>Start Outlook Express.</li><li>Attempt to send and receive mail. An error message is displayed stating that the server cannot be found.</li></ul>
3. Resolve the issue.	<ul><li>Refer to the topic Guidelines for Troubleshooting E-mail Issues.</li><li>The issue is considered resolved when the user is able to successfully send and receive mail.</li></ul>
4. Close all windows and log off of both virtual machines.	

Exercise 2
Troubleshooting Issues Related to Outlook Express Data

In this exercise, you will troubleshoot a situation in which one of the default mail folders is corrupt.

Scenario

A user calls and says she cannot delete a message from one of her folders. She has already saved a copy of the message elsewhere and does not need to back up the mailbox—she wants just to delete the message and ensure that her inbox is functioning properly.

Tasks	Guidance for completing the task
1. Using Acapulco, log on to the domain as **Samantha** with a password of **P@ssw0rd**.	
2. Start Outlook Express and send yourself (Samantha) a message.	■ Although this message can be deleted individually, we will use it to simulate the corrupted mailbox. Do not resolve the issue by simply deleting the message.
3. Create a subfolder in the inbox titled My Project.	
4. Restore Samantha's inbox to its default state.	■ Refer to the How to Repair a Damaged Default Mail Folder topic.
5. Resolve the issue.	■ This issue is considered resolved when you have restored the inbox to its default state. The message you sent to yourself will disappear, but the My Project subfolder must still be present after you restore the inbox to its default state.

Exercise 3
Configuring Outlook Express for Newsgroups

In this exercise, you will help a user configure Outlook Express so that he can read newsgroup messages offline.

Scenario

A user calls and states that he is unable to access newsgroups using Outlook Express. After you help the user regain access, he would like to read newsgroup information offline.

Tasks	Guidance for completing the task
1. Using Acapulco, log on to the domain as **Max**.	
2. Open Outlook Express to reproduce the problem.	▪ Attempt to access the preconfigured newsgroup.
3. Resolve the newsgroup connection issue.	▪ This issue is considered resolved when Max is able to download messages from the newsgroup.
4. Resolve the offline issue.	▪ This issue is considered resolved when Max is able to disconnect from the server and still read and create responses to newsgroup postings to be uploaded at a later time.
5. Close virtual machines and delete changes.	

Lab Discussion

After you have completed the exercises in this lab, take a moment to answer the following questions. When the entire class has finished the lab, the instructor will facilitate a lab discussion based on students' answers to these questions.

1. How did you determine the cause(s) of the issue(s)?

2. How did you resolve the issue(s)?

3. What are some other ways the issue(s) could have been resolved?

Course Evaluation

Your evaluation of this course will help Microsoft understand the quality of your learning experience.

To complete a course evaluation, go to http://www.CourseSurvey.com.

Microsoft will keep your evaluation strictly confidential and will use your responses to improve your future learning experience.

Notes